BAFTA award winning Lee  most recognizable and celeb and stars in his own multi-*Going Out*, is a team captain on *Would I Lie to You?*, and frequently appears on *Have I Got News for You*, *Live at the Apollo* and *QI*. He has performed many stand-up tours across the country, and has released two stand-up DVDs, *Lee Mack Live* and *Lee Mack – Going Out*.

Lee lives in London with his wife, Tara, and their three children.

MACK THE LIFE

LEE MACK

CORGI BOOKS

TRANSWORLD PUBLISHERS
61–63 Uxbridge Road, London W5 5SA
A Random House Group Company
www.transworldbooks.co.uk

MACK THE LIFE
A CORGI BOOK: 9780552166553

First published in Great Britain
in 2012 by Bantam Press
an imprint of Transworld Publishers
Corgi edition published 2013

Addresses for Random House Group Ltd companies outside the UK
can be found at: www.randomhouse.co.uk
The Random House Group Ltd Reg. No. 954009

The Random House Group Limited supports The Forest Stewardship
Council® (FSC®), the leading international forest-certification organisation.
Our books carrying the FSC label are printed on FSC®-certified paper.
FSC is the only forest-certification scheme supported by the leading
environmental organisations, including Greenpeace. Our
paper procurement policy can be found at
www.randomhouse.co.uk/environment

Printed and bound in Great Britain by Clays Ltd, St Ives plc
Typeset in 11/14.5pt Life by Falcon Oast Graphic Art Ltd.
4 6 8 10 9 7 5

For Tara, Arlo, Louie and Millie x

CONTENTS

The visits to the psychiatrist in this book are genuine. Some scenes have been edited for the sake of brevity, but other than that are taken directly from recordings of the actual conversations.

Having said that, the rest of this book is totally fabricated.*

*Joke.

PSYCHIATRIST'S OFFICE

Lee is sat talking to a woman. Having finished his autobiography he has had the idea to ask a psychiatrist to read it, then meet with Lee and analyse him, to see if she can offer up any thoughts about what makes him tick.

BRIAN: You do realize that if I agree to do this, that we can't really class it as psychiatry, don't you?

LEE: Why?

BRIAN: Because this is not really how psychiatry is done.

LEE: That's fine, it doesn't have to be actual psychiatry. As long as you prod me a bit. Not literally.

Lee is worried. Will his last comment be read as overly sexual, even though it was just a joke?

BRIAN: Well, if it doesn't have to be psychiatry why choose a psychiatrist?

LEE: Well, because I did a random search on Google . . .

Lee pauses. He thinks about cracking a joke about usually

using Google for other things, *i.e.* porn, but decides not to as she might think that the joke is to mask the truth. She might think he **does** use Google to search for porn, especially after the 'prodding' joke.*

LEE: . . . and I had three choices: psychiatrist, psychotherapist and psychologist . . .
Lee realizes his mistake. He hasn't got three choices. He only has one choice. He has three **options**. *He is about to correct himself, then realizes she will not be judging him on his grasp of the English language. She will be judging him on his use of sexual jokes about prodding and excessive searching for porn on the internet.*

LEE: . . . and, not knowing anything about this field, I figured a psychiatrist was the most qualified. Psychologists sound like they're only used for catching serial killers, and as for psychotherapy, that sounds a bit too much like anyone can do that, even if you're not properly qualified. Any old person can claim to be one of those people, I bet.

Lee panics. What if she is also a psychotherapist. He is annoyed with himself. He only said this because

he was trying to ingratiate
himself with her, assuming that
there was probably rivalry between
these factions. Lee is convinced
he has said the wrong thing. He
wouldn't mind but it's not even
his opinion, it's the opinion
businessman Sir Alan Sugar gave to
psychotherapist Pamela Stephenson
when Lee did The Graham Norton
Show *with them both. In fact, at*
the time, Lee defended the honour
of Pamela Stephenson on the
subject. After Sir Alan Sugar had
claimed 'anyone can buy headed
notepaper and call themselves a
psychotherapist', Lee had butted in
and said 'No, Sir Alan, it's not
everyone that can buy
a title.' This had got a laugh and
a round of applause at the time
(but was annoyingly edited out due
to not wanting to upset Sir Alan).

LEE: (*trying to be light-hearted*)
          Please tell me you're not also a
          psychotherapist.

BRIAN: Well you can be both.

          Brian doesn't let on if she is
          both. Lee doesn't push it any
          further and decides to just get
          paranoid instead.

BRIAN: Won't it be hard to distil these
          one-hour sessions into a two- or
          three-page script?

LEE: Don't worry. I'll edit it down to
          the highlights. I might even use
          it as an opportunity to crowbar in
          some anecdote that happened on a
          chat show, but then subsequently
          got edited out. So, will you do
          it?

BRIAN: OK.

          Lee is pleased she has agreed.

BRIAN: But I'd rather remain anonymous if
          that's OK.

LEE: No problem. I won't mention your
          real name, I'll just call you
          Brian.

          Lee goes to exit.

BRIAN: By the way, I'm a cousin of
          Jedward.

          *Lee is unsure why he is being told
          this, but likes this odd fact and
          decides he will include it in the
          book. Even though that surely
          means her anonymity is blown.
          Unless of course Jedward have
          loads of cousins that are
          psychiatrists.*

CHAPTER ONE

My great-grandfather was a transvestite

When I read other people's autobiographies I am often a little disappointed at the start. Do we really need to have three chapters on their parents, or in some cases grandparents? The first hundred pages always seem to be about how their granddad, a South American immigrant, was smuggled aboard a cargo ship to Britain to escape certain execution at home for his strong political beliefs, and I'm always left with a sense of 'this is all fine, but when are you going to get to the really weighty stuff, like the time you got hammered with Kerry Katona?'

But I'm also very aware that to some a person's roots are interesting because it may give clues as to how you ended up doing what you do, which, let's face it, is probably what most people are waiting to find out at the start of an autobiography. So let's get that out of the way, and then I can tell you about the time I got hammered with Kerry Katona, who I've never actually met.

First things first, I don't really come from a showbiz family. I say 'really' because my great-grandfather, who I never knew, was a variety hall comedian by the name of Billy Mac. You'll notice the lack of 'k' at the end of his name, which his son, my Granddad Jack, was not happy about when I failed to do the same. In fact when my mum sent him my first publicity photo he immediately Tippexed the 'k' off 'Mack' to show me how much better it looked without it, and sent it straight back. I immediately wrote back saying 'Thanks Granddad Jac' (sic).*

But I always felt that 'Mac' looked abbreviated whereas 'Mack' was like a surname in itself and wouldn't look like I'd created a stage name, as I always thought changing your name a little too showbiz. So why didn't I just keep my real name? Because it's McKillop, and that is a name which is just too hard to remember or spell. And, to be honest, it would feel very odd getting on stage as 'Lee McKillop' as that's me, whereas, to some degree, the person on stage is someone else. I suppose it's a sort of self-defence mechanism. It's probably the same reason I won't do stand-up gigs in my hometown of Southport. It would feel too weird, like doing stand-up to my family over Christmas dinner:

'What's your name, and where are you from?'

* 'Sic' as in 'deliberate mistake' – I don't mean he was ill, or really cool, or in bed with his sister.

'I'm your Auntie Betty, and I'm from upstairs, now sit down and eat your turkey, you annoying little tosser.'

I know very little about Billy Mac. In fact, what little I do know has been learned since I started doing stand-up, so it's not as though the knowledge of this was an influence on the career I chose. All I do know about him is from the three publicity photos I have. He used to occasionally dress up as a woman in his act (either that or my great-grandmother was very unattractive) and he used to sing a song about 'Cabbages, Ca Beans and Carrots'. I have absolutely no idea what 'Ca Beans' are. I have had many a debate about whether they actually exist, or whether the gag was the fact that the other two words begin with 'ca', so the forcing of 'ca' in front of beans is what makes it supposedly funny, but if that was the case then surely the rule of three in comedy would make 'ca beans' go at the end of the sentence. You see, that's what comedians talk about on long car journeys. It really is that interesting.

I suppose it is a bit bizarre that completely independently I have chosen the same profession as a man I never met, or knew much about. I suppose it invites the question, is comedy, or performing, genetic? I suspect it isn't. Maybe other things are genetic that perhaps then lead to comedy. For example, maybe it's possible to pass on, genetically, an inability for the brain to develop in certain areas, and so a certain part of the brain is stuck in a childlike state, which perhaps leads to 'joking around', which then leads on to making a living out of it. Being childlike is common amongst comedians and it's a fact that a very high proportion of them were bed wetters until very late in life. Well, I say fact, more of a thought I had at the start of the last sentence.

Anyway, who cares? I'm not a great believer in studying comedy in an overly academic way. It's like finding out how magic tricks work. Or why Simon Cowell's TV shows are so unbelievably popular. I'm not sure I want to know how or why.

Although the performing 'gene' skipped a generation, my dad John (Billy Mac's grandson) was keen on a bit of amateur dramatics when he was younger. Later in life, when I started doing stand-up, he was very quick to point out to people this was where I 'got it from'. In fact this was literally his opening line on meeting my new girlfriend, now wife, Tara. It was promptly followed by him turning the other way to 'get into character' then turning back to her and reciting his Bill Sykes part from *Oliver Twist* – 'Have you heard the noise a chicken makes when you're wringing its neck, Fagin? It squawks, it squawks.' My dad, who was partial to the odd tipple (for those that knew him I know you'll appreciate this is a massive understatement, but that in itself could fill a whole book and there really isn't time), had maybe had a little too much of the loopy juice that day and perhaps slightly misjudged the moment as he proceeded to throttle her as part of the performance. I was just glad he hadn't gone for his opening line to my previous girlfriend, who was a dancer. Before he'd even said hello he had sat beside her, grabbed her leg, given it a little bit of a wobble and said 'A bit bloody weighty to be a dancer, aren't you?'

My dad had met my mum, Christine, in the mid-sixties and very soon they were married and had their first child, my brother Darren. This was all by the ridiculous age of twenty-one, which nowadays seems unbelievably young, but really was absolutely normal for the time. Two years later I came along and was immediately named after Lee Marvin, the actor. It's hard to imagine nowadays but there was a time when the name Lee was actually considered a bit cool, a bit American, a bit exotic. I am acutely aware it is now the name given to someone in a comedy or drama if he is a gobby plasterer from Essex or a glue sniffer. Luckily they went for Gordon as a middle name, so at least I still had some coolness to cling on to. By the way, singing 'Gordon is a moron' when you find out someone's middle name is really tiresome. I appreciate that only applies to the over-forties, but you know who you are.

My dad worked in the family business of panel beating. Due to this being a bit of a dying industry I should explain to younger readers that a panel beater is someone who fixes dents on cars, and not someone who turns up to *Question Time* to punch politicians. Actually, to the younger reader I should also explain that *Question Time* is like *Mock the Week*, but without the knob jokes.

As well as the panel beating, my dad, alongside my mum, used to work in local bars and it soon became my dad's dream to have his own pub. Actually, I suspect that my dad's dream was still to be a performer of sorts, but at this point he'd stopped the amateur dramatics, and as any show-off will tell you, if you can't show off on stage then get your own pub and show off there. Or take up darts.

My dad was a keen darts player, and very good. Due to my parents' break-up and me subsequently living with my mum (don't worry, I'm getting to that bit in a minute), I haven't got a great deal of stories about growing up with my dad after about the age of eleven, but one thing that has always stuck with me is the story of his darting excellence during a match. It may have been exaggerated to me by my dad, or may not even be true at all. Like the time he told me Father Christmas had broken down on the roof of the garage he worked in (my dad had helped to fix the sleigh and Father Christmas had told my dad that for us to get our presents that year we had to be my dad's slave for the day). But as a mad darts fan myself (and pretty good even though I say so myself) I'm willing to accept the darts one to be true. Whilst panel beating in the garage my dad would practise playing darts in his spare time, and his party trick was to play with six-inch nails. They obviously don't have flights in them so had to be thrown the way a knife thrower would, with the nails spinning round in the air. He got very good at this over time. One night during a match, and with my dad needing bull's-eye for the game with his one remaining dart, his opponent tried to put him off by announcing to the crowd 'He's going to bottle it.' My dad calmly took the flight out of the dart and threw it knife thrower style like he did with the six-inch nails. It spun in the air and promptly landed in the bull. Which is amazing when you consider how small the bull is. Although I suspect, like the Father Christmas story, it's actually a *load* of bull.

Finally my parents got their own pub, and so when I was seven years old we upped sticks and left our hometown of Southport to start a new life in the Dog and Partridge pub, Rochdale (now L'Italiano according to Google street maps. I say this not as a way to promote the restaurant, but as a way of trying to get a blue plaque put up. I'll even pay for it. And screw it in if you like). Upping sticks was something I was to get used to, as moving house became a regular part of my childhood. In fact, by the time I was twelve years old I had lived in eight houses or pubs. The pub in Rochdale is a little bit of a distant memory now as I was only there for about two years. In fact, many years ago I went back to the pub for the first time in my adult life with Johnny Vegas, a man who I still consider gave the funniest stand-up performance I have ever seen. It's quite weird being in your childhood living room, but which is now part of an actual pub. It's even weirder when you've got the most unusual-looking man in showbiz with you, rasping away about some incoherent nonsense, and random strangers shouting 'Monkey' at you. Even weirder was that this was before he'd done his famous ads.

The best things about growing up in that pub were that Cannon and Ball played there (Bobby Ball then went on to play my dad in my sitcom *Not Going Out*, so

I love the idea that both 'dads' met), the greatest dog in the world turned up on the doorstep (Sheba, a stray, who became our childhood pet), and the locals were allowed an afternoon lock-in to do séances, which, having the liberal parents we had, me and my brother were allowed to join in. I say 'liberal'; I do of course mean 'a bit mad'.

My other memory from that period of my life was of my first ever appearance in the national newspapers. We had all gone for a family day out to a shopping centre in Preston, because we knew how to live the dream. Me and my brother decided it would be fun to slide down the middle section of the escalators: a common form of entertainment for children before Alton Towers took over. A passing security dog took exception to this and bit me on the leg. A quick trip to the hospital and, three stitches later, it was all soon forgotten about, because in those days suing people wasn't the pastime it is today.

Many moons later – but still way before Rottweilers and pit bulls had been invented – the press decided that the devil-dogs of the time were going to be Alsatians, and on this particular week they singled out security dogs, whose handlers were apparently only given two days' training. Clearly health and safety was covered on day three, and the security guards had missed this, so they didn't know that letting dogs bite children was deemed 'risky'. The *Sunday People* ran a story and I became the poster boy of the campaign. Well, the only kid who agreed to do the photo shoot is probably more accurate. For the purposes of this book the publishers kindly found the original newspaper article, which I've included in the photo section. It was funny seeing it again after thirty-odd years, and it brought back memories of the press photographer telling me to stop giggling and smiling, as I was supposed to be looking 'traumatized'. You can see on my face that I've still got half a smile, which was the best they could get from me that day.

Very soon afterwards we were in our second pub, a brand-new establishment called the Centurion on the Roman Road Estate in Blackburn. It was massive, or certainly felt that way after the pub in Rochdale. This new one was set next to some woodland, and living in such a large place felt like we were squires of the land with our own estate. Admittedly it was a council estate, but an estate nevertheless.

I made friends very quickly at my new school. I am under no illusions that this was largely down to the fact that the other kids found our pub very exciting. It had a pinball machine, a pool table and a dartboard, and, more importantly, if you were a visitor it had free crisps and Coke. There were no other pubs on the estate, and very little to do, so the other kids were keen to visit. It got so busy with my mates coming round that my mum had to limit me to one friend at a time in the house. I remember being outside the pub with a load of mates and having to pick which one was allowed in. I'd like to say that the decision made me feel racked with guilt and that I shouldn't have been put in such an awkward position. But it didn't. It made me feel a bit special and that we had the coolest house in the world. I remember thinking how lucky we were that we lived in such a great place, whilst the others lived in much smaller, run-down houses on the estate. I didn't realize it then, but very soon we'd have to leave the pub and join them on the estate after my parents' break-up made it impossible for us to stay there. (Don't worry, doom-mongerers, the break-up bit's coming. Blimey, what's the matter with you?)

It's weird growing up in a pub. In one respect you see your parents all the time as they work pretty much from home (we lived in the flat directly above the pub). But conversely it's such an all-consuming job that you never see them. Particularly my dad, who was more of the driving force behind running it. He worked so much I literally only have one memory of sitting down and watching TV with him. It was a Saturday afternoon in 1979 and we watched the FA Cup final together. Arsenal beat Man Utd 3–2 and it's still the greatest FA Cup final I've ever seen. In fact, I subsequently bought the whole match commentary on a vinyl LP (bizarre, I know, but brilliant). I'm sure the obvious conclusion to draw from this is that that one moment of a shared father/son experience embedded itself in my mind and made it very special to me. But what actually embedded itself in my mind was John Motson's commentary on what must be the greatest last few minutes of any football match in history: 'There's a minute left on the clock . . . Brady for Arsenal . . . Right across

. . . Sunderland! . . . It's there! . . . It's 3–2!' If you ever get to hear the Radio 5 commentary, which is what I own on vinyl, it's even more amazing. No? Oh, OK, please yourself.

Nowadays I see similarities with my own work life, and how often I see my own kids. I spend months and months working from home writing *Not Going Out*, which on the face of it is very conducive to family life as I'm at home all the time. But the reality is that it's so all-consuming and a painfully slow process that I actually feel I'm seeing – well, engaging – more with my kids when I'm on tour (or when I'm not working at all, which is obviously much better). Because when I'm on tour home time really is home time where I completely shut off from comedy. Whereas when I'm writing the sitcom it's a constant presence in my head, like an unpaid electric bill that never gets sorted. (What do you mean 'direct debit'?)

My mum was with us a lot more, and she went downstairs to the pub a lot less. Actually that may be my memory playing tricks on me. I suspect what actually happened was she made our tea and put us to bed and then went downstairs to the pub, as I have quite a lot of memories of her getting ready in the bathroom. That's one of the problems with running a pub, you're constantly in a state of 'getting ready' to go out. Oh yeah, and the limitless amounts of alcohol you have access to, that can be a drawback as well.

In fact, running a pub has got quite a lot in common with comedy.

Both my parents were party people. Often after a long day of working in the pub all day they would have 'lock-ins' with the locals. Lock-ins were very common in the 1970s and 1980s as pubs were still restricted in when they could open, an archaic law that had been passed in 1914 to help the war effort. Basically you were only allowed to open between about twelve and three, then again from about six to eleven. This made lock-ins a valuable commodity, and they always felt a little exciting, like we were part of a community of prohibition American drinkers in a speakeasy. You'd have thought that if you were working from the crack of dawn in the cellar to eleven o'clock at night you'd be ready to stop. But I think the biggest appeal for my parents about the job was the social side, so many a night would end with the locals staying and drinking after hours with my mum and dad in their element as the genial hosts. Basically my house was often one big party, where it was instilled into me that life was about having a laugh rather than working your socks off in a dead-end job that you hate. Words I obviously forgot when I once spent a summer stacking shelves at B&Q. I was sacked after telling the supervisor to 'Do It Yourself'. Don't worry, he didn't laugh either.

I've heard a few comedians talk about the fact that they had to announce to their parents that they were giving up their serious career of being, say, a doctor or a lawyer as they wanted to get into comedy. And how their parents were disappointed with them for throwing away their career for the pursuit of some silly dream.

Well, my parents were the opposite. If I'd ever told them that I was sick of titting around for a living trying to make it as a comedian, and I was going to knuckle down to a more academic career, I think they would have genuinely been disappointed in me. Life was about not taking things too seriously.

The great irony of this of course is that running a pub is extremely hard work. On the surface it looks like it's just about having fun, but what goes on beneath the surface can sometimes be a lot harder than it looks. Again, very similar to comedy. Getting up at seven in the morning and working in the cellar all day, doing the accounts, cleaning the beer pipes – that's like the writing in comedy. That's the bit people don't really see. Opening the pub doors and putting on your best 'host' face, when actually all you want to do sometimes is curl up on the sofa and watch *Match of the Day* – that's the on-stage performance when you've already done a hundred shows and you're ready to stop. A bloke's had too much to drink and smashes a bottle against your head – that's the heckle.

Soon it all became too much for them and my parents split up. It came to a head on holiday. Four of us went, only three of us came back. Oh well, it could have been odder, it could have been the other way round.

Going abroad in the 1970s, especially if you were living on a council estate, was not the norm and we were very lucky that we could afford it. Before my parents ran a pub our holidays consisted of going to Butlin's or Pontin's, as they did for many working-class kids growing up in the sixties and seventies. But now through hard work, not to mention every scam known to man when it comes to running a pub, my mum and dad could afford to take us abroad. We had three foreign holidays in total, and all three were a disaster. One ended with a broken leg (more to follow), one ended with a broken marriage (more to follow), and one was in Magaluf ('nuff said).

One of them was a skiing holiday in 1979 when I was eleven. Skiing was something very rich people did. We could not believe that here we were in the Pyrenees. It was like the Beverly Hillbillies going to . . . well, going skiing in the Pyrenees. On day one we all went to ski school. By the end of the day I had decided that I knew all there was to know about skiing and was going to spend the rest of the holiday whizzing down the mountain like the bloke from the Milk Tray advert. How hard could it be? After all it was just a case of sliding down a hill.

As I lay there on the snow with a broken leg, I thought 'Note to self: must remember that not every-thing is as easy as it looks so don't just dive in at the deep end, assume you know better than everyone else, and ignore the advice of those more experienced', a lesson I soon forgot and so I carried on as normal for the rest of my life. My mum and dad were behind me in the proper ski-school party and they soon caught up with me. I was crying my eyes out and my mum tried to calm me down, whereas my dad went for the more direct approach of saying 'Get up, you tart.' When my mum realized I had broken my leg she got a bit panicky and needed to be calmed down. What happened next didn't help, and if it had been an idea I'd had for *Not Going Out* I would probably have dismissed it as too coincidental to be true.

On chairlifts at ski resorts there is the occasional seat which is designed to carry people with injuries. These are more like beds than seats. Because one of these beds had arrived at the ski station nearest to where I was injured, they had to stop the chairlift and wait for me to get taken to it by stretcher, otherwise it may have been another half-hour before it came round again. So as my mum was holding my hand and starting to panic, the brakes were applied to the chairlift above her. At that moment she heard a scream, and as we all looked up we saw my brother Darren sitting on a chairlift, but he'd been unable to pull down the safety barrier. Because the brakes had been applied quite sharpishly the whole thing began to rock backwards and forwards with my brother screaming and gripping on for dear life eighty feet in the air. Our family has always had a sort of aura of sitcom about them.

I spent the next two weeks sitting in the hotel bar whilst the rest of the family skied and the barman, who was the spitting image of the actor Peter Lorre, used to carry me to the toilet three times a day. This was the 1970s and leaving your kids alone, even with a stranger, was not only acceptable, it was the law. In this modern age it's hard to read that last bit without thinking that my parents were neglectful. But they weren't. The problem lies with what we have all become now (paranoid lunatics easily influenced by tabloid paranoia), not what was happening back then (trust in humanity).

When I got home to England the plaster that the Spanish hospital had put on had completely disintegrated, and the English doctors blamed the shoddy workmanship of the Spanish. We never told them it was more likely due to the fact that my mum, not wanting me to be left out, had let me join them when they had a sauna.

Another family holiday abroad was a Pontinental holiday. That's not a spelling mistake, it's what they were called. It was Pontin's, but abroad. Because Pontin's and Butlin's were a regular holiday destination for us before the pub money rolled in, it seemed an obvious thing to try these new, fancy foreign versions in Spain. And after the skiing debacle I suspect they felt they were on safer ground. I mean, it's good old Pontin's, for God's sake, what could possibly go wrong?

On the last night before we were due to fly home my mum and dad had a huge argument and my dad stormed out. About what, I have no idea, but I could hear shouting through the adjoining wall where me and my brother were sleeping. To be honest, rowing wasn't that unusual as they were both quite argumentative people who found it hard to back down (that *is* genetic). The next morning, as my mum hurriedly packed our things, my dad still hadn't returned. She told myself and Darren to go and look by the swimming pool in case he'd fallen asleep on one of the sun loungers. You see, whereas lots of people search their hotel room for a pair of shoes or glasses when they are doing last-minute packing, with us lot we had to look for family members. He wasn't there. My mum asked if we'd actually looked in the pool to make sure he hadn't drowned, but we decided if he had it was too late anyway, so we'd check later before we boarded the coach.

I found out many months later that he'd simply had enough, and couldn't face returning to the stresses of pub life, and so had hitchhiked through the night to a friend's somewhere in Spain. Clearly there were other marriage difficulties otherwise they would have stayed together, left the pub and done something else. It's hard to say what those difficulties were, but I think my dad's access to so much free booze certainly didn't help with the stresses of running a business and bringing up young kids. Plus he had permed hair for a while, which is a form of disability.

You see my dad was a very funny bloke, a very popular man who was always very generous and helpful to those around him. Sadly, and in his own words, he wasn't what you'd call textbook 'dad' material. In a lot of ways I saw him as not so much a father, more of an errant older brother. Which was a shame, because I already had one of those.

PSYCHIATRIST'S OFFICE

BRIAN: Why did you choose a female
        psychiatrist?

LEE: I dunno. I just did.

BRIAN: It's just that there was part of
        me that wonders if, as a result of
        your father leaving home when you
        were young, you trust women more.

LEE: I don't think so. To be honest I
        think the main reason was that I
        once had the character of a female
        psychiatrist in *Not Going Out* and
        I really liked the scenes we did
        together. Plus there was a female
        psychiatrist in *The Sopranos* and I
        thought that was really good, so
        hopefully this will be the same.

        *Lee is worried. He has only seen
        one series of* The Sopranos *but
        from memory the lead character
        ends up having an affair with his
        psychiatrist. Lee is concerned that
        Brian will think the phrase
        'hopefully this will be the same'
        is Lee suggesting they too could
        have an affair one day. Hopefully
        she hasn't seen* The Sopranos.

LEE: Have you seen *The Sopranos*?

BRIAN: Yes.

Shit.

LEE: I always go for opposites when writing. Opposites are funny. Fat and thin. Posh and working class. Men and women. So I suppose it's just a device to make it entertaining. Well, hopefully.

BRIAN: This is one of my concerns about this whole idea. It is *you* that has to be here, in this room. Talking to me with as much honesty as you can. Yet the end result, the book, is for the reader.

LEE: Don't worry about that. Forget the reader completely.

BRIAN: Will you be able to do that?

LEE: Of course.

Lee knows that isn't completely true. In fact, during the session she tells Lee she is from Limerick. Lee is very close to saying that he was once mugged in Limerick, the city not the style. This is an old stand-up routine he used to do which was followed by Lee acting out being mugged in the style of a limerick:

*'Hello, my name is Pete
I'm standing in the street
Give me your cash
Don't be flash
Or I'll kick you in the teeth'*

*Lee would never even think of doing something like this normally as he would never usually dream of using any of his material unless he is on stage. But he sort of hoped the awkward reaction of the psychiatrist to Lee doing it would make good reading. So he clearly **does** have one eye on the reader. Then again, he didn't actually do it, so maybe he is able to 'be in the room'.*

LEE: Don't get me wrong, I'm not saying my dad leaving home didn't have *any* effect on me. Of course it did. I've heard it said, 'Show me a comedian and I'll show you a man whose mother died when he was a kid.' The absent parent is a common theme with comics, I know that. It's just not a conscious thing with me. And to be honest even if I did think that, I'd be reluctant to talk about it in a book.

BRIAN: Why?

LEE: Because I just think there's too many comedians who talk about their personal issues, and I don't really want to be one of them. Some things aren't for sale. Aren't comedians supposed to tell jokes? When did they suddenly start going on telly to do other things? Like learning to dance, or

telling people they used to have
eating disorders?

BRIAN: It feels like there's a conflict
         in you - you don't want your book
         to talk about things too
         autobiographical . . .

LEE: Exactly. I want it just to be
         about getting into comedy.

BRIAN: Yet you appreciate that wanting to
         get into comedy started in
         childhood, so your childhood is
         relevant.

LEE: Yeah. In fact, by coming here to
         see you I sort of get the best of
         both worlds. Touch on the
         personal, without looking like I'm
         opening up too much. Basically I
         want to have my cake and eat it.
         That's not a joke about eating
         disorders by the way.

BRIAN: Do you know Freud said there was
         no such thing as jokes?

LEE: He obviously hasn't worked with Tim
         Vine. Trust me, sometimes there's
         too many.

CHAPTER TWO

Rock on, Tommy

Although my mum fought on to try and run the pub on her own for a while, it proved impossible and soon we had to move out of the pub and on to the estate. Suddenly we were no longer the kids with the cool house. We were now the kids that used to have the cool house. Which is actually worse than being the kids who never had the cool house. We didn't last long in our role as recently deposed squires of the land and very soon my mum decided it was time to move back to our hometown of Southport to be nearer the rest of our family. It was decided that my brother Darren would live with my dad, now settled back in Blackburn having returned from his extended Pontinental holiday, and I would live with my mum. My brother was (and still is, and probably will continue to be) two years older than me and was in his third year of secondary school in Blackburn, and so was a lot more settled in this school than me. He was also a lot more academic than me and doing well, so staying with my dad and keeping at the same school seemed to make sense at the time, whereas I had only just started secondary school so moving to a new one felt less of an issue. So now four had become two (but at least me and my mum got custody of the dog).

It was now 1980, I was twelve and I was living back in Southport and at my new school, Stanley High. To this day I'm still not sure who Stanley is, or was, but I like to think he was the man who invented the box cutter. I joined halfway through the second year, which, in new money, I believe is now year eight. If I had to trace my stand-up comedy career back to a starting point I think that this would be it.

Having spent the last few years living in the industrial Lancashire towns of Blackburn and Rochdale I arrived back in Southport with a very strong Lancastrian accent. Southport, although in Lancashire,* has a much softer accent than other Lancashire towns and is a sort of hybrid of Lancastrian and very soft Scouse (some of the snobbier golf club members of Southport won't forgive me for saying that, but live with it, Hyacinth Bucket, it's true). My accent may have been strong, but

* Actually Southport is in Merseyside and has been since Merseyside was created in 1974. But this has been a bone of contention with some Southport residents, who still insist on writing 'Lancashire' on their letters. Although I'm more than happy to write 'Merseyside' on letters, I consider myself from Lancashire because that's where Southport was when I was born. If there's anyone reading this from my local county council and you want to complain, then please feel free to write to me under my new name of 'Frankie Boyle', a name I adopted in 1974.

I didn't have a physique to match. I was one of the smallest, and certainly skinniest, kids in my year. It's a great mystery to me, how I could have moved from one town to another, less than an hour away, and gone from being average size to suddenly the little kid. The only explanation I can think of is the sea air of Southport made kids a lot healthier than the industrial mill towns of Blackburn and Rochdale. Basically it felt like I'd gone from the film set of *Kes* to *Land of the Giants*. Suddenly, I was surrounded by bigger people. Much bigger. Especially the girls. They towered over me like Amazonian goddesses, and added to the fact that I was a bit of a late developer, trying to go out with one of them was like asking Kenneth Williams to take on Lennox Lewis.

I needed another way to win them over.

I noticed that the other kids were fascinated by my accent and used to tease me about it. It was clear that this was good-natured so I totally embraced it, and probably exaggerated it. At the time Cannon and Ball were big on the telly, and it was pointed out to me that I sounded like Bobby Ball. Again, I embraced this, and learned how to do an impression of him and before long I was doing what I still see as my first ever 'performance'. I stood on the roof of a Portakabin (quite a high 'stage' admittedly, but needs must) and a crowd of kids gathered round as I spent five minutes giving them all the Bobby Ball catchphrases I could remember. 'Rock on, Tommy!', 'You've got my skin!', 'You piggin' hate me!', they were all there and I stormed it. Well, that's how I like to picture it anyway – the reality was probably that a few kids just stood around as the lunatic shouted on the roof, but it garnered me a few laughs and I remember thinking 'Yeah, I like this.' From then on I was the archetypal class clown. Up until this point I was quite a studious child, with fairly good grades. Not as academic as my brother, but certainly more in the 'swotty' gang rather than the 'trouble' gang. Looking back at my school reports, which I still have, you can clearly see a steady decline from this point onwards, which culminated in me failing all but two of my 'O-levels', English and geography. These two subjects have come in handy over the years as it means I always know where the Boggle set is.

Passing geography was a particularly proud moment for me, as a year earlier my mum had kicked up a huge fuss about which exam I would be taking. In those days there were two exams, O-levels for the bright kids, CSEs for the less academic. Brutal streaming that told you from the outset what they thought of you. A year before your exams you took 'mocks', a sort of pretend exam to find out how you were getting on. Although I scraped through my 'mock' geography O-level it was decided that I was on the steady decline downwards (as the rest of my reports prove) and that I was never going to pass the O-level the following year. So I was relegated to CSE, but my mum wasn't having any of it. She went to the school to complain, arguing that whatever they thought of me, I had just passed the 'mock'. After a long stand-off where she wouldn't back down (genetic), it was agreed I would stay in the O-level class. I'd like to tell you that I spent that year proving my mum right and really knuckling down to work, but the truth is I carried on messing about and getting into trouble, but somehow, miraculously, I scraped a pass. Years later my mate's younger brother started at the same school and apparently the geography teacher had a little saying that he used to repeat to the new pupils each year: 'If Lee McKillop can pass his O-level geography, then anyone can.' A fact that came up in *Would I Lie to You?* many years later.

In fact, if I'd have known when I was at school just how valuable 'truths' would be on *Would I Lie to You?*, bearing in mind I need at least two or three every series, I'd have probably spent my schooldays doing things like learning to play the trumpet with my arsehole.

The same person who tried to demote me is also the same teacher who wrote my favourite comment of all in my school reports: 'Sooner or later Lee will realize that joking around in class will get him nowhere.' I have mentioned this in many an interview, and the obvious reason I like it is that joking around has not only got me somewhere, it's actually led to the only proper career I've ever had. But the other reason I like it is because he was actually right. Without my ability to be more focused on the more mundane academic side to comedy, i.e. the writing, I really would have, like he said, got nowhere. So if you are reading this Mr Taylor of Stanley High School 1984, it did go into my brain at some level and wasn't wasted words. Having said that, my mum was right about the geography O-level and you were wrong. So, one-all.

One of my more bizarre experiences at Stanley was the video nights. The video nights consisted of one of the teachers putting on films for the kids to watch after school, in exchange for twenty pence, which went towards the new minibus fund. This practice was, and I'm sure still is, highly illegal as you were effectively setting up an unlicensed cinema. But what made it even more bizarre were the films we watched. Over the course of three weeks we watched *The Texas Chainsaw Massacre*, *The Exterminator* and *Shogun Assassin*. All these films were not only X-rated (in new money that's an 18 certificate), they were all actually banned for many, many years shortly afterwards. I remember walking home with my mate Cleggy, two twelve-year-olds utterly terrified at what we'd seen. This to me is so odd I sometimes have to check with my old school mates if it really did happen, but it did. I wouldn't lie to you. Well, I would, but only within a BBC-formatted panel show and for a reasonable fee. You'd have thought our parents would have complained (actually mine would have laughed), but you have to remember that the concept of video nasties hadn't been coined by the press yet, as video films were in their infancy, so it wasn't on the 'agenda'. X-rated films were just never seen by children, as they weren't on the TV, and in the pre-computer, pre-DVD, pre-YouTube age, there simply was no access to them. So whether children should or shouldn't be watching them wasn't even a debate at this point, it just didn't happen. Well until the head of physics at Stanley High changed all that in 1981.

During this period of my life, other things were happening away from school. My mum had a couple of new relationships, some terrible, some really terrible, eventually leading to a new permanent man in her life. Two had now become three, and we were heading towards getting a full squad again. But, to keep the football analogy going, the new striker couldn't adapt to the system he was expected to play in, and the fifty-million-pound signing was soon barracked by the crowd for his inability to gel with the team. After a lot of boardroom disputes, the new striker was eventually asked to leave, and the squad was back to its depleted, but thankfully calmer, self (if any libel lawyer can sift through that and win the case, you deserve the money).

Shortly after they split my mum fell ill and needed to go into hospital for a while, so now not only had three become two, two had now become one, and not in a good way like the Spice Girls' song (actually, thinking about it, if I was talking about 'two becoming one' in relation to me and my mum in the same way as the Spice Girl song it wouldn't be good, would it?). There was no way I was going to keep in the Premiership with only one man on the pitch, I needed to look to the January transfer window (I might stop this football analogy now). I ended up staying with my Auntie Frances (my mum's sister), my Uncle Jim and their daughter Alison. It was supposed to be a temporary thing whilst my mum was ill, but when my mum returned home from hospital, despite the pleas of the fans, she had decided to re-sign the striker on a trial basis (I promise that's the last one). I really, really didn't want to go back to what I considered the madhouse. I was now fourteen and I decided I was enjoying the stability that this new 'family' was giving me. This was a traditional nuclear family set-up that I wasn't used to and having had a fairly turbulent few years I asked if I could stay where I was for a while. It was agreed, and although I probably didn't appreciate it at the time, now I've got three children myself, I can see just how much of a sacrifice taking on someone else's child must be. I let them know how much I appreciated them at the time, the best way I knew how. I went shoplifting.

I wasn't a particularly wild child, but it's fair to say that due to the upheaval of the previous few years I had a waning respect for authority, be it parents, teachers or shop-owners. As far as I was concerned if Woolworths were going to price me out of the market, I would have to just take it. To this day I cannot believe that I thought it was a good idea to try and steal a poster that was wrapped in a four-foot tube. Where the hell was I going to hide it? And the weird thing was, I didn't even know what the picture on the poster was. I just saw the rolled-up tube and grabbed it. I like to think that there was a policeman somewhere unrolling the evidence to discover a massive picture of a My Little Pony and thinking 'This lad's got issues.' Before long I was let off with a caution and was hauled in, with my auntie and uncle, to see the Sergeant for my official telling off. He asked me what exactly I intended to do with my life, especially now my school grades were slipping and I was acting in a criminal manner. I replied 'Become a policeman.' This was an attempt at being rebellious and sarcastic (and funny) but was taken at face value, and the Sergeant was delighted. He spent the next half an hour telling me what a great career it was and how it offered a fantastic pension. To this day I'm convinced he might have done it deliberately just to bore me to tears, and it was him that actually got the last laugh. It obviously worked as I've never been in trouble with the law since, and hopefully it will stay that way, providing no one goes sniffing round Epping Forest with a spade.

So if there is a 'starting point' to me being a comedian, I guess it was these formative years at Stanley High School. Obviously it could be argued that it wasn't just my new school, strong accent and puny body that had brought out the 'comic' in me. This all happened at the same time as my parents splitting up, my mum's new relationships, and me going to live with my auntie and uncle. All of which, I'm sure, must have had some influence in making me start joking round more. But the truth is, I don't have any conscious recollection of deciding that joking around was a way of coping with the trauma of a family break-up, the same way as I *do* have a conscious memory of joking around as a way of ingratiating myself with new friends at my new school. So, in my head, I always think of my comedy beginning with my change of schools, and *not* my parents breaking up. But who knows?

So there you go, that's how I started thinking 'I know, I might become a comedian.'

I'm glad we've got that out of the way. Now, did I ever tell you about the time I got hammered with Kerry Katona . . .

PSYCHIATRIST'S OFFICE

BRIAN: When you were at school, or ever
          for that matter, was it suggested
          to you that you might have ADHD?

          Lee knows that ADD is 'attention
          deficit disorder', but is not
          aware what ADHD is. Lee has never
          heard that phrase before. Or maybe
          has, but wasn't listening properly.
          He was probably thinking about
          chickens or monkeys.

LEE: No. What does the 'H' stand for?

BRIAN: Hyperactivity.

          Lee doesn't like this. He doesn't
          mind 'attention deficit disorder'
          (although it's the first time it's
          been suggested that he might have
          it) as he knows that most people
          are boring, so why listen anyway.
          But hyperactivity suggests he acts
          like a seven-year-old after too
          much Sunny Delight.

LEE: No. Why, do *you* think I've got it?

BRIAN: I think it's possible.

LEE: I doubt it. To do the amount of
          writing I do I have to be
          completely focused. Almost
          obsessively, otherwise it wouldn't

get done.

BRIAN: A symptom of it can be hyper-
         focus. It's not just a disorder
         that manifests itself with people
         being unfocused, it can also mean
         the opposite, that people can
         become really, *really* focused on
         things.

         Lee is sceptical. To him that is
         like saying an alcoholic is
         someone who drinks loads, or they
         don't drink at all. He thinks
         about saying that to Brian, then
         realizes in fact that that is a
         perfect description of an
         alcoholic, and so will be
         supporting her argument, not his
         own.

LEE: Well it's never been said before.
         Maybe it hadn't been invented in
         the 1970s.

BRIAN: But you were the class clown at
         school.

LEE: So?

BRIAN: That is a classic sign of ADHD.

LEE: What other signs are there?

BRIAN: Inattentiveness.

LEE: Surely that's every child. That
         means all my kids must have it.

*Lee is suddenly worried. Despite
the fact that on the outside he is
slightly dismissing the idea, on
the inside he thinks he probably
does have it. He's never thought
this before – in fact, up until
twenty seconds ago he hadn't even
heard of it – but now not only is
he convinced he has it, he assumes
it will probably kill him. That's
if his wife doesn't kill him first
of course, because it might be
hereditary, and he is already
responsible for passing on the
bad-eyesight gene.*

LEE: Is it hereditary?

BRIAN: Highly.

*Oh crap. 'Highly' – that's worse
than 'yes'. Fingers crossed; maybe
Lee's bad northern diet will be
passed on too, and so his kids
will get obese, and this will
cancel out the hyperactivity.*

BRIAN: You said yourself earlier in the
         book that maybe it's possible to
         pass on, genetically, an inability
         for the brain to develop in
         certain areas, and so a certain
         part of the brain is stuck in a
         childlike state, which perhaps
         leads to 'joking around'. You
         could have been talking about ADHD
         without even realizing.

LEE: If you have it, do you have it for
           life?

BRIAN: Sixty per cent of people grow out
           of it by their late teens.

LEE: Maybe I was one of those sixty per
           cent.

BRIAN: I don't think you are.

LEE: Oh.

BRIAN: Don't worry, it's been around
           since the caveman days. Nature
           selected individuals with this
           predisposition to be the ones who
           often were the risk takers,
           impulsive and on the lookout for
           danger.

           *Lee now hopes he has this brave
           condition.*

BRIAN: Unfortunately, in the caveman days,
           the ones with ADHD were usually
           eliminated first, but at least it
           gave the rest of the tribe a
           chance to escape.

           *Lee wants rid of this crippling
           disease.*

CHAPTER THREE

My name's Ben Elton, goodnight

During my school days, and the 1980s in general, something major happened in the world of showbiz; no, not Keith Harris branching out from Orville and developing Cuddles the monkey (although that was big, and I (genuinely) still say 'I hate that duck' each time I sniff), the birth of 'alternative comedy'. And I loved it.

Old-school comedians, who at the time were being pushed to the side, have often used the tired old quote of 'Alternative? Yeah, it's an alternative to laughing' as a way of dismissing the new wave of comedy that happened around this time, but for me it was far from this. It was gut-wrenchingly, hilariously (I'm almost tempted to say life-changingly, but is that too much?) brilliant. I talked before about how moving to a new school was probably the starting point for me becoming a comedian, but alternative comedy was also a major, major factor. But alternative comedy in the early 1980s was very much a London thing. There were certainly no alternative clubs in the north, and even if there had been I was twelve and there was no way I would have been allowed to go. Even my liberal, party-loving, laid-back parents drew the line. So everything I saw was on the telly.

If I had to pick two TV shows that had the most influence on me at the time, it was *The Young Ones* and *Saturday Live* (which went on to become *Friday Night Live* when it moved to . . . well, I'm sure you can work it out).

The link between both these shows is Ben Elton, who co-wrote the former and hosted the latter. Nowadays many people – surprisingly a lot of comedians – have a go at Ben Elton for 'selling out'. This is mainly due to him going from ranting, leftie stand-up comedian to West End theatre man, hob-nobbing with Andrew Lloyd Webber and writing a musical about Queen, a band who were happy to play in South Africa during Apartheid when many other bands refused to go (bizarrely Queen themselves seem to have found it a lot easier to shake off this stigma than the bloke who wrote the musical about them, which I've always seen as a little odd). I've never had a problem with Ben Elton; in fact I think he's bloody brilliant, and finding out a bloke who once did left-wing, anti-Thatcher rants, but who is now a little more 'establishment' than his gags suggested, is about as shocking as finding out Bernard Manning's mother-in-law was in fact of average weight. To me it was, and still is, very clear. He was a stand-up comedian telling jokes, and anyone who saw him as a political influence, and therefore now a sell-out, should probably look towards politicians for a political steer rather than speccy, shiny-suited light entertainers. Because I wasn't looking at Ben Elton the political activist, I was looking at Ben Elton the 'front man' of alternative comedy, which I loved. Because alternative comedy was my punk.

As I get older I now realize the 'alternative' comedy scene also had its drawbacks, the main one being its absolutely dismissive attitude towards anything that preceded it. The alternative scene was very much the Khmer Rouge of comedy, counting itself as year zero with a new fresh start. All the other comedians, Jimmy Tarbuck, Brucie, Cannon and Ball, they were all rounded up, taken into a field and shot by Pol Pot (Alexei Sayle).

Obviously I had watched comedy before this 'revolution'. In fact, there was one show that, looking back, must have made a real impression on me. It was the Royal Variety Performance and a comedian I didn't even know, or indeed cannot now even remember, was on the bill. I didn't take much notice of his act, but I did see him meet the Queen afterwards and I remember thinking he must be famous. Because to be a comedian who meets the Queen you must have to be really, really successful, and really, really funny.

I still haven't met her. But I've met Duncan Goodhew.

There were other shows too. Thursday nights were the nights me and Darren had a Curly Wurly and watched *It Ain't Half Hot Mum*, a show which somehow managed to be brilliant and terrible at the same time. There are many things in life that seem to fit into this unusual category, and I highly recommend compiling a list. It's a great game. Mine currently stands at *It Ain't Half Hot Mum*, 'Stay Another Day' by East 17, my parents' mentality to life, fame, fudge and juggling.

Then there were shows like *Fawlty Towers*, *Morecambe and Wise*, *Steptoe and Son*, *Some Mothers Do 'Ave 'Em*. But although I've grown to think of these shows as 'classics', at the time they weren't the thing that ignited my desire to be a comedian myself. That all came after 1980. Again, it's to do with my slightly anarchic parents, I think. Loads of comedians talk about sitting round with their mums and dads watching *Morecambe and Wise* when they were younger, but I've got far more memories of sitting with my mum watching Vyvyan in *The Young Ones* shoving six-inch nails into people's heads. It's odd, and also very pleasing, having a mum whose favourite television show of all time is *Bottom*.

When I say I wanted to become a comedian, it still very much felt like an abstract concept when I was at school. It wasn't really ever going to happen. It was very much a dream, in the same way as wanting to become an astronaut, or a professional footballer. It was one thing wanting it, but you knew in the back of your mind it was an unrealistic aim. I'd seen people on *Saturday Live* performing comedy, but that wasn't in real life, that was on the telly. And being on the telly was as alien as being on the moon or playing at Old Trafford. It's hard to imagine nowadays, but there was a time, and I think my generation will be the last to grow up with this, where seeing yourself on a TV screen never happened. Nowadays with video cameras and video phones, seeing yourself on a screen is a completely normal concept. In fact people often ask what my kids think when they see me on the telly. And the truth is, not much (a bit like the *Observer*). Because they see themselves on a TV screen all the time, because we're always filming them, or they're filming themselves, like all kids do nowadays. But when I was growing up, video cameras didn't exist. So seeing yourself on a TV screen just didn't happen. And this all just added to the notion that television was for 'other' people. For the select few. For the famous and 'special' people. That's why, when I was called in to see the careers officer, I didn't say I wanted to be a comedian. Because I didn't really think that was realistic, I thought that would be the overly ambitious ramblings of a teenager who hadn't thought things through properly. It was a silly dream.

So I said professional golfer instead.

This wasn't me trying to be cocky or a joke, it was a genuine career option as far as I was concerned, as I'd spent that summer learning to play, and was getting OK at it (well, I'd stopped losing so many balls, and with a bit of practice who knew what could happen). She asked me what my handicap was, and I told her that I didn't have one, as I wasn't a member of a club. But at a guess I'd say it was thirty-six, the maximum allowed. She made it clear that if I was playing off the maximum handicap at fourteen years of age, it was extremely unlikely that I was going to make it as a professional. This irked me and I was determined to prove her wrong. I think I may have even used the phrase 'we'll see about that' in a way that they would in a Hollywood film, where they would then immediately hard cut to the hero putting a twenty-footer for the US Open Championship. But this wasn't a Hollywood film, it was a pipe dream, and a British pipe dream at that, and British pipe dreams always have a smaller budget than American ones. So the hard cut was actually to a year later, with the same careers officer, and with me still playing off the maximum handicap. But being the stubborn person I am who wouldn't be proved wrong, I said 'I've decided to become a caddie.'

But I didn't become a caddie, in fact I didn't really become anything for quite a while. My first proper foray into stand-up comedy was in 1994, but I left school in 1984. So what did I do in those ten years? That's me trying to be literary and introduce the next bit, it's not me having a breakdown and forgetting. I can remember exactly. I pretty much did every job that is not really classed as a career, and you earn less than a hundred quid a week doing.

On leaving school most of my mates went to the local A-level college, but I'd failed most of my O-levels. My mum thought of going down to the college to try and convince them I should be accepted, like she did with the geography O-level incident, but this time it wasn't going to wash (the pleading, not my mum).

I was sixteen and now living back at home with my mum and Fernando Torres (you'll really have to read the earlier bit otherwise that might sound a little odd). It was clear that her and Fernando were staying together and he wasn't getting a move to Inter Milan any time soon, so I'd better just get used to it. Also, now I'd left school, I couldn't really expect to impose on my auntie and uncle any longer, due to the fact that I was now a 'man'. It's one thing taking on a nephew, another taking in a lodger, especially one that hasn't got a job or any particular prospects.

I sat at home one day and realized that being a golfer, or a caddie, was not a realistic career. And I definitely wasn't going to become a comedian because I didn't even really know what that actually meant. The 'special' people on *Saturday Live* weren't like me. They were . . . well, they were comedians. Surely that was something you were born with. So having rejected being a golfer, and a caddie and a comedian . . . oh yeah, and an astronaut (it was pointed out that I'd probably have to go via the RAF, and I hated flying) . . . I decided I had to be more realistic. I had to be grown up and sensible, and I had to realize that my pipe dreams were exactly that: dreams. It was time for a reality check.

I know, I'll become a jockey.

PSYCHIATRIST'S OFFICE

LEE: I've been having a think about this ADHD thing.

Lee hasn't just been 'having a think', he's been looking it up online all the time since it was suggested. It's now his new obsession. But by saying 'having a think' it suggests Lee is not that bothered about it. This is also helped by adding the word 'thing' at the end. It suggests a casual attitude towards this disorder, almost like he hasn't quite decided if he's going to have ADHD or not.

LEE: You said it's been around since the caveman days.

Lee suddenly starts thinking about Captain Caveman and wonders if this is because of the ADHD, or simply because he used to watch too much television.

BRIAN: Yes.

LEE: And that it was a kind of benefit to the group. It was 'needed'.

BRIAN: Exactly. It wouldn't have survived as a gene if it wasn't needed.

LEE: Almost like it was all part of
           evolution.

BRIAN: Yeah.

           Lee suddenly becomes aware what
           he's doing, as he often uses this
           technique when talking to people.
           Basically getting people to admit
           to things that have been said, a
           sort of recap of all the things
           which suit his argument, before he
           pounces with the killer statement.
           Lee is convinced he would have
           made a good lawyer and so decides
           to reconsider that voiceover he
           was offered which starts with
           'Have you had an accident at
           work?'

LEE: So if that's the case, why is it
           seen as a 'disorder'?

           Boom. Lee has proved his point and
           now the world of psychiatry will
           have to reconsider its complete
           teachings.

BRIAN: It's an interesting debate.

           Lee is annoyed. She's not supposed
           to act like she's agreeing. What's
           the point in trying to subtly lay
           down the bait of an argument if
           the recipient isn't going to bite?
           He may as well have taken the
           maggot of subtlety from the hook
           and hit the catch with a big club.

*Like the one Captain Caveman used
to have. Lee starts thinking again
about Captain Caveman and tries to
remember his catchphrase. Lee then
realizes he hasn't been listening
to Brian for the last minute or
so.*

BRIAN: It brings up the whole debate
about 'What is mental illness and
does it actually exist?' People
could argue it's just society's
way of viewing things.

*Lee assumes that when she says
'people' she means herself, as Lee
also uses this technique when
debating things. If Lee wants to
sell something as a fact he will
say 'many people' so as to give
credence to his argument. Although
he occasionally misjudges this and
uses it about things that aren't
actually debatable, like the time
he mixed up the names of two
famous astronauts and followed it
with 'Actually, many people believe
that the first man on the moon **was**
Buzz Aldrin.'*

BRIAN: If you were in some lost tribe
somewhere that wasn't in touch
with our consumer society you might
view things differently. For
example, if someone was hearing
voices or seeing visions, we might
label it as schizophrenia, whereas
they might see it as gifted and in

touch with the Gods.

Lee wonders if he is now going to be told he has schizophrenia as well, and this is Brian's way of trying to put a positive spin on it before breaking the news. Like a vet saying 'First the good news, you're going to be saving a lot of money on cat food.'

BRIAN: Basically it's seen as a disorder when it's causing significant impairment. It really can be a major stumbling block. You're not going to be able to pay attention. Your mind's everywhere and it can interfere with learning.

Lee suddenly remembers what it was: 'Captain Caaaaaaaavemannnnnn!!!!!!!'

BRIAN: But having a mild degree of it can be very beneficial in certain cases. Particularly in your job, I would imagine. It can certainly help in having a quick mind.

Lee still can't make his mind up whether he will have ADHD or not, but after weighing up all the pros and cons decides to take it.

CHAPTER FOUR

Wiping Red Rum's bum

To some Red Rum will always be the thing that the child says in the film *The Shining* when he is able to foresee the death of himself and his mother (Red Rum is 'murder' backwards by the way, he wasn't just randomly mentioning Grand National winners from the 1970s). If I'd been that child's mother I'd have sat him down afterwards and said 'If ever you have another premonition that your father's going to run amok and kill us all with an axe, probably best to say the word the right way round. That really wasn't the time for word games.'

But to the many, including myself, Red Rum was the greatest racehorse that ever lived, being the only horse to win the Grand National three times. In fact, since his last win in 1977, no horse has even won it twice, which shows just what an amazing achievement this was. I actually think of him as being one of the greatest sporting heroes this country has produced. But I'm probably a little biased as not only did he come from my hometown, he was also the first horse I ever rode.

I had been sitting at home questioning what I was going to do with my life now I'd left school, and failed most of my O-levels. I couldn't decide, so I did what I often do when I'm unsure about something, I made a cup of tea and put the telly on. Horse racing was on. I'd always liked horse racing, mainly because my Granddad Jack enjoyed a flutter, and I used to love the weird bets he placed. 'Yankee', 'Heinz 57', 'Canadian': all bets where you picked different horses in different races, and if a few (or even better all) came first, you'd win money. (My mate and fellow comedian Sean Lock refers to money you make in comedy as 'winnings' and he's right, that's what it often feels like.)

Plus I'd always loved the Grand National. When we were kids, having this once a year annual bet was very exciting, even though I think our stakes were no more than ten pence. To me, the Grand National was up there with the FA Cup final or Christmas Day. Days that, certainly when I was kid anyway, were about the nation stopping and uniting in a shared experience. Nowadays these days only seem to happen if a princess dies or Andrew Sachs gets a dodgy answering-machine message.

As I watched the horse racing that day on the TV, I suddenly had a realization. Surely it was the only sport where you could get involved at the relatively late age of sixteen and yet still make it as a professional. As long as I was skinny and small (and I still was at sixteen), surely I could make it as a jockey. Even if I grew a bit it wouldn't matter as National Hunt jockeys (i.e. over fences) were bigger than the flat ones. I mean flat as in 'not over fences', I don't mean squashed ones. Obviously everyone is bigger than that type.

And how hard could it actually be sitting on a horse? After all, I'd almost made it as professional golfer/caddie/astronaut and they were much harder to do surely? They involved skill/lifting/flying (respectively), but this would only involve sitting. And if there was one thing I loved more than the Grand National, it was sitting. I decided, there and then, I was going to become a jockey. But not only a jockey, a Grand National-winning jockey, like John Hurt and Elizabeth Taylor (Taylor was later disqualified for not staying in the saddle until reaching the weighing enclosure – if you don't know what I'm talking about get on Wikipedia).

Like every resident of Southport, I knew that Red Rum was trained in our hometown by the legendary Ginger McCain, a man who got his name from his love of oven-ready chips (not sure where the 'Ginger' bit comes from though). His achievements were even more remarkable, because instead of being in the countryside and having fancy gallops like virtually every other trainer in the country, he operated from the back of a secondhand car lot on a fairly busy road. He would train his horses on the beach at Southport, and many attribute his walks in the sea as the 'magic formula' that fixed his injury-prone hooves (Red Rum's, not Ginger's). When I was sixteen, Red Rum was seven years into his retirement, but was still at the stables and still quite a celebrity in the town. So I immediately found the number and phoned. A woman answered, and the conversation went something like this:

Me: Hello is that Ginger McCain?

Her: No.

Me: I mean the stables . . . I know you're not Ginger.

Her: I might be.

Me: Are you looking for any jockeys?

Her: Well, they're quite small, but I think we've got them all accounted for.

(She didn't say that, but I wish she had. She actually said 'No'.)

Me: What about stable boys?

Her: Have you got any experience?

Me: No. But I like horse racing. And I'm very sporty. I almost became a professional golfer/caddie/astronaut.

Her: How heavy are you?

Me: Seven and a half stone.

(I wasn't, I was about nine stone, but I thought I'd try it on.)

Her: That's very light.

Me: Well, you can see why I'd have struggled with a bag of golf clubs.

Her: Come to the stables tomorrow and we'll have a chat.

The next day I went to the stables and I tried to work out which horse was Red Rum. I couldn't tell, they all looked the same. I know, racist. Much easier to spot when they've got their nosebands and jockeys sat on top in distinctive colours. The woman from the phone call looked me up and down, which considering my height didn't take long.

Her: You're not seven and a half stone.

Me: I might have slightly exaggerated.

Her: It doesn't matter. You can be much bigger if you're a National Hunt jockey. Certainly bigger than the flat ones. I don't mean squashed ones, everyone's bigger than those.

Me: Nice one. If I ever write a book can I use that?

Her: Sure.

It was decided, I was going to be the new stable boy on a trial basis where I would work for nothing, and if I proved myself over the next few weeks I would reach the heady heights of YTS* boy and be paid £26.50 a week by the government.

My main job was to muck out the stables and prepare the horses' beds whilst the others took the horses to the beach. It was like I was working at some sort of equine B&B.

On day one Ginger taught me an important lesson. Whilst chatting to me next to a horse, the horse, as horses often do, decided to do a big poo. Ginger told me to chuck it on the manure pile, so I walked off looking for a spade. He immediately called me back and told me that that I needed to get used to using my hands otherwise I'd be spending all day looking for garden tools. He

* The YTS was the 'Youth Training Scheme' and was a way of training sixteen- and seventeen-year-olds in vocations they may have otherwise not been skilled enough to do. Like shovelling horse shit for eight hours a day.

demonstrated the move: you put your hands underneath the straw that the poo is sitting on and lift it so your hands aren't actually touching the poo. Imagine you're looking at horse dung sitting on a plate of straw. If you can't imagine that, order a starter at a Heston Blumenthal restaurant. You then chuck it straight on the manure pile. That might sound disgusting, but you very soon get used to the smell of the stuff as it's an all-day occurrence. The same way you very soon get used to drunken hecklers. A few hours later Ginger spotted some dog poo that the stable mutt had left in the yard and asked me to get rid of it. Now I had a dilemma. Surely now I should get a spade. It was on concrete, so no straw to separate my hand from touching it, but more importantly it was dog poo. And surely no living human being, even a kid not quite ready to go on a YTS, should be asked to do that. But he had made it clear early on that I had to get used to this, and that looking for a spade each time would be a time-consuming act. I stood looking at the poo, then looked at Ginger, who was looking back at me. Maybe this was a test, like Willy Wonka's test on Charlie when he asked him to leave the factory, and Charlie returned the everlasting gobstopper instead of selling it on to Slugworth, which resulted in Charlie inheriting the factory. Maybe if I passed the test Ginger would say 'Well done, son, you're the one! Get your silks on, you're riding in the 3.40 at Kempton tomorrow.' Maybe this was my one and only chance to one day be a future Grand National-winning jockey. I'd made my mind up. I was going to show the great Ginger McCain that I had listened to him, that I learned from him, that I was ready to be the great Sorcerer's apprentice.

'Not with your bloody hands! That's disgusting!'

'But you said—'

'That's horses! Dogs are filthy little things.'

Everyone was looking. It was day one, in a new job, and I had just been chastized for the crime of picking up dog shit with my bare hands.

'I'm just going to go and wash my hands.'

Very soon after starting work there, one of the other stable lads, 'Spider', decided it was time I learned to ride. 'Spider' was obviously his nickname (I have no idea why, maybe he was a Siamese quad that was separated at birth). All stable boys had nicknames. Mine was 'Bruce' (as in Lee), which very soon changed to 'Curly' as I wore round glasses like the character from *Coronation Street*. Apart from the odd donkey at Blackpool, and a bit of pony trekking in Spain, I'd never actually sat on a horse in my life. Certainly not a racehorse. Spider put me on top of one and walked me up and down the stable yard. He then informed me I was sitting on Red Rum. It was only a few steps, and lasted about thirty seconds, but it did mean I could then spend the rest of my life saying 'The first horse I rode was Red Rum.' Which, even though I say so myself, is quite a good claim to fame, and yet another 'truth' that came up on *Would I Lie to You?* many years later.

This story has often been told back to me in many a bastardized version, my favourite being a local reporter who once asked me 'Is it true you rode Red Rum in the Grand National?' I said 'No, you're getting confused. That was Alan Carr. I rode Nijinsky in the Derby.'

The second time I sat on a horse, or as I now think of it, the last time I ever wanted to sit on a horse, came a few weeks later. I was taken out of the stables and on to the road to learn some basic riding skills with one of the Irish jockeys at the stables, 'Murph'. 'Murph' was short for Murphy, not one of the most inspirational nicknames in the history of stable lads, but much more inspired than the other Irish jockey working there, Kevin Doolan, whose nickname was 'Kev'. Murph and Kev had already taught me many things. How to muck out stables; how to tie a bale of hay; how to groom a horse (this was pre-internet, so nothing untoward); how to drink beer; how to stop a horse from kicking you* when you're cleaning out its anus with a sponge (I know, imagine doing it for £26.50 a week); how to socialize with girls much older than you, girls that see *you* as a boy and *themselves* as women; how to leave your hometown, indeed country, and start a new life somewhere else in order to pursue your dreams; how to clean the end of a horse's penis with a sponge (26 pounds bloody 50 a week); and how to speak extremely quickly and almost incomprehensibly in a strong Irish drawl, a skill I would put to the test many years later in one of my favourite sketches from *The Sketch*

---

* You lift one of its legs up. A horse can't kick you when it's stood on three legs. It's like you trying to kick someone whilst you're stood on one leg.

Show. This is a bit of comedy I enjoyed doing so much I'm willing to break my ban on promoting the dubious, copyright-infringing website YouTube by including this link: www.youtube.com/watch?v=TR5yDZO4nZE.*

Murph put me on a horse and decided to teach me some of the basics of riding. I learned, almost immediately, something very important, and probably the most important thing about riding (and comedy). A horse (audience member) knows if you are scared. And if it senses you *are* scared, *it* gets scared, and it runs off with you (not the audience member though). This would be terrifying in the normal circumstance of being on a gallop, or in a field, but to be on a fairly busy street with buses and cars around you, it becomes the single most scary thing that will ever happen to you in your life.

As the horse ran into a fairly quiet suburban street, I thought the worst was over and at least I wasn't going to be hit by a truck. But then I saw that the street had a very sharp left turn at the end and the horse didn't seem to be aware of it. It was like he was going to run straight through the living room of the house we were approaching. When we reached the turn, the horse suddenly realized we had no choice but to turn left, and so despite the ridiculous speed he was travelling, tried to

* It's only after I wrote this that I realized this link won't work because you are probably reading this from the printed page. But I decided to keep it in as I wanted to demonstrate my slightly Catweazle approach to technology. If you don't know who Catweazle is, then here's a link: http://www.youtube.com/watch?v=XUUW4PobzyQ.

turn at a right angle. Horses' feet and concrete are not designed to go together. It would be fair to say that concrete doesn't have much 'give'. In racing terms the ground that day would have be considered 'fast', when in fact only a minimum of 'good to soft' was going to save my life. What happened next is extremely hard to describe, but I can only describe it thus: you know that thing in *Scooby-Doo!* that Scooby and Shaggy do when they're turning a corner, it's a sort of running on the spot combined with a slip, like they've suddenly realized they're running on ice. Well that's what the horse did (and he would have got away with it too if it wasn't for that pesky new jockey). Somehow, and to this day I'm not quite sure how, he didn't fall over and kill me, and instead achieved the heroics of a horse performing in the musical *The Canal Turn on Ice* (a joke only aimed at people who enjoy horse racing). But now I had bigger problems. We were heading towards a field separated by a very large hedge. I was a novice to this jockey game, and I knew nothing about horses, but even I knew that the horse had one intention, and one intention only: to jump that hedge. As we got close to it I'd like to think I thought of something dramatic, like my whole life flashing before me, but to be honest I have absolutely no idea what I was thinking. I suspect it was something along the lines of 'Just how heavy can those golf club bags actually be?' We reached the hedge and the horse seemed to do a sort of crouch as if ready to spring up and over the fence. Then for some reason it stopped and froze. It obviously realized there was an idiot steering the ship, and best to abort mission. It slowly rose from its 'crouch' and stood motionless. I took the opportunity to dismount and seriously review my new ambition to become a jockey.

My confidence never really recovered from that, and although there were many other attempts by me to try and ride, usually involving a horse freaking out and sprinting off down the road with me on its back, I realized very quickly that being a jockey was utterly life-threatening and terrifying. I often get people telling me that stand-up comedy is the bravest, most scary thing a person can do. And they are wrong.

I spent almost a year at McCain's, even though I had virtually given up any ambitions to be a jockey. I'm not sure why I stayed really, but I suspect it was something to do with not knowing what I wanted to do next. I probably aged about five years in that one year, and with the risk of using a literary cliché, I probably started as a boy and ended up leaving as a man. An extremely immature man both physically and mentally, and one with a broken wrist (I'd fallen off a hay wagon), but a sort of man none the less.

I have many fond memories of that time, including sleeping with the one horse I was given to look after, Citrus. I mean literally sleep, in his stable. This hasn't suddenly become the most confessional book in the history of comedy. It would be a very unusual man who skirted round the issue of his mother's relationships by using a football analogy, only to follow it with 'Did I ever tell you about the time I shagged a horse?' There was also the time I took Red Rum for a walk to my grandma's house ('Get that bloody thing off my lawn'). Or the time I took an amorous horse for a walk, and his huge erection took the wing mirror off a Ford Anglia. Or selling 'Red Rum Manure' door to door for fifty pence a bag. And even though all I did was muck out the stables and develop a fear of horses, the year I spent there has always made me feel, however tiny, connected with Red Rum, and for that I will always be grateful. And it was with real sadness when I heard of the death of Ginger McCain in 2011.

If you're looking down, Ginger, you taught me one of the greatest lessons in life. Hands for horses, spades for dogs.

PSYCHIATRIST'S OFFICE

BRIAN: You use the phrase 'self-defence mechanism' throughout the book. Too much in fact. I'd look at that again.

Lee is not happy as he takes that as a criticism. He appreciates that he did say to Brian early on that she must say whatever she thinks and not hold back, but Lee is in showbiz and thus people must understand that this is never meant. Like when a wife says 'Be honest, do I like look nice in this dress?' the number one rule is 'Forget she said, "Be honest".'

BRIAN: 'Self-defence mechanism' is a bit of a label. You've got to be careful with using psycho-babble phrases. It reminds me of an NLP therapist I recently met . . .

Lee doesn't ask what NLP stands for. He's sticking with ADHD and doesn't want anything else.

BRIAN: She was talking about a patient and said 'I used some clean language intervention.' But that phrase meant nothing to me. I thought 'What does that mean? You didn't call her a cunt?'

*Lee is surprised to hear a
psychiatrist swearing. He wonders
if the usual is happening. The
'usual' being that since becoming
a comedian he notices people swear
at him much more. Particularly
people who wouldn't normally do
it, like mums in the playground
who he hardly knows. Lee assumes
this is because they see him
swearing on television and assume
that this is how Lee talks all the
time, so they are trying to do
this as a bonding thing. Lee
always finds this odd. He then
decides that Brian isn't actually
doing this for effect though, and
her swearing is more to do with
the fact that she is Irish,
because in Ireland it is not only
acceptable for people to swear,
it's actually compulsory.*

BRIAN: When we use defence mechanisms,
         they are there to protect our
         vulnerability. Maybe you should
         actually be talking about those
         vulnerabilities rather than the
         fact you're covering them with
         defence mechanisms.

LEE: OK, let's talk about those
         vulnerabilities.

BRIAN: OK.

         There is a long pause.

LEE: Actually, we'll do it next time,
         I'm running out of memory on my
         Dictaphone.

         *Lee knows that isn't true, and
         realizes that he said it as a
         self-defence mechanism.*

CHAPTER FIVE

Darts, dole and bingo

I was fast approaching eighteen years old. Although I still had this vague notion, and that's all it was, a very vague notion, that one day I might become a comedian, I still didn't know what that meant, or more to the point what it involved. All I knew is that I was still, like my school days, joking around with my mates and making them laugh and having a sense that people hopefully did find me funny.

I say 'hopefully' because if there's one thing comedy has taught me, it's that people can pretend to find you funny, even when they don't. When I was at school there was a girl I really fancied. She was taller, much more mature, and in the league table of looks was Premiership as opposed to my second division face. Please be aware though that when I was at school the second division of football was exactly that, one league below the top flight, which meant that, although not exactly in the league of this particular girl, I still had

Championship looks, although some would dispute that and say Vauxhall Conference.* My memory tells me that for years she found me extremely funny and it was a possibility, perhaps when I grew a little taller, that we would go out together. If you'd asked me a couple of years ago how she would describe me back then, I would have guessed something along the lines of 'Very, very funny. Much funnier than the older-looking more developed boys of his age, and despite the fact he wasn't what I would have classed as "my type", his wit and humour won me over and I always secretly liked him.' I say a 'couple of years ago', because she turned up, out of the blue, to one of my stand-up tour dates. I hadn't seen this girl since we were at school. She said to me backstage 'I'll always remember you as the really annoying little kid. You were constantly trying to crack jokes and I found it really irritating.' This wasn't her trying to be cocky, or making 'friendly' banter with the person who'd just been on stage for the last hour and a half and therefore could take the 'ribbing'. I could see this was the truth. I'd misinterpreted her polite laughs at school as genuine admiration. Even if she *had* found me funny (which I suspect she actually did sometimes, he says desperately), she may have also found me irritating as well. That's the thing that many comedians,

* As every football fan realizes, the new name for the top flight of non-League football is in fact the Blue Square Premier. But as every comedy fan knows, having a face like the Vauxhall Conference is funnier than having a face like the Blue Square Premier.

either professional or just the pub joker, can make the mistake of thinking: 'funny' is everything, and no other personality traits count. It's very easy to get a skewed perspective on reality, and certainly about how much you are liked. You can put all your likeability eggs in one basket, the 'funny' basket. You start convincing yourself that if someone finds you funny, you've nailed it, nothing else matters. You're invincible to this person. Likewise, if they don't find you funny, it's game over. So being 'funny' becomes the be all and end all of your thoughts. It starts to matter too much, to the point where you've got too much invested in it. Or put more simply, you go mental.

I've heard women describing their husbands as 'not funny', sometimes even in front of them. I suspect, to all comedians it's the ultimate insult. It's as if they've just said 'This is Peter, my husband, he's OK, I suppose, but he does have a very small penis', whilst Peter looks on, smiling inanely like it's all just friendly banter. Although they might not be funny, they might have other massively appealing facets that comedians might not particularly rate as important, like being very kind and loving. Or great dads. Or good in bed.

I've always had a fear of comedy giving me an artificial view of things. It's probably why I avoid things like Twitter. Often people in the world of showbiz will convince others (and themselves) that they like Twitter because 'it's a "marketing tool"', or 'it's a way of engaging immediately with my audience' or 'it's a great way to share information with like-minded people' or many, many other justifications for it. To some extent these factors are all true. However, the single most overriding reason why most of them do it, and I have very good friends who do Twitter who will hate me for saying this, is so they can be told how great they are on a regular basis. And it works, they *are* told this. This is what leads to the skewed perspective. If 95 per cent of people tell you you're brilliant, or hilarious, or amazing, and 5 per cent call you an unfunny prick – and that's the problem with Twitter, a maximum of 140 characters doesn't attract moderate opinions – then it's easy to conclude this is a fair demographic representation of the nation; that 95 per cent of people love you and 5 per cent hate you – which is actually quite a good statistic for the performer if it were true. But it's not. The real truth is most people, actually a very, very large proportion of people, feel nothing towards you. In fact a lot more people than most comedians would even want to acknowledge haven't even *heard* of you. And that doesn't sit well with a lot of comics, because that's what joking around was about in the first place, to get noticed.

Twitter is shit. I have tried to dip in to see what it's about, but it is woefully dull. I looked at various people's tweets but found none of them in the slightest bit engaging. I'm starting to wonder if 'less than 140 characters' refers to the amount of interesting people using it.

I don't want any more of a skewed perspective than being on stage already gives you. If you're making three thousand people laugh, or hopefully most people in the audience anyway, it's easy for the brain to convince itself that 'Most people think I'm hilarious.' But they don't. Most people in your audience do, but that's not the same thing. Most people in the real world are actually very, very indifferent about most performers.

However, that is the perspective of a 43-year-old comedian writing an autobiography, not the perspective of a lad approaching eighteen who still thinks that if people laugh at him, he's invincible. I did know, however, that it was all well and good making your mates laugh, but it wasn't a career. That's what I needed now. I had already put to bed the idea of golfer/caddie/astronaut, and there was now room in the bed for 'jockey' (there's always room in a bed for a jockey). 'Comedian' hadn't been put to bed, because, like I say, 'comedian' wasn't even a viable option. I couldn't put 'comedian' to bed any more than I could put Kim Wilde to bed, or the girl at school who I thought found me funny, but actually found me irritating. Remember, at that time, me becoming a comedian was so far off the spectrum of thought that 'astronaut' genuinely was more of a viable option in my head. I felt there was more chance of me going to the moon than being a comic (some critics will say NASA's loss is comedy's loss).

So I was approaching eighteen. I needed a job and money. It was time to grow up and forget such lofty ambitions and ground myself once again in the world of reality. Even I was starting to see that to think you can start riding a horse at the late age of sixteen, and still make it as a professional, was the rambling thoughts of a dreamer.

I know, I thought, I'll become a professional darts player.

Darts was something I'd always been quite good at, mainly because I grew up in a pub and started at an early age. The same applied to pinball, but that wasn't a professional sport. Darts has recently had a major facelift, and once again, thankfully, it's on the up. A lot of this is due to the money and coverage Sky TV has given it, which sadly means that only a relatively small amount of people actually watch it on the telly, but in the mid-eighties it was different. Darts was massive. So I thought, yeah, I'll have a go at that. Now when I say I was good at darts, what I mean is, in relation to other sports. That possibly says more about how good I was at other sports. Remember how good I was at golf, and I still thought I could make it as a professional? Well, apply that logic to darts. I wasn't in a team, I didn't play regularly and I didn't own a dartboard. What I mean is, when I was a kid growing up in the pub, I was good. And even then, only for my age. I decided if I was going to be World Champion (and that's what I had decided, like winning the Grand National; just becoming a professional wasn't enough), I'd better start practising.

The next year was spent on the dole, playing darts in my bedroom. All day, and I mean all day, locked in my bedroom chucking arrers (as we professionals call 'em). If you'd walked past my bedroom in 1986 all you would have heard is three thuds, followed by a long pause, followed by three thuds, followed by a long pause. All day, every day. It would have sounded like a teenage boy discovering the pleasure of self-abuse, but without the energy to really get the job done.

For a short time I got good at it (darts, not self-abuse). And when I say good, I mean really good. Hitting one hundred and eighties became a regular thing, and I remember once, at my peak, hitting ten consecutive sets of arrows which amounted to: three one hundred and eighties, four one hundred and forties, and three one hundreds. That, I thought, is the standard of a professional player. But, of course, it isn't really. Top players are throwing practice arrows like that, all day, every day, for *years*. More importantly they can do it in tournaments. I'd had an extremely good few minutes in my bedroom (no, we're *still* not talking about self-abuse). The reality was I was way off the standard of being good enough, and I mean *way* off. However, I had something that most other people didn't have: blind optimism, bordering on the delusional.

I joined a local team, which was in the pub I'd started going to next to McCain's stables, The Upsteps. This was just a stopgap of course, I was planning on being World Champion in, say, two to three years, but I figured I'd better join a team to keep me going until then. I was rubbish. Once I was out of the bedroom I couldn't perform (I usually have the opposite problem). One of the reasons I put it down to at the time was the lack of bed between the dartboard and myself when I was playing in the pub. In my tiny bedroom I had to throw the darts, then walk round the bed, retrieve the darts, and do it again. If you do that for eight hours a day suddenly it feels very weird when there's no bed there. There's no actual written rule in darts that says you can't place a bed between you and the board, so maybe that's what I should have done. It certainly would have been the best 'walk-on' of any darts player in the game. It's all well and good Phil Taylor getting the crowd going with his walk-on music of 'I've Got the Power', but it counts for nothing if the crowd has just witnessed the far more impressive spectacle of a man dragging his bed on to the stage with him.

The bigger problem I had was nerves. As soon as people were watching I went to pieces. Of all the things that feeling nervous doesn't suit, it's darts. I cannot think of a single activity that a shaking hand is more brutally unforgiving towards, apart from brain surgery, bomb disposal, microscopic anatomy, heart surgery and all the other ones I *can* actually think of when I use a bit of common sense. Oh yeah, and comedy.

If the audience can see you're nervous, it's game over. There are a few exceptions of course. I've seen Lee Evans starting his set with lines like 'I'm bricking it', and then spending the next hour or so nervously pacing round the stage wiping the sweat off his brow. That, however, is different because he's magnifying that aspect of his character and playing on it. He took years to hone that skill. Most comics, including myself, have a stage persona of looking, to a degree, in control, so once the cracks of nerves show through, the game's up. A lot of performers believe it is good to be nervous on stage. They say it releases endorphins and makes you the performer you are. I don't believe that. I think this is something that really nervous performers convince themselves of so they can justify the horrible feeling they get before they go on stage. Comedians hate nerves because it reminds them that deep down they think they are crap. And yet they have to walk out on stage like Billy Cocky Pants and pretend the opposite. This is a stressful way to live, which leads to heavy drinking, self-abuse and brothels. Just remember that next time you're watching the Chuckle Brothers.

There are basically three feelings I have had on stage (and just before, backstage). The first, and best, is absolute confidence, where I know, even before I go on, that things will be good, and I will be on form. That is only a minority of times though. The majority of times I feel a second way – slightly nervous. This is not as good as the first, but infinitely better than the third feeling, which is the worst: apathy. If I'm feeling apathetic before I go on, and there's no rhyme or reason why this seems to happen, but it does happen, probably about as much as the 'absolute confidence' feeling (but still in the minority in comparison to the 'slightly nervous' feeling), I know it's going to be a tough night. I suspect the audience may not notice it, but I sense the night slipping sometimes, as I feel I simply don't care enough. Like I say, this is a very unusual state to be in, probably once or twice on the whole of my last 135-date tour, but it still happens. It used to happen a lot more when I was on the circuit, and doing sometimes up to five gigs a night. I don't know what causes it; tiredness, boredom, maybe even *over*-confidence, but it happens, and when it does I know I'm in trouble unless I suddenly snap out of it. I am ashamed (well, only a bit) to admit that once, on tour, I seriously contemplated setting up a hidden TV screen at the front of the stage so I could watch an England football match whilst doing the show. I definitely think that is under the 'apathetic' heading. I know, not great, but in my defence it was Croydon.

It soon became clear that professional darts was not an option. Well, actually what I mean is, being the World Champion in two years wasn't an option, as that was the actual goal. I still think that if I had carried on, locked in that bedroom for years and years, I could have made it as a professional darts player (but bear in mind I'm slightly delusional). It's one of the biggest thrills of my life that a couple of years ago I got to play a game against the legendary Eric Bristow in front of a packed crowd of twenty-six people, and beat him. I think by Eric's own admission he's not the player he used to be after suffering from 'dartitis', a condition which can stop the thrower releasing the dart, but it was a victory none the less.

After the darts player had jumped into the bed and joined the orgy with the golfer, the caddie and the astronaut, I needed to once again seriously review my career options. A visit to the job centre was needed, and before long I was working in the Top Rank Bingo Hall in Southport. I'd finally stopped dreaming of un-attainable goals. Or maybe I hadn't.

Looking back I'm not sure if I was simply growing up during this period of my life, and so wanting ridiculously grand career paths seemed ludicrous, or I was having the first, more grounded realization that actually I really *did* want to become a comedian. So until that day arrived, and that's exactly how it felt, that one day it would just magically be somehow offered to me, then literally any old job would do. I felt I was just biding my time until a famous film director would overhear me making my mates laugh in a pub and say 'You're hilarious, fancy becoming a famous comedian?' – you know, that sort of grounded view.

It was 1987 and I was now 'checking the claims'. This involved standing amongst four hundred or so people, predominantly old women, and when they shouted 'House!', I would run over with my microphone and check that they did indeed have a winning claim. It was not even close to the world of comedy, not even remotely in the ballpark of doing what I thought (or at least had some vague notion of thinking) I wanted to actually do, but at least I was making some sort of start, I was using a microphone. Oh yeah, and I was wearing a dickie bow. I was halfway to being a light entertainer. Actually, if you've seen some late-night shows on ITV2, I was ready for action.

I look back on my bingo hall days as being the first few steps towards 'performing', albeit in a very, very small way. Certainly not an intentional move on my part towards some sort of grand masterplan. I didn't have a plan. Being a comedian at this point was as much a distant, unobtainable dream as it had ever been. What it also gave me was my first proper wage packet (fifty-five quid a week) which enabled me to leave home and get my own place for the first time (twenty-five quid a week). Well, I say 'own place' – it was a bedsit round the corner from the bingo hall that was just about big enough for a human being to live in, providing they didn't own a cat and they weren't partial to swinging it. It was difficult living off such a small wage packet, and probably the reason that I soon moved from 'checker' to 'barman' in the bingo hall as at least I then didn't have to budget for beer any more. This wasn't technically stealing, as I was told that after the pipes had been cleaned it was important to taste the beer to check it was OK. It was never specifically stated how much beer constituted a 'taste'. Plus, if you pay peanuts, you get monkeys. If you pay less than peanuts, then you get robbing monkeys (Buddah, 1973).

The year and a half I spent working at the bingo hall were happy times. It was an all-consuming job where you start work early and go home late. This was particularly true when I realized that, even with free beer, the thirty quid a week I had left after my rent wasn't enough to live off, and so I subsidized my income by working for the contract cleaning company that used to get the bingo hall ready for the day. It meant I was arriving at work at about 7.30 a.m. and leaving the building sometimes way after midnight if we all stayed for drinks, which we often did. Especially when *I* was serving, as people liked the staff discount I offered for loyalty cardholders (100 per cent to close friends). Unlike Nectar there were no *actual* loyalty cards, but then again, unlike Nectar, they *were* actual decent rewards. What the bingo hall gave me was a sense of independence. I was now no longer living with my mum and Fernando Torres and I had my own place. I still had this constant nagging doubt that I should be doing something else. Something more fulfilling. Something to do with comedy. But I didn't know how. Also that director hadn't suddenly come over to me in the pub and offered me that film role. I'd even started raising my voice more and started talking really loudly. Either he wasn't hearing me, he didn't think I was funny, or he wasn't actually there.

Still, at least my next job, although not comedy, was finally sort of in the area of 'showbiz'.

After my dad not returning home from holiday, you'd have thought I'd have had enough of Pontin's wouldn't you?

PSYCHIATRIST'S OFFICE

BRIAN: I think you may be eliciting in me
          some sort of protective instinct.

          *Lee assumes she means an instinct
          to protect herself, which must
          mean she thinks Lee, to some
          extent, is being aggressive towards
          her. Lee doesn't like this, as
          he's not aware of it, and so he
          thinks he's being misjudged. He
          wants to tell her in no uncertain
          terms that she's wrong, but he's
          worried that this kind of outburst
          will bring out the protective
          instinct in her.*

LEE: I do that to people.

          *This is Lee being light-hearted,
          although it is actually true.
          Sometimes Lee's passion for
          something has been mistaken for
          aggression when in fact he's
          simply being 'enthused' by his
          train of thought, and Lee feels
          that these people need to realize
          that he is not being 'aggressive',
          the fucking idiots. Lee lets Brian
          talk for a while longer, but it's
          playing on his mind, so he's not
          listening properly (or is that the
          ADHD again?). After a while he
          picks her up on it.*

LEE: Can I bring you back to that thing you said earlier. Why do you feel 'defensive'?

BRIAN: I didn't say defensive. I said protective. And I meant protective over you.

Lee has totally misjudged her comment. Far from being an accusation, it was in fact a nice thing to say. Lee decides to keep his dignity by not showing any remorse on his face. Instead he keeps the 'What did you mean by that?' face on, as though she has still said something wrong. Lee is an idiot.

LEE: What did you mean by that?

BRIAN: It's to do with transference and counter-transference.

Lee changes his look from 'What did you mean by that?' (defensive) to 'What did you mean by that?' (confused).

BRIAN: It means how you relate to me, and how I relate to you. And I'm finding myself becoming protective towards you. I think my protective instinct may be connected to your own relationship with your mother. I notice in the book you talk in much more detail about your father but you don't really talk about your mother. Your mother seems more of an important influence in your life, yet you seem to skirt over certain issues.

LEE: Well, my dad was more like a wayward older brother, and I didn't grow up with him, so he's more detached and so easier to joke about.

At this point Lee wants to say 'He was a really funny man. The kind of man that could read out a telephone directory and it would be funny. To be fair, he used to do it with his cock out. And it wasn't quite as funny when he started phoning people.' Which is one of Lee's old gags. Lee likes this gag because he thinks it's funny, but also it's true. His dad **would** *have been capable of getting his cock out whilst reading the telephone directory to get a laugh. He never did (and certainly would never have then phoned people) but he was capable, and comedically that's enough in Lee's eyes. In fact, that's how Lee judges a lot of people in the world of stand-up comedy. He often asks 'Could they suddenly get their cock out and blow a rapsberry for no reason whatsoever in the middle of their act.' If the answer is yes, then Lee already likes them. It's the*

reason why Lee will always like
comedians such as Johnny Vegas
slightly more than comedians such
as Jerry Seinfeld.

LEE: Plus I was closer to my mum, and
          so if I write about her it might
          start getting mawkish. I don't
          want this book to be overly
          personal or sentimental. Some
          things are too private, even for
          an autobiography. It's not all
          'for sale'.

BRIAN: Why? Would that feel like you were
          prostituting yourself?

LEE: Well, it would feel like I was
          prostituting my mother. And there's
          no way I'm doing that. Not for
          £18.99. If I did prostitute my
          mother, it would need to be for
          nothing less than £19.99.

CHAPTER SIX

Happy camper

When I tell people I worked as a Bluecoat, people usually get confused and think I'm talking about Butlin's. Or sometimes Maplin's, which isn't even a real holiday camp, it's the fictional one in the sitcom *Hi-de-Hi!* It would have been very difficult for me to do a summer season at a BBC One fictional holiday camp set in the 1950s, ten years before I was actually born.

The other mistake is that people assume me going to Pontin's was about fulfilling some sort of dream to become an entertainer. The reality was that I was the only non-performing Bluecoat when I started my summer season in Great Yarmouth in 1988. The rest of the Bluecoats all came from a sort of *Fame*-type performing-arts school where they were taught that fame costs, and this is where they had to start paying in sweat (and their parents' cash).

I had been working at the bingo hall with a guy called Kevin. He left to set up an entertainment agency for children's entertainers and DJs. One day I popped in to see how he was getting on. When I walked in the door he was on the phone trying to get one of his acts an audition for Pontin's. He gestured for me to wait for him to finish the call, then just before he hung up, he put his hand over the mouthpiece and said to me 'Fancy being a Bluecoat at Pontin's?' I thought it was pointless going for the interview because I didn't have any performing skills. 'What can *I* do?' I was probably hoping he'd tell me he'd spotted something in me and that he knew I was destined for great things. Maybe he'd heard me singing at work and knew I was a talent that needed nurturing, or I had the natural physique of a dancer. Or, even better, he thought I could become a comedian.

'Be the sports organizer, they don't go on stage.' Oh.

The next day I was at Pontin's in Blackpool watching children's entertainers and singers get up one by one and audition to get their summer season booking. I sat there waiting to be called over thinking I didn't have a hope. I couldn't do anything. I'd never been on stage in my life, apart from a bit of bingo calling and the odd nativity. I wasn't even that good at sports. I decided to do what I always do in these situations. Lie.

I told the man who interviewed me that although I wasn't able to perform, I was an extremely proficient sportsman. I told him I was a county-level snooker player. Not only was that a blatant lie, I'm not even sure it makes sense. I don't think snooker players play at 'county level'. Luckily he knew less about snooker than I did, which meant he knew less than nothing. He was also probably glad of the break (that's honestly not a snooker joke), as me not performing meant that he didn't have to watch, for the twentieth time that day, a fully grown man asking him, another fully grown man, if he'd like a poodle or giraffe (balloon modelling, not a bribe). Although he accepted I couldn't offer anything performance-wise, he did tell me that I would be required to take part in the big Friday night Bluecoat show, where I would have to 'skip around like a twat and wave my hands like an idiot'. He didn't say those words obviously, but if he'd been more honest than I was being about my snooker abilities, that's what he'd have said, because that's what you have to do when you're a Bluecoat at Pontin's and you have no performing skills.

So I got the call a few days later to tell me I had got the job and was starting in a few months' time at Pontin's in Hemsby. I asked where Hemsby was, and was told 'Great Yarmouth'. I asked where Great Yarmouth was and was told 'Norfolk'. I asked where Norfolk was and was told to 'buy a map'. That last bit of the conversation never actually happened, but it's a fair reflection of my lack of knowledge at the time, despite my O-level geography.

When I found out where Hemsby was it was a bit of a shock, as it was the furthest Pontin's from my home (Pontinental had closed at this point. Hardly surprising, bloody marriage wreckers). So now I had to tell my then girlfriend that I was going to be going away for the summer season to work. She'd assumed that when I'd gone for the interview I was going for a job at the Pontin's in my hometown of Southport. I remember sitting with her in a pub. The conversation went like this:

Me: I got that job at Pontin's.

Her: That's brilliant.

Me: The only thing is, the place they've offered me is a long way away.

Her: What do you mean? I thought it was here in Southport.

Me: No, it's in Hemsby.

Her: Where's Hemsby?

Me: Great Yarmouth.

Her: Where's Great Yarmouth?

Me: Norfolk.

Her: Where's Norfolk?

Me: I'll show you on this map I just bought after my conversation earlier that never actually happened.

Her: But that's miles away.

Me: I know.

Her (casually): That's a shame, isn't it?

Me: Yeah.

Her: You really wanted that job, didn't you?

Me: What?

Her: Never mind, I'm sure something else will come up.

(Long pause of realization by me.)

Me: I'm taking the job.

(Long pause of realization by her.)

Her: I thought you loved me.

Me: So did I.

I didn't want to settle down. I was only nineteen. I wanted to make something of my life. I wanted to see the world.

Her: You mean you want to be a sports organizer at a holiday camp in Great Yarmouth.

Me: All right, no need for sarcasm.

Looking back I feel bad the way I casually ended our relationship. I was a nineteen-year-old who didn't really give a crap about anyone but myself, like most nineteen-year-olds. If the person in question is reading this, I'm sorry. I should have been a lot nicer.

Her: I'm not reading this. To be honest, I barely remember you.

So, soon I was off to Pontin's in Hemsby, Great Yarmouth, Norfolk. I remember the day I arrived walking into the ballroom where the entertainments manager was rehearsing with the Bluecoats for the Friday night Bluecoat show. All the Bluecoats were laughing and joking and there was a real sense of camaraderie, which considering it was day one was a really good sign that everyone was going to get on great. What I didn't realize at that point was that they all knew each other already, coming from the *Fame* school previously mentioned. I remember their laughing immediately stopping as the door slammed behind me and I crossed the ballroom dance floor. It was like that scene in *American Werewolf in London* when they enter the pub. I was almost expecting one of them to say 'You made me drop my juggling balls. I've never dropped these juggling balls before.' (If you haven't seen the film, trust me, that's a good joke. If you have seen it, then it's actually a very average joke.) After a walk that seemed like a lifetime I finally reached the group. 'Hello, I'm Lee, I'm the sports organizer. I'm not like you lot, I can't perform, so probably best to ostracize me for a few days and see me as very much the outsider of the group. Probably best if you see me as the lowest rung on the ladder and make me regret leaving Southport in the first place,' I didn't say, but may as well have.

Her: Serves you right. Not that I can remember you.

They immediately put me in a chalet with Gavin. Gavin was the camp comic. I was very impressed. He was doing what I wanted to do. An actual comic. Amazing. But it turned out he was neither camp nor a comic. It was clear that he'd been given this title because, like me, he couldn't really do anything else. Maybe all 'comics' have at some point made this decision. They can't do anything else, so falling over for cheap laughs will have to do. But despite his lack of performance skills, he was still part of the 'gang' – he knew them all and he had been on stage and performed with them. I hadn't, and this made me very much the outsider to begin with. It also didn't help that I was older. They were all seventeen years old, whereas I was almost twenty. Not a major difference on paper, but at that age it seems like a big difference as those three years can make someone a lot more mature and wiser.

Her: Is that right?

Above: Despite what my right hand looks like, my dad was not a lobster.

Below: I don't know what I was being accused of, but I was clearly guilty.

Left: Supporting photograph for my application to join the Merchant Navy.

Right: Mum and Dad. The bottom photograph of my dad is either sexual gratification or a Bruce Forsyth impression. Not sure which.

Right: I think it's fair to say I burnt easily in the sun.

Left: My dad showing off my broken leg on a skiing holiday. Luckily the soft focus and dark background is hiding his perm.

Right: Aged five, with a sinister smile that says 'I've just planted a bomb'.

Left: Me (*left*) and my brother, Darren, on our way to a beatnik poet convention.

Right: Me (*right*), Darren (*left*), Mum (*centre*).

GUARD DOG SCANDAL

A STARTLING admission by Britain's biggest security firm is arousing concern among dog experts.

The company, Securicor, says that its dog handlers receive only two days' full-time training before going out on duty.

"Two days are inadequate for people in charge of potentially dangerous dogs," said Mr. Peter Doig, M.P.

He is calling on the Home Office to examine the law on the training of guard dog handlers.

Chief Inspector John Simpson, head of Greater Manchester Dog School said: "It is just not possible to train a man properly in two days, even if the animal is fully trained.

"Such a combination of inexperienced handler and trained dog is fraught with danger.

Dangerous

"Our minimum is 13 weeks as laid down by the Home Office, and then it is a continuing process after that."

Colonel John Clifford, commanding officer of the Army's Dog Training Depot at Melton Mowbray, said: "You are dealing with a very dangerous piece of equipment.

"A man would learn very little in two days. It takes that length of time to get to know an animal.

"A dog handler must be trained to such a degree that he carries out certain procedures by reflex or he will lose control.

"It is only by practice that you learn to keep a dog under control.

"It is easy to be caught off balance by a big dog. The animal and his partner should practise together many times."

Securicor have 800 guard dogs based all over the country. They are used to patrol premises on a lead with a guard.

A spokesman for the firm claimed that a two-day course was appropriate.

He added: "We believe our record, which is good, proves this.

"Commercial considerations don't apply as far as the company is concerned on how long training should or should not be.

Lee McKillop... bitten.

Sam Perrie... worried.

Two-day training scheme shocks experts

By CLIVE ENTWISTLE

Bitterly

But ex-Sergeant-Major dog instructor Sam Perrie, who used to run Securicor's dog training centre at Merseyside, claimed that he has a record of more than 40 incidents of Securicor guard dogs biting employees and members of the public.

Mr. Perrie said: "The handler's course used to be four weeks but over the years it has been steadily reduced.

"I complained bitterly that two days was tolerably insufficient but the powers-that-be kept overruling me.

"The company have what they call a multi-handling policy. This means that different men handle different dogs every time they go on duty.

"This makes the combination even more potentially dangerous. An inexperienced man will soon lose control of a dog he doesn't know well.

"What I am afraid of is that one day a dog will get free from its handler because of his inexperience and badly maul someone.

"In my time with Securicor I dealt with a number of complaints where dogs had escaped. Most of them should

never have happened."

A current employee of Securicor said: "I would like to see a minimum of a month's training. This two days worries me very much.

"I don't think a man is capable of handling a dog safely and correctly after such a short time. The dog is as good as its handler.

Kiddy

Mr. Perrie added: "Most of the time the dogs are in empty premises with the guard. There isn't much danger then.

"The time that worries me is when the handler is getting a dog out of his van to go into the premises.

"It only needs a kiddy to run round the corner for an inexperienced handler to lose control."

In one incident five-year-old Lee McKillop was bitten through the calf by a dog on a lead in a Preston shopping precinct.

Teeth

In May 1975 a Securicor dog sank his teeth into the arm of Mr. Dennis Boyd while he was jogging to work along a fleet in Ulverston, Cumbria.

The company paid compensation in both cases. And Mr. Perrie claims that in other incidents Securicor employees have been attacked.

My first bit of press. It wasn't a publicity stunt, honest.

Above: Aged eleven, in glasses that I thought were cool, but made me look like a welder.

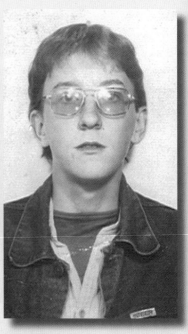

Right: Aged sixteen. I thought if I put tints in my glasses I would look less like a welder. It backfired.

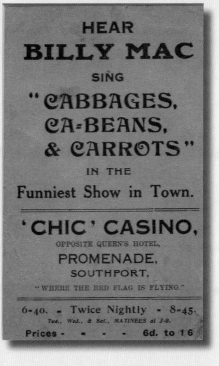

HEAR
BILLY MAC
SING
"CABBAGES,
CA-BEANS,
& CARROTS"
IN THE
Funniest Show in Town.

'CHIC' CASINO,
OPPOSITE QUEEN'S HOTEL,
PROMENADE,
SOUTHPORT,
" WHERE THE RED FLAG IS FLYING."

6-40. - Twice Nightly - 8-45.
Tue., Wed., & Sat., MATINEES at 3-0.

Prices - - - - 6d. to 1/6

My great-grandfather Billy Mac.
Maybe it does run in the family.
I mean show biz, not dressing in
women's clothes.

Above: My Bluecoat days. Where's Wally?

Right: They are shadows; I'm not on my way to a Mickey Mouse convention.

Me: Will you please stop interrupting.

So there I was, feeling a bit sorry for myself, wondering if I was the only person in the world who not only couldn't sing and dance, but didn't actually want to. Surely there must be someone else out there who just wants to have a laugh and get drunk, someone who I can share the experience of a summer holiday camp with. Someone else who's got two left feet and has the physical coordination of a tree on roller-skates.

Entertainments manager: There's a new Bluecoat called Saul starting tomorrow. You two are going to share a chalet. Apparently he likes a drink. You two will get on well.

Saul was from very near my hometown. Actually almost an hour away, but now I was a world-travelling free spirit on the other side of the world (Great Yarmouth), an hour away seemed like round the corner. Within a few days of him starting he had taken the legs off my bed as a practical joke, written random words around the chalet in chalk (mainly swear words, but the odd 'tractor' or 'squirty' just to add to the confusion), and put a huge red sheet on the ceiling so the chalet looked like a harem. Imagine if Ted and Spike in *Hi-de-Hi!* had actually been Arabic. And they had set the show in Morocco. And one of them had a form of Tourette's syndrome that only manifested itself with words written in chalk on the walls. That's what it was like.

On Saul's second night we sat outside our chalets drinking Taboo and smoking Consulate menthol cigarettes (we were real men's men) and Saul, within earshot of the other Bluecoats shouted at the top of his voice that the others were a bunch of showbiz twats. I knew we were going to get on. If you'd told me that twenty-four years later he would still be my closest friend, that we'd be godfather* to each other's children, and that we would be best man at each other's wedding I'd have said . . .

Her: I can't imagine getting married, I'm not the marrying type.

Me: Is this going to carry on throughout the book?

Most comedians will tell you that the funniest person they know isn't another comedian, it's actually a mate. Mates are always funnier than comedians. Because comedians talk about comedy. And comedy is never as funny as lying on a bed that suddenly collapses, and as you lie on the floor, pissed out of your head, you look up and see the word 'cock' in chalk on the side of the cupboard. I think this is one of the reasons I have never truly, properly loved being on stage as much as some. I've heard people say it's the greatest feeling ever making thousands of people laugh. But it's not. Laughing your head off with a mate is always better because you're the one that's laughing too, not just

---

* Although both me and my wife are godparents to their children, Saul and his wife Tracey are actually only godparents to our children in spirit, as we have not had our children christened. This is mainly due to the fact that my atheist wife finds the practice laughable. I, on the other hand, am more spiritually connected than her, and would find the experience a right good piss-up.

telling the jokes. Don't get me wrong, it's brilliant being on stage and I really like it (most of the time), but I'm not sure it's 'better than sex' as I've heard many a comic say. Although my wife disagrees with me on this. She's never actually stood on stage and told jokes but she told me it *has* to be better than sex, surely? (Although I have made myself the victim in that joke, I wrote it. So any laughs are mine, and not my wife's. She did not really say this. She's not even in the room with me as I'm writing this. She's probably having sex.)

That summer of 1988 was brilliant. To many people, certainly the post-alternative comedy world that consigned places like Pontin's to the cultural dustbin, these holiday camps are seen as naff dinosaurs that no longer have any relevance. But to a nineteen-year-old lad who was suddenly away from his hometown it was another world.

A typical day went like this:

I would wake up and my first role of the day was to dress as Captain Blood and hide from the kids, whose job it was to find me and throw me in the swimming pool. Captain Blood was a pirate who had committed an unspecified crime and each week he was considered 'guilty' and punished in a way that many would describe as a kangaroo court. There were some weeks when the kids would discover me hiding and go absolutely ballistic. Although seven-year-olds aren't that big, if you've ever been chased by about a hundred it gets a bit scary. Especially when you know that some weeks they are really going to start laying the boot in. There were days when the kickings I got were so bad I assumed that a rumour had got out that the crime Captain Blood was supposed to have committed was more untoward than simply stealing treasure, and perhaps involved phrases like 'register' and 'C-Wing'. Getting beaten up by a load of violent children might sound like a terrible job, but it felt very 'showbiz' and I loved it.

Lunch, as always, was served in a café very similar to a motorway service station. If, like me, you are in your forties and have spent far too many hours in service stations up and down the country, this might sound hellish. But ask any nineteen-year-old and they'll tell you that actually motorway service stations are very exciting. Eating in one every day, for free, was like a dream come true. And a dream sponsored by Ginsters at that.

In the afternoon I would organize the staff versus holiday-makers football match. This was one of the highlights of the week, and was taken very seriously, mainly by me. I would spend the week hyping it up so that we always attracted a small crowd, and I was often the scorer of the winning goal. This was less to do with skill, and mainly down to the fact that I was both goal hanger *and* referee. It was fair to say that the power of the job was getting to me. I even awarded a small trophy to the winning team, and on the weeks the staff won it, which was the majority of weeks, I would keep it in my chalet. Basically, I was a sad bastard. But a happy sad bastard.

Then in the evening I would put the red dickie bow

on, don the blue coat, and go into 'host' mode. This involved going from table to table and talking to the guests, making sure they were having the time of their lives. Which usually they were. I mean, after chucking a bloke dressed in a £6.99 pirate costume into a swimming pool what's there not to love. The rules for 'hosting' were that you had to spend as much time with the elderly as you did with people your own age, you weren't allowed to stay at any one table for more than fifteen minutes, and if you were offered a drink you were only allowed a half. But I had my own rules. Talk to the table with the eighteen-year-old daughter, always ask for two halves, and stay as long as you like.

Being a Bluecoat was great, and importantly it gave me an insight into what 'fame' was like.

It might sound odd saying 'fame' and 'Bluecoat' in the same sentence, but that's exactly what it felt like. There was something about wearing that blue coat and red dickie bow that suddenly made people want to come up and talk to you. To this day, I have never signed so many autographs in a day, or had so many people asking to have their photo taken with me. Bearing in mind I didn't really perform like the others (apart from skipping like a twat), this felt very odd. Especially when it was on the first day of their holiday so they didn't even know you from Adam. It was as if roles had been assigned: they were the holiday-makers, you were the 'stars', and so they wanted to talk to you. And that's pretty much what 'fame' feels like now. It all feels just a little bit pointless and a bit fabricated. A bit like reading the *Observer* (I'm not bitter, honest).

You see, although some people genuinely want to say hello and how much they enjoy your comedy, there is still a part of me that thinks that many people are simply giving out 'roles', like they were when I was back at Pontin's. At some point, virtually everyone who is considered famous has had the following experience. You're signing an autograph, then a different, random person asks 'Is he famous?' When the autograph hunter says 'Yes', they then ask if they too can have your autograph, even though they just made it clear they've never heard of you, never mind like you. It's utterly insane and shows that just being famous is enough for some people. What they're famous for is irrelevant.

Don't get me wrong, having a bit of fame has many, many advantages. And trust me, I only really do have a bit. I realize I am not a Premiership footballer (I wish) or a Hollywood actor (I don't wish), I am a bloke with a sitcom who crops up on panel games and does the occasional live stand-up tour. My life is not so consumed by being recognized that it's affected in a negative way, or a massively positive way (if indeed that is possible). But, for me, it's enough. Any more and I think I would say 'forget it' and get out of the job. For me fame is like fudge. I totally get why people want a little bit, but once you've had a taste why the hell does anyone want any more? (Actually I always do want more fudge so bad example. Maybe Beef and Tomato Pot Noodle is better.)

So there I was, a Bluecoat at Pontin's in 1988 living

the dream and enjoying my bit of fudge (if you've just opened this book and randomly turned to this paragraph please read the previous bit, otherwise that will sound like either a sexual innuendo or a non sequitur).

I was even the host of my own television show. Admittedly it was Pontin's Television, and we only broadcast to the chalets, but I once interviewed Duncan Goodhew, and as retired swimmers who do the holiday camp circuit tour go, he was one of the most well known. I'd even got myself a new girlfriend who was one of the dancers. The sun was shining, life was perfect. What could possibly go wrong? My first attempt at stand-up comedy, that's what.

PSYCHIATRIST'S OFFICE

BRIAN: You say being recognized doesn't really mean too much to you one way or the other, but it must bother you sometimes.

LEE: It depends who's doing the recognizing, to be honest. I have this theory that there are basically three types of people . . .

Lee wants to say 'Those that can count, and those that can't', which is one of his old stand-up gags. But Lee doesn't crowbar his stand-up material into everyday life. He is happy, however, to occasionally crowbar it into a book.

LEE: There is person 'A', as I like to call them.

Lee doesn't really call them this. Lee has never called any set of people 'people "A"' in his life, but he's trying to offer a theory up, and when Lee does this (which is often, and about anything), Lee feels it's always best to sound like what he's saying he's said before. That way it sounds a little more thought through than it actually is.

LEE: Person 'A' is the person you know well, your friends or relatives. They don't massively care that you're on the telly, and although they may ask you about your work and even watch what you do, you know that they'll always know you as the person you actually really are.

Lee says 'person' but actually means 'chancer'.

LEE: Then there's person 'B'. They have never met you in their life, they only know you from the telly. These people will often ask for a photo . . .

Lee daydreams for a millisecond (which in his head is about five minutes) and remembers the time he met the legendary Peter Fonda and asked him for a photo. When Peter agreed, Lee gave Peter the camera, stood next to a random girl and asked Peter to take the shot. This was Lee trying to be funny, but Peter Fonda didn't really bat an eyelid and took the photo anyway.

LEE: . . . or an autograph . . .

Lee daydreams again. About the time he was asked to sign a girl's breast. He agreed (he felt it was the only civil thing to do), but the pen didn't work properly.

*Without thinking he did that thing
people do when a pen doesn't work,
when they scribble on the corner
of the page. But Lee didn't do
this on a piece of paper, he did
this on the girl's other breast.
Bizarrely, and like Peter Fonda,
she didn't bat an eyelid.*

LEE: Person 'B' is fine. Often very
         polite and hardly ever an
         inconvenience. But then there's
         person 'C'. Person 'C' is
         somewhere between person 'A' and
         person 'B'.

         *Lee is annoyed. Saying person 'C'
         is somewhere between person 'A'
         and person 'B' is confusing. Why
         on earth didn't he call person 'B'
         person 'C', and person 'C' person
         'B'? That way person 'B' would
         have much more simply slotted in
         between 'person A' and 'person C'.*

LEE: Person 'C' is someone that doesn't
         really know you, but they have a
         connection with you. It might be
         that they serve you regularly in
         the shop . . .

         *Lee daydreams. He remembers a
         checkout girl who once recognized
         Lee and spent the next five
         minutes telling him that the actor
         Keith Barron used to be her
         cousin. Knowing that Keith Barron
         was still alive and well, Lee*

*couldn't understand how he 'used'
to be her cousin. After he had
paid and was about to leave he
felt he had to ask. 'How is that
possible?' asked Lee. The reply
was so bizarre Lee had to double-
check it is what she had actually
said. 'Sorry, not cousin . . .
customer.'*

LEE   . . . or they might be your
mechanic, or the friend of a
friend that you've only met a few
times and you don't really know
that well. Occasionally, and it is
only occasionally, these people
don't know how to act. They don't
want to act like someone who only
knows you from the telly, because
that isn't quite true, and yet
they also don't want to act like
they know you on a personal level,
because that isn't quite true
either. This makes them feel a
little confused and sometimes act
a little odd. Often rudely.
Basically they resent being a 'C',
being wedged between an 'A' and
a 'B'.

*Lee realizes that he has basically
confused his argument with his
categorization technique, and feels
that if Brian was marking his
theory she would give him a 'D'
which would be wedged between an
'E' and an 'F'.*

CHAPTER SEVEN

First gig (that doesn't really count)

Every Friday night at Pontin's was the Bluecoat show where Saul and I were given the role of flag wavers at the end of the show behind the talented, beautiful people (it was Pontin's so obviously beauty was relative). The beautiful people sang 'I Wish I was in Dixie' and Saul and I were supposed to wave the American flag. The show had nothing whatsoever to do with America but no one seemed to mind. Then again, when you've just spent ten minutes dancing along to Agadoo whilst copying the moves of a six-foot crocodile called Captain Croc, themes don't seem important.

Unfortunately the flags never actually turned up, so for that summer season we had to wave our hands instead – both hands at the same time. Never a good look, but when you're waving goodbye to your dignity it's always good to use both hands so your dignity can clearly see you as it disappears over the horizon.

Straight after the show the other Bluecoats (all except

me and Saul) performed in another show in the adults-only bar – the 'Naughty But Nice' show. This was supposed to be a more adult-themed show, but given the family nature of holiday camps 'adult' meant the girls did the can-can instead of the usual dance routine, and the children's entertainer did an act aimed at the grown-ups that involved maybe smoking on stage, or the odd bit of very mild innuendo. In other words, by today's standards it would still be tame enough for *CBeebies*, and it would take an idiot to misjudge this and go on stage drunk and start swearing at the audience. I'm sure you can see where this is going.

One night the entertainments manager told me he wasn't going to do his usual and host the 'Naughty But Nice' show, and would I like to do it? Up until this point all I'd ever done was bit parts in the main Bluecoat show, and the odd lighting and sound cue for the 'Naughty' show. Now I was being asked to front it and to do all the links. Actually that's not completely true. I'd also done the odd hosting of competitions at this point, like 'Miss Silver Lady', a beauty competition sponsored by the sparkling wine of the same name (imagine Miss Asti Spumante – that was the standard). The rules were simple: you had to wear something silver. I would ask them what was silver, and each week an old granny would get up and think she was the first to crack the joke, 'My hair'. This would always lead to a round of applause and eventually victory, and each week I was always one bite of the tongue from saying 'It happens every week, you cretins!', but abusing the audience on stage would be the work of an idiot. And no way was I an idiot (can you still see where this is going?).

I was very nervous about doing this hosting role for the 'Naughty' show as for the first time ever it involved comedy. I was being asked to be funny. However small my role was, it was still 'comedic'. I was utterly terrified, but also full of adrenalin as maybe, just maybe, this would finally lead me to being a 'comedian'.

So, first things first – material. I didn't have any jokes. Each week I'd watched the comedians who played at Pontin's, and the first thing I noticed was that they shared a lot of gags. The first question these comics would ask me on entering the backstage area was often in relation to the previous night's act. 'Did George do the gag about the penguin in the desert?' If George had, then Kenny wouldn't do it (for some reason every comedian who has played Pontin's is called George or Kenny. Apart from some who aren't, but let's not allow small details to ruin decent observation). So what I thought I'd do was use the lines I'd seen them use, as they didn't actually seem to be owned by anyone, they were just lines and gags that were bandied around. Of course they probably *did* belong to someone once, and that's the saddest thing about gag theft: gags soon become 'everyone's' when in fact they were once someone's. But I was nineteen and scared, and the last thing on my mind was the ethics of comedy. So I decided to get my 'act' together by copying other people's jokes. Morally wrong, and fatal for a comedian. But I wasn't a comedian. And I certainly didn't know the 'rules'.

The first thing I considered doing was something I'd seen a comic doing the previous week. He'd said to me before the show 'When I ask you to dim the lights, don't do anything. Even if I ask you twice, just ignore me.' In the middle of his act he turned to me and said 'Dim the lights.' As instructed I didn't. He asked me again. As instructed I ignored him. He then turned to the audience and said 'Great . . . three million unemployed and I get a dick-head doing the lights.' The audience wet themselves and they all stared at me. I sat there thinking 'You utter twat.' I remember thinking there and then, if I ever become a comic, I'd never treat anyone like that. But this was a week later and I *was* going to be a comic, so I thought 'I'll use that.' Then I remembered there was no one doing the lights, because I was having to do both jobs, host *and* lighting operator. And as any decent comedian will tell you, asking yourself to dim the lights, then ignoring yourself, then calling yourself a dick-head is comedic suicide. (If there are any new comedians reading this, write this advice down, it's all free.) Plan B.

There was a children's entertainer working that year called Stuart, a Scottish bloke who seemed to know what he was doing, and would always do a bit of an adult act for the 'Naughty' show. He very kindly gave me one of his gags to use on the night. Each week he would open his 'Naughty' act by putting a handkerchief over his hand and asking the audience if anyone had not enjoyed the entertainment this week. When someone (and there was always one) shouted 'Me!', Stuart would get the band to do a drum roll. ('What the hell's that? Sounds more like a ham roll?' was the line that always followed – I always liked that line, even though it means absolutely nothing.) Then Stuart would say to the gobby audience member 'Well, this magic trick is just for you.' He would then pull the handkerchief off his hand and he would be holding two fingers up. This was as rude as it got, and was considered a little risqué for the Pontin's crowd (that was about to change; they would soon be seeing his risqué act as the halcyon days of clean comedy). This gag always worked, and so I decided to do that one. I now had my first 'bit'. I also decided to do the 'Kent' bit, but more of that hellish frickin' nightmare in a moment.

As for the other bits I planned to do, I genuinely can't remember what they were, mainly because I never got that far.

Backstage I was absolutely petrified. Years of wanting to be a comedian, but not really knowing what that meant, and here I was about to actually do a 'turn'. I decided to have a drink to settle my nerves. Then another drink. And another. And then another. And then one more.*

I have only ever been drunk on stage three times. This first time at Pontin's, my second ever gig six years later (which I've always considered my first ever proper gig, hence the title of this chapter) and a show in Edinburgh

---

* This is supposed to be for dramatic effect. I *can* count.

in 1998. What I learned from those three experiences is: if it's your first gig, never drink to calm your nerves; if it's your second gig (which you actually then subsequently consider to be your first gig), never drink to calm your nerves; and more importantly never, ever, go on a lunchtime bender with The Mighty Boosh and Al Murray when you're doing a show that night.

So it's August 1988, and although I'm not quite sure how it's happened, I'm stood with the microphone in my hand in front of four hundred or so people hosting the 'Naughty But Nice' show.

As I've said, it wasn't the first time I'd been on stage at Pontin's, far from it. I'd hosted all sorts of competitions and games. But this was totally different. Before, it was all about other people, kids dressed as pirates, or grannies saying 'I've got grey pubic hair, does that make me a "Silver Lady"?' (They never really said that of course, but it would have been a novel twist to the usual line.) Now it was all about me for a few minutes, and what's more they were expecting laughs. Before now it had all just been big smiles and 'Let's hear it for Dorothy's pubic hair!' (See, ladies, how much funnier it would have been.)

I remember, even before I opened my mouth, thinking 'Blimey, I'm thirsty', and the realization was that I was drying up with fear. I learned an important lesson at that point, and ever since I have never been on stage without a glass of water. Oh yeah, and another little tip I picked up that night was never get steaming drunk and abuse the audience with a tirade of filth for no apparent reason.

So I was holding a microphone and four hundred paying holiday-makers wanted entertaining. It suddenly dawned on me I was utterly, pant-wettingly terrified.

I decided to kick straight in with Stuart's handkerchief gag.

Me: Has anyone not enjoyed the entertainment this week?

Stuart (backstage, to himself): Not as your opening line, you dick-head! Say hello first!

Audience member: Me!

Me: Right, get up here.

Stuart (backstage, to himself): Don't get them on stage! Just say it!

The man slowly walked on stage. It seemed to take an age, and I had nothing to fill the silence with apart from 'Hurry up' and 'Come on' and 'Where is he?', none of which will go down in the annals of history as 'great improv'. He finally approached the stage. I reached in my pocket to take out the hankie. It wasn't there. Lesson number two, young comedian reading this book: if you are doing a gag involving a hankie, make sure you've got a hankie.

Me (to self): Oh God.

I reached in the other pocket, and there it was.

Me (to God): Thank you.

I think I may have used it to wipe the sweat from my head.

The audience member was now on stage with me, and he was a cocky little shit. And that's coming from a nineteen-year-old lad who thought he could do stand-up comedy with no real material, whilst drunk, and hadn't even bothered to double-check he had his props, so you can imagine how cocky he was.

Me: OK, you haven't enjoyed the entertainment this week then?

Man: No.

Me: Well this trick is especially for you.

I turned to the band.

Me: Ham roll.

They looked confused, then did a drum roll.

I slowly placed the hankie over my hand and mimed some 'magic' business as if I was going to make something amazing appear. Whilst I was doing this, the cocky shit turned to the audience and started acting out a huge yawn to show them he was bored. This got a laugh from the audience. That wasn't right. Surely that wasn't right. *He* had just got the first laugh of the night, and at my expense. If I'd wanted that to happen I'd have told myself to dim the lights, then ignored myself, then called myself a dick-head. I was now panicking, and ever so slightly annoyed with him and the audience.

There are some entertainers who spend the latter years of their life despising their own audience, as if they are in a long-term marriage that they are trapped in and want out of, but can't. Once you feel like this it's pretty hard to ever enjoy the job again. Lesson number three: Never have this feeling after thirty seconds of your first gig.

I removed the hankie, and started to stick two fingers up at the cocky shit . . .

Stuart (to himself, backstage): Perfect. Just stick the two fingers up and you're home and dry. It will be seen as 'edgy' given the usual Pontin's conservative policy on adult humour, but given that you're only miming the gesture it will be seen as 'cheeky' rather than aggressive. As long as you leave it at that, you'll have got your first laugh and you'll be off and running. And the whole night will then go smoothly, and you'll have garnered enough confidence to then seriously start pursuing your dream to become a comedian. Just leave it at that, Lee, please, for the love of God, just leave it at that.

As my fingers made the two-fingered salute and began to rise, I saw the cocky shit still 'yawning' to the crowd and still getting laughs for his actions. I looked the cocky shit in the eyes and decided that to accompany my two-finger salute I would do my first ever bit of improv.

Me: Why don't you just fuck off?

There is a moment on stage when you tell a gag where there is an eerie silence. It's usually after a gag that you consider important. It can be because the set-up is extremely long so there's a lot hanging on it. It can be the first time you tell a joke and you're desperate for it to work. Or it can be a bit of information that explains a whole episode of a sitcom, and if it doesn't work you feel the whole episode collapses. I recently filmed an episode of my sitcom *Not Going Out* where there was a line right at the end: 'When are you lot going to start dogging?' If this line worked and got a big laugh it meant the whole episode made sense, if it didn't it meant the audience didn't accept that as a feasible explanation of the story that had just been presented to them. Bearing in mind I'd spent a month writing it, and almost two weeks filming it, there was a lot at stake. When the location clip was played in to the studio audience I actually closed my eyes and prayed for it to get a laugh. That's when the eerie silence happens. Because your brain is working overtime, everything is slowed down, so a split second of silence for the audience to take in the information and digest it can feel like an age. You want and need it to happen so much that you literally feel like time has stood still. That's why when it does happen it's such a great feeling and why when it doesn't it's such an empty feeling. There are times when there's so much invested in the result that the eerie silence before the laugh, or lack of it, lasts for ever.

This is especially true if it's the first ever joke you have told on stage in your life and you are the friendly Bluecoat whose job it is to look after the children of the holiday-makers, and smile all week, and be polite and courteous at all times, and your job is to make them feel that nothing is too much trouble because you are a family entertainer who just wants everyone to have fun. And you've just told a member of the audience to 'fuck off'.

The eerie silence ended. To this day it's still the longest eerie silence I've ever had on stage. In reality it was probably about a second. But it felt like about five seconds. That might not sound long, but imagine you're doing a eulogy at your grandmother's funeral and you've forgotten your speech. So you panic and get your cock out. The whole of your family are staring at you. Now count to five.

Then something brilliant happened . . .

The whole crowd erupted into a huge laugh, then a cheer, then a round of applause. (At Pontin's that is, not your grandmother's funeral. You would have been sectioned for that.) It was an amazing feeling. The audience were on my side, and I officially got my first 'laugh' as a comedian. The man skulked off back to his seat, and on a high I introduced the Bluecoat girls who were going to do the can-can.

As the Bluecoat girls danced to the backing tape the house band popped backstage for a quick drink. They were wetting themselves. Bluecoats just did *not* swear on stage, and they'd loved it. Even Stuart told me the gag had never worked that well before. I was on a real high. The lead singer of the house band, a girl called Wendy, told me 'This is what the audience want. They want a bit of edge. Give 'em some more of that.' She was right . . . surely. She must know about comedy, she was the lead singer of a covers band called L'Escala that knew every Black Lace song going, and she was quite pretty. She must be right. I also noticed that she was showing me the slightest bit of interest for the first time. I liked this comedy malarkey. My only other memory of any sort of interaction with her up until this point was her telling me to stop picking my nose as it made her feel sick. Thinking it would make her laugh I turned to her and stuck my finger as far up my nose as possible and she puked in her glass of beer. It was fair to say up until this point she wasn't interested.

So clearly swearing was the way forward. Plus I'd been listening to Ben Elton on his *Motormouth* album that afternoon, and he swore loads, and his audience loved it. So, decision made, if in doubt, swear.

This wasn't a million miles away from the advice I was given many years afterwards by the late, great Malcolm Hardee. Malcolm, a man who may not be remembered by the wider general public (apart from maybe his naked balloon dance seen on such shows as *O.T.T.* with Chris Tarrant) was, and still is, loved by the comedy circuit for being an absolute anarchic, lunatic, hilarious, alcoholic nutter, the like of which seem to be a dying breed. His advice to new comics was simple: 'If in doubt, wobble about. If that doesn't work, fall over. If all else fails . . . cock out.'

Before long I was back on stage ready for the 'Kent' bit. I should have been using the time backstage rehearsing exactly how it went. But that sort of nervous attitude was for the newer comic, I was now a seasoned professional who had had his first (and only) laugh, and there wasn't time for that. I was busy celebrating my new 'bloke who can talk to Wendy without making her puke' status. Plus a few more drinks wouldn't do any harm.

Before long the Bluecoat girls had finished the can-can, which for some inexplicable reason seemed to go on for twenty minutes or so. Surely the audience didn't want this rubbish? They wanted me to tell them to fuck off.

I strutted back on stage, Wendy peering through the curtains thinking 'I'll marry him one day.' Or did she pop out for some chips? I forget, it was a long time ago. I said hello to the audience – a new bold move. No longer straight in with a 'bit' – time for some banter. A few people shouted hello back, but it was apathetic. My mouth went slightly dry. Oh crap, I hadn't brought a drink on stage. I suddenly remembered that being on stage was nerve-racking and I wasn't a seasoned professional after all. It was like being transported all the way back to that first gig I'd done all those minutes ago. Quick, do the 'Kent' bit.

The 'Kent' bit was based on watching other comics at Pontin's. I noticed that one thing all comics used to do was ask where people were from, and when the audience member told them, they would crack a joke about it. The first time I saw this I was impressed, but the reality was that these were stock lines that could be shared around, e.g. Scotland, or anywhere northern, was greeted with the reply 'Who paid for your holiday?' Or Wales was greeted with the sound of a sheep suggesting they liked to have sex with them. It was all terrible stuff of course, but all that mattered to me at that time was that it worked and people used to laugh. I'd seen enough comedians working at Pontin's at this point to know a line pretty much about anywhere in the country. And anyway this was all just padding, because what you were really looking for was the answer 'Kent'.

Because as soon as the audience member said it, the comedian would always say 'What did you call me?' It always got a huge laugh and round of applause. And because of the close proximity of Great Yarmouth to Kent, there were always loads of audience members from there. It was a cert. Surely.

Me (to random audience member): So . . . where are you from?

Man 1: Wales.

Me: . . .

I'd gone blank. What was the gag about Wales?

Me: Hi.

Man 1: Hello.

Me: Hi.

I started to panic. Quick, find someone from Kent.

Me (to different random audience member): Where are you from?

Man 2: Scotland.

Me: . . .

What the hell was the Scottish gag? Why couldn't he be from Kent? Why was he ruining this? If I wasn't careful Wendy was going to start puking again. I really, really, really needed to find someone from Kent, and quickly.

Me: Anyone in from Kent?

Man 3: Me!

There's a moment in a gag when you realize you've messed it up and you have to make a split-second decision. Bail out and make a joke about its collapse (preferred), or hope you can think of a new ending (not recommended). I went for the second option:

Me: (to man 3): Well then, you're a cunt.

Just to be clear, when I say the previous eerie silence was the longest I've ever had on stage, I meant the longest silence that is then greeted with a laugh. If you count the eerie silences that don't get a laugh, then this is the longest I've ever had, as that eerie silence still exists today. Pontin's in Hemsby is now sadly closed and has been for a few years. The Norfolk bar, where the 'Naughty But Nice' show was performed, is now just an empty building which if, like me recently, you ever get to visit you'll see is just one long eerie silence. Well, that eerie silence . . . it's mine. I created that.

The next few minutes have been slightly blocked out by my brain, but it basically involved asking people where they were from, then telling them they were wankers, regardless of where they came from. The audience reaction was a combination of shocked silence and occasional jeers. I really hope Wendy went for those chips.

The next day I was called into the manager's office. Not the entertainment manager, the general manager. This had gone to the top. He showed me a 'smiley form'. The 'smiley form' was the customers' assessment of the holiday. On it they were asked a series of customer satisfaction questions, and for each they had to draw a smile if they were happy on an already printed face (picture a child's drawing of a face, two circles with dots for eyes and a small circle for a nose; that was the 'smiley form'). For the question 'What do you think of the Bluecoats?', instead of a smile someone had drawn a speech bubble that said 'I thought of the Bluecoats what they thought of me, PTO', and on the back they'd drawn a huge hand sticking two fingers up with the caption 'They can fuck off!'

I was immediately sacked and within an hour I was back on the train up north. My brilliant new job, my career as a TV presenter on Pontin's Television and my glamorous dancing girlfriend all now behind me.

PSYCHIATRIST'S OFFICE

BRIAN: I think we have a bit of a dilemma, which is something you identified at the beginning of the book. There's Lee McKillop and there's Lee Mack. Lee McKillop has to write a book about Lee Mack, but Lee Mack is the funny one who tells funny anecdotes about Lee McKillop.

Lee is pleased. She said 'funny'. If she'd just said amusing that would have been terrible. Lee realizes he didn't listen to the other words properly, just 'funny'. And so he has to listen back later to the tape to see what else she said.

BRIAN: I sometimes feel like I'm playing a game of 'Where's Wally'. Don't worry, I'm not saying you have a split personality.

Lee wouldn't mind a split personality. At least that way maybe only half of him would have this ADHD he's supposed to have.

BRIAN: But I *would* like to talk to you about 'personality'. One of my professors summarized it as 'who you love and what you do'. And what you do is stand-up. I think a lot of people buying this book will want to know how you have the balls to do it.

Lee is surprised she said 'balls'. Lee wants to say 'Maybe your use of male sexual organs to express bravery is due to a fascination with your own father's genitalia.' Then realizes that it probably won't get a laugh. And, as ever, without that, what's the point (of anything)?

LEE: I actually don't think it's as scary as people think. A fellow comic, Ivor Dembina, once said to me the biggest secret in comedy, that only stand-ups seem to be aware of, is just how easy it is to keep people entertained for twenty minutes. To some degree I think I agree with Ivor.

Lee is not completely sure that what he has just said truly reflects how he really feels, so makes a mental note to blame his friend Ivor Dembina in the book, despite the fact that in the psychiatrist's office Ivor was not actually really mentioned. In fact Lee's not 100 per cent sure it was Ivor who said it in the first place, but feels that Ivor will be too tight to buy Lee's book, so won't find out anyway.

BRIAN: As a comedian you have an ability
           to communicate the funny side of
           situations which for someone else
           could be seen as a total disaster,
           like it was for you when you did
           your first comedy show at
           Pontin's. In a sense, what
           happened after that experience is
           you were doing your own CBT.

           *Oh Christ, more letters. Lee is
           unsure what she means. Lee has
           already done a CBT on his moped,
           but that was 'compulsory basic
           training'. Surely she can't mean
           that. If a policeman stopped Lee
           on his moped and said 'Have you
           done your CBT?' and Lee replied
           'In a sense, yes. Because I have
           an ability to communicate the
           funny side of situations, which
           for other people could be seen as
           a total disaster', Lee would
           surely be collared by the fuzz.*

BRIAN: I'll explain more about CBT next
           time.

CHAPTER EIGHT

Magic, bands and close encounters

Going back home to 'normality' after leaving a holiday camp is hard, especially when it's happened so suddenly because you've been sacked. I no longer had my bedsit, so there was no choice but to move back in with my mum and Fernando Torres, who I have to say had now started to settle into his role as striker a little more, and was now bagging a decent amount of goals a season, albeit he still wasn't the most prolific scorer we'd all hoped he would be. A bit like that Chelsea striker, you know, Fernando Torres.

It's particularly difficult because as a Bluecoat you hardly ever leave the holiday camp, so the bubble you're living in becomes even more insane. Again, a good lesson in working in showbiz. I still look at some comedians and think 'You need to spend a little less time on camp, and a little more time on Great Yarmouth High Street.' If they could hear my thoughts I'm sure they'd ask what the hell I was talking about, but I'd simply reply, 'Your fame is like Pontin's and your kids and family are like Great Yarmouth High Street', which wouldn't help.

I rang the man from Blackpool who'd originally booked me and begged for my job back. He eventually relented and said I could go back to work (hooray) but I was going to be transferred to Morecambe (boo). A week after my sacking from the sunny east coast of Hemsby, where I had a beautiful dancing girlfriend and a new best mate, I woke up in rainy Morecambe in my new crappy chalet looking at Heysham nuclear power station. They hadn't even bothered to write obscenities on my chalet wall in chalk. Soon after I left Morecambe it closed down, and Her Majesty's Prison Service was genuinely considering turning it into an open prison.* Nice.

I spent the winter in Southport trying to get my job back at Hemsby for the '89 season, desperate to get back to the bubble. Although I'd spent that season as a 'non-performer', I'd clearly been swayed towards the stage a little more, as during that winter I joined a band. A friend of mine asked if I'd be the lead singer in his group based purely on the fact that I had been a Bluecoat and so therefore was used to being on stage. I had never sung in my life, but, like being a golfer or an astronaut, I thought 'How hard can it be?' So, without any formal audition or talent, I was now lead singer in the seminal soft rock band The Appraised. Again, I was

* Gospel.

not trying to fulfil any ambitions, I still sort of thought I might one day somehow be a comedian, maybe (whatever that meant). But I thought being in a band might be a giggle. You know, the same reason that people like Morrissey, Nick Cave and Leonard Cohen got involved in music. I didn't realize it at the time, but what it showed was that I had started to develop, possibly from my experience of trying (and failing) to do stand-up at Pontin's, a very thick skin. So thick was it that, despite having no singing ability whatsoever, we booked our first gig right next door to the bingo hall where I used to work, the same pub I broke the news to my then girlfriend that I was leaving town. Plus I invited all my old work mates to come and see us. What the hell was I thinking? But then again, I look back at my first few years of stand-up and think the same thing, so maybe this was all part of developing a hide as thick as a varnished rhino. Or at least convincing myself I was anyway, as a self-defence mechanism.

I turned up to the gig and saw that the band were all dressed like . . . well, like a band. Leathers, dark clothes, T-shirts. I think the correct description would be 'grunge'. I, however, much to the despair of the band, turned up in a suit with a white polo neck underneath, and my then customary highlighted quiff with accompanying two big gold-hooped earrings (hi, girls!). It could have been worse: a few years earlier during my bingo hall days I'd actually had a perm. This was during the time of course that men from the north considered the perm a viable manly option, usually accompanied by a moustache. In fact so 'manly' was it considered that when I expressed doubt to my father (who had one) about getting it done myself, he uttered the immortal line 'Just get your bloody hair permed, you poof.'

We played mainly cover versions, Billy Idol's 'White Wedding', that sort of stuff, and the gig was passable. Possibly even good. But then again I spent the first few years of my stand-up career thinking I was 'passable, possibly even good' and I look back now and think 'It was awful, possibly even abysmal.' Rhino skin, you see.

Soon my short-lived singing career was over. The second and final gig ended with me being hurriedly escorted from the building after I was threatened by a local who insisted we turn the music down. What I learned that day is, if a psychotic-looking man with a swallow tattoo on his neck ever asks you to do something, you do it. You do not say, on the microphone, 'Sorry, madam, is it too loud?'

Another example of my thick skin starting to develop was my one and only attempt at being a children's entertainer during this time. Having done a summer season at Pontin's I quickly realized that the best-paid Bluecoat was the kids' entertainer. This was because he had an actual cabaret act, and he came with all his props and magic tricks. Again, I thought, 'How hard can it be?' I thought I'd get myself some tricks, do some parties, then, when the new summer season came, if I got my job back at Hemsby, I'd be the new children's entertainer and earn more money. I didn't for one minute stop to think that even if I did get my job back, then maybe, just maybe, the person who was sacked for telling the audience to 'fuck off' and that they were 'cunts' would possibly not be employed in the role of children's entertainer.

I rang my entertainment agent mate, the one who'd got me the interview at Pontin's, and told him my plan. Owing to the fact that agents are the only people in showbiz who are more delusional in their belief in their clients' abilities than the clients themselves, he booked me straight into a gig.

The big problem I had in being the next Charlie Chuckles was a lack of tricks (oh yes, and experience and ability and talent and desire, but that kind of thing never really bothered me). I'd seen that a lot of the magic tricks were pretty much self-working, so all I needed to do was buy them. But that was the problem, I was skint. So I decided to make them. OK, I'd never actually made any magic illusions, and I had no basic knowledge of carpentry, but how hard could it be? Luckily Fernando Torres had a work shed at the bottom of the garden so I went straight down there and started work. I was in there for many, many days.

If it had been a film, there would have been a wide shot of the shed, some upbeat music, and the sounds of hammering, sawing, drilling, screaming, shouting and occasional bad language. In the film, this montage would carry on for about a minute, then the music would suddenly stop, I would exit in close-up, then remove my welding goggles from my dirty face, wipe the sweat from my brow and smile. And I would be played by Jim

Carrey. And I probably would fail dramatically, but fall in love with a waitress and so actually end up 'winning' after all. The audience would exit happy, having laughed heartily for an hour and a half, then remember how mawkish the ending was and vomit in their popcorn.

Two weeks later I arrived at the 'gig'. It was for the child of a landlord of a pub, and the venue was the pub itself. About twenty kids sat on the floor, and ten adults watched from seats behind them. I arrived with my three homemade tricks. The plan was to pad out the 'act' with some very cheap tricks I'd managed to buy, then hit them with these 'big' three illusions, which would be spread throughout the act.

The first of these big homemade ones was a trick I'd seen at Pontin's and had copied. It was a wooden, two-dimensional robot with detachable head. The idea was you take the head off, get rid of it, then put a balloon over the space where the missing head was, then as if by magic the balloon pops and the head has reappeared. This was achieved (spoiler alert) by the fact that there was a second head on a spring that folded back, and when you let go it sprang back up. Due to it having a small pin on its nose, the balloon popped and it looked like the head had magically reappeared. If you still can't picture what I mean, imagine what some of the adults were imagining when they watched my act that day; a man with his throat slit and his head folded right back so it was hidden behind his body.

The second trick was my real pride and joy. I'd actually come up with the idea myself rather than copied it. Yes, that's right, folks, I was so confident/ assured/creative, call it what you want (delusional/ idiotic/mentally ill), I was inventing tricks. This involved me throwing a pack of playing cards on to a small table, then covering it with a huge box, saying 'Ali Kezzam',* then when I removed the box the cards had magically arranged themselves into a card tower. This was achieved by the whole table top flipping round on itself when I released a switch, thus revealing a pre-made tower of cards that I'd glued together and hidden on the underside of the table.

The third trick I genuinely can't remember, perhaps because I never actually got to do it. Suffice to say, going by the previous two, it was most likely ill-conceived and shoddily made, and probably had brightly coloured stars stuck to it.

I opened with the 'silk hankie disappearing into the hand' trick. A trick easily bought (secret plastic thumb) and it looks very impressive once mastered. It even looks good if you haven't bothered mastering it, but just scrape by, as I proved that day.

It got a round of applause. See, I knew this was going to be a doddle. I then did a very simple card trick with giant cards (again cheap to buy, and easy to learn), which was mainly an excuse for loads of kids' gags I'd seen all the other kids' cabaret acts share/copy/steal – 'Pick a card [they do]. Do you want to change your

* If you're trying this at home, 'Ali Kezzam' is optional and not essential to the trick.

mind? Or are you happy with the mind you've got?'
Laughter ensued. I was storming it. My summer season
had given me the confidence to stand on stage, and
bearing in mind the last time had ended in disaster, this
was proving much easier. It was time for a big (homemade) illusion – the Mysterious Reappearing Head of
Fu Manchu (I'd decided the robot's face I'd drawn
looked more like a Chinese man than a robot, so I'd
renamed the trick). Everything was going well, then
suddenly, when I let go of the hidden head, it didn't
spring up. Disaster – the internal spring mechanism
switch* had come off and instead of it magically reappearing it just hung limply behind its body, almost
like it was too ashamed to show its face and be seen as
part of this woeful double act. I panicked, and tried
to subtly flip the head up using the body of the
robot/Chinese man as leverage. But it wouldn't flip. It
was too heavy. So I put down the bag in the other hand
(which contained Fu Manchu's other head), and used
this hand to manually flip his head up. The balloon
popped, but not loud enough to cover the sound of a
child saying 'That was stupid.' I had to do something
quickly, but what? I could move on and not acknowledge the heckle. Bad move, that would be an admission
of defeat. I could get him on stage, put a hanky over my
hand, reveal two fingers, and call the child a cunt. No,
that had failed me at Pontin's. I could agree with
him that it was stupid, and smash the robot/Chinese

* i.e. elastic band hooked over a drawing pin.

man's head against a bar stool, pretending I was angry, but hopefully looking 'wacky'. Yes, I'll do that.

As I was smashing its head against the stool and shouting 'Die! You nasty evil Chinese man, you've ruined it for everyone', I remember thinking 'Note to self: you're an idiot.' But it sort of got a half-laugh, and I'd just about got away with it because the previous two tricks had worked, and because I was a bit manic anyway I think they felt it was all part of the act. I should have then calmed it down and stuck with the plan, and padded it out again with some pre-bought (i.e. working) tricks. But I panicked. I needed to show them I had big illusions, not just card tricks and a few gags. It was time to hit them with the 'Amazing Card Tower of Cairo' – I'm not sure why I picked Cairo, but my theory was, if you can get an image of a pyramid or a Fez into someone's imagination, they'll think something is more mysterious than it actually is. It was going fine until the reveal. Again the switch to the internal spring mechanism* failed. I lifted the box off and the cards were still spread out on the table. I told the children that this was because they had not shouted 'Ali Kezzam' loud enough. This is common practice to whip up the crowd in children's entertainment, but because of the slightly manic state I had worked myself into, I think there was a chance that I actually believed this to be true, and was starting to blame them. I put the box back over the cards and asked them to shout it again as I

* See previous footnote.

fiddled with the mechanism. But it wouldn't shift. I was going to ask them to shout it again, then I had a thought; maybe it wasn't the volume of the kids that was to blame, but my shoddy carpentry skills. I panicked (again), then I remembered what I'd done last time. I removed the box and promptly jumped on top of the table, smashing it to pieces and hurling abuse at it for letting down the 'lovely ladies and gentleman'. The audience assumed it, again, to be part of the act, but I knew in my heart there was some truth in it, and I was slightly losing it. I then got all the kids to join me and rip the tricks apart, and when this seemed to go down well, I got them to do it to the other trick that I hadn't even tried yet, the one I've now forgotten. It was a scene of chaos. Kids getting splinters and magic tricks flying everywhere. I assessed the mess that was happening around me and realized that they were actually loving it, although some of the parents were bemused/ frightened/phoning social services. I had just about got away with it apart from one big problem. I was booked for half an hour and I'd only done about ten minutes. There was nothing left to smash. I immediately turned to the cassette player that I'd brought for my walk-on music, pressed play and the sound of the Proclaimers echoed round the room as I got all the kids to perform a series of party dances I'd learned at Pontin's. Seeing loads of kids spend twenty minutes performing dances like the locomotion to the Proclaimers is an odd sight, but one that helped add to the notion that I was a deliberately 'crazy' act, as opposed to the reality that I was having a minor breakdown. Eventually most parents looked like they thought I'd done a good job, although I suspect many wished I'd go and 'walk five hundred miles, and then walk five hundred more'. And to play safe maybe even another five hundred.

Eventually the telephone call came that I was waiting for.

After my punishment of being sacked at Hemsby, they had changed their minds and were having me back for the summer season of 1989. I could go back to that bubble, where I was recognized, my autograph was sought, I was respected and photographed, and I didn't have people saying things like 'Call me "madam" again and I'll rip your gold earrings out and stick them up your arse.' Or 'I bet you're not in the magic circle, are you?'

That summer season of 1989 was mainly about me trying to re-create the magic of the previous year. But, ironically after being sacked, I was the only person on the Bluecoat team to go back and, although still a really great year, it was not quite the same as that first magic summer season. Saul had gone back home to be a gravedigger (he should be the one writing the autobiography) and now I didn't even have anyone to write obscenities on my wall.

I did, however, get a new 'dancing' girlfriend, and after a short stint at a caravan site the following year, where I resigned after an argument, and as revenge hid a fish in a sofa so it would stink the place out (I'd go into more detail but I've got to save some of these stories for *Would I Lie to You?*), me and my new girl-friend ended up living together in London. We'd gone there because she had decided she wanted to get into acting, and was soon enrolled in the Italia Conti theatre school, and I went with her. I'd like to tell you that I was the perfect boyfriend who was supporting her dream of becoming an actress, and so I was happy to give up everything in her pursuit of that dream. But the reality was we'd spent the last two years at holiday camps and caravan sites and having no fixed abode as such, so moving somewhere else seemed like nothing new. It wasn't like I had a job, or a particular desire to go back to Southport. I didn't really have anything to 'give up'. I didn't say that in rows obviously. I'm a bloke. In rows I said 'Have you any idea what I've given up for you?'

So in 1990, at the age of twenty-one, I found myself living with a girl in London, renting a room from another couple who owned the house. But I didn't have a job. And I needed money, fast.

But what could I do? I had no real discernible skills, I had no real academic qualifications (two O-levels just doesn't cut it at interviews, even if you take your mum with you) and my only real ambition was to be a comedian. But what that actually meant was still a bit vague in my head.

I put an advert in the newspaper *Loot*, which was like eBay before the days of Bill Gates ruining our lives and making things you can actually touch become a thing of the past. And as anyone who has worked with me will know, I'm a massive, massive fan of touching things.

I have done many, many stupid and naive things in my life, but how I didn't realize that putting the following advert in the paper could and would cause problems is beyond me:

'Male, twenty-one seeks work, anything legal considered'.

In my head, I was showing initiative and a strong work ethic, but to many it meant 'I will indulge in sexual practices/intercourse with men at the right price.' The phone didn't stop all day. What was intriguing was the repeated use of the word 'genuine' during these phone calls. 'Is this a *genuine* ad?' In my head it was genuine. I would do anything, work on a building site, wait on tables in a café, clean cars. So yes, it was genuine. The first phone caller asked me 'In that case would you be willing to . . .' He described an act that I genuinely didn't know was a sexual practice, but suffice to say, and in the words of Meatloaf, I would do anything for cash, but I won't do that. What is even more bizarre is that despite this experience, I *still* managed to replicate the mistake a few years later. This happened when me and my then girlfriend, now wife, Tara, were students and we put a similar advert in the magazine *The Lady*, looking for work for the summer holidays as a 'couple' in posh stately homes. We were hoping for gardener/maid or chauffeur/waitress-type positions, but we ended up with only one offer, which was to fly to Kenya and have a man watch us having sex. If I catch a glimpse of myself in the mirror during a 'performance' I get thrown, so you can imagine what that would do to me. Plus the money was crap (oh yeah, I got that far in the conversation).

So I was without skills, and not willing to have sex with men for financial reward. But what I did have was some experience of DJing at Pontin's. I'd heard that if you had your own equipment and a car, the money was pretty decent (actually, quite like male escort work). It was also sort of like being on stage, which wasn't exactly being a comedian, but a lot more like it than working in a factory. That was it, decision made. I would like to write at this point, in keeping with the running theme of the book, 'I mean, how hard could it be?' Which, like the other times I've said it, would be a self-deprecating way of showing that I thought I could do pretty much anything, even though it turns out I couldn't. But in my humble (I say humble, I mean accurate) opinion, anyone really can be a DJ. As long as you can lift a needle on to a record. Or press 'play', as I believe would now be a lot more topical. Unlike 'jockey', 'disc-jockey' is money for old rope* and any-one who has ever uttered the phrase 'brilliant DJ' are probably the same people who say things like 'brilliant shoelaces'. So decision made, DJing it was.

If you were living in London in the early 1990s and you celebrated your twenty-first birthday, or your Bar

* This is a dig at the massively over-rated art form of club DJing, and not the kind of DJ that works on the radio and does things like interview me about my upcoming projects, e.g. a book I might be promoting. That lot are brilliant.

Mitzvah, or your wedding, there's a possibility that you were entertained by the wonderful sounds of the Close Encounters Mobile Disco Roadshow (available with bubble machine at extra cost, 10 per cent deposit required).

I would travel around with my equipment stuffed into the back of my then girlfriend's battered old Datsun Cherry, much to the annoyance of her mum, who felt I was wrecking it. But then again her mum was still angry at my doing what I did to her daughter's other cherry, which was to make her lose it (not true, but as any comedian will tell you, never let the truth get in the way of a half-decent joke).

My equipment was shoddy to say the least (I'm not still on the subject of making people lose their virginity, we're back to mobile discos). I hadn't learned from the children's entertainer incident the previous year, and there were a lot of homemade props. My 'laser show' was in fact the cheapest known laser beam affordable on the market, which was then gaffer-taped on to the top of an old fan (I mean the things that cool you down, not someone who asks for your autograph, that would be too much to expect). The fan would then oscillate from left to right, whilst the red beam flew across the floor and children would try and look directly into the beam, in a fashion that I would describe as science fiction meets disco, but a health and safety officer would describe as irresponsible meets illegal. This kind of casual approach to the welfare of the customers was further highlighted by my bubble machine, a device which sent thousands of beautiful bubbles cascading over the dance floor when the ballads were playing, an effect that was, even though I say so myself, tacky as fuck. If you've ever listened to 'Lady in Red' by Chris de Burgh and asked the question 'Could this get any cheesier?', well, the answer is yes. I decided that the fluid that was used to generate the bubbles was far too expensive at ten quid a pop, and surely cheap Tesco's washing-up liquid would do the same job. I mean what was the difference? That question was answered, very shortly afterwards, by a waitress carrying a tray full of glasses across the dance floor. She slid across it then crashed to the ground like Jane Torville on a hen night. In fact I think it was a hen night.

But litigation was the least of my worries. I had far bigger concerns. My then girlfriend, after just two months of our moving in together in London, decided she didn't want us living together any more. I suggested we tried living in separate places, but still carried on our relationship. But she didn't want that either. Nor did she want us to meet up for drinks occasionally. In fact she thought it better if we didn't actually see each other at all. Looking back now I think there might have been a chance she wanted to end the relationship.

It was all completely understandable in hindsight: she was eighteen and surrounded by a load of Bonnie Langford wannabes, and I was the slightly older boyfriend. I think she didn't really want to be living with someone, when everyone else around had just left home for the first time and were living the student life.

The writing was on the wall the one time I was introduced to these new mates. She asked me if I wouldn't mind not doing my usual shaking of hands when I was introduced to them. This was a telling moment. She obviously saw me as the slightly older, possibly stuffier 'husband' and probably thought it embarrassing if I shook their hands, like I was a granddad at a golf club. So I respected her wishes, and instead I grabbed their tits.

So now I was living in London on my own, and due to the fact that I'd spent the short time living there setting up Death Trap Mobile Disco Roadshow, I hadn't really got to know anyone apart from my two flatmates, and we didn't really get on owing to the fact that we were different types; they were arseholes and I was perfect.

I very shortly moved out and found myself living on the floor of a woman's house in Neasden. She had advertised looking for someone who could help run one of her many, many businesses she ran from home. Everything from a place to leave your pet when you went on holiday, to watching porn videos to check their classification (swear to God). It was the single most messiest, craziest, mental house I have ever lived in, and bearing in mind I now have three children, that is saying something. Waking next to a caged rat that wasn't there when you went to sleep, and knowing that when you go down for breakfast porn will be on the telly, is an unusual way of starting the day. Honestly, it was enough to make you just want to get up and go down for breakfast.

I still didn't really know anyone in London, and it was fair to say I was getting lonely. I was totally ready to pack it all in and go back up north, when a chance encounter happened which made me stay in London, and subsequently see it as 'home' for the next twenty-odd years, right up until the current day. I was still doing my DJing at nights, and I got a phone call from a guy called Terry Dillon who also ran discos. He wanted me to fill in for him that night. He asked me to meet him at a train station so he could give me the cash. As I approached him on that dark and isolated platform, I really, really hoped he hadn't seen my advert in *Loot*.

The next day he rang to see if it had gone OK, and before you know it we were meeting for a pint, which shortly led to me going ice-skating with all of his mates. It's an unusual way to make new friends, holding the hand of a six-foot-two African gentleman who's scared of the ice, but I'm delighted to say that all these years later I am still very close friends with all the people I met that day, and as a result of meeting Jude, Terry, Tim and Fiona I stayed in London and started to consider it home, without which I may never have gone to The Comedy Store a few weeks later.

PSYCHIATRIST'S OFFICE

BRIAN: After your various performance disasters, like the magic and what happened at Pontin's, most people would have given up. But you didn't because you were able to do your own version of CBT, albeit without knowing you were actually doing it.

LEE: So what is CBT?

BRIAN: Well, put simply . . .

Lee is relieved.

BRIAN: . . . Cognitive Behavioural Therapy is based on the fact that the way you think influences the way you feel. It's used to treat, for example, depression. Most people who are depressed have negative or distorted views which make them feel bad, and when they feel bad they think even more negative thoughts so they get caught in this vicious cycle and they can't move on. It basically breaks down to ABC. 'A' is the Event, 'B' is the Belief, 'C' is the Consequence . . .

Lee wonders if she realizes that 'event' doesn't start with an 'A'. She obviously does because she's

clearly highly intelligent, so
evidently the fact that the 'B'
and the 'C' represent things that
start with the same letter is just
a coincidence and is not a system
as such. Then Lee finds himself
daydreaming, which he has been
doing a lot more of lately, as he
now feels as though he is
officially ADHD and thus allowed
to not focus on what is being
said. Indeed he should be given an
orange sticker for his car and be
allowed to park anywhere he likes.
His daydream involves his
psychiatrist going through her
whole life thinking that 'event'
begins with an 'A', and it's been
going on so long that no one has
the heart to tell her she's been
wrong all these years. In the same
way Trigger in Only Fools and
Horses *thinks that Rodney is*
called Dave.

BRIAN: . . . your coping strategy, Lee.

Lee is worried. He zoned out for a
bit and hasn't been listening.
Luckily he has his Dictaphone and
fills in the blanks later at home.
What she actually said was:

BRIAN: . . . and in your situation 'A', the
           Event, was Pontin's and having a
           really bad show. 'B' is the
           Belief, and for you clearly the
           belief was positive. You clearly

felt that something good had come
from it, your first laugh, or just
the experience, or whatever. 'C'
is the Consequence, and the
consequence for you was that you
didn't then give up. You didn't
follow that first show by going
into what is known as the black
and white . . .

'Minstrel Show'?

BRIAN: . . . thought process. Whereby it's
all or nothing. You realized there
were positives and negatives, and
concentrated on the positives. And
all of this is a form of CBT. It
was your coping strategy, Lee.

*Lee secretly hoped she had called
him Dave.*

CHAPTER NINE

The special people

On 23 November 1990 I visited my first ever comedy club, The Comedy Store, Leicester Square, London.

I'd like to pretend to you that I have an amazing ability to remember the exact dates of all the things that have happened in my life, but the only reason I was able to find out the date for this book is that I remembered it was the day after Margaret Thatcher resigned, as one of the comedians did a joke about it. Something along the lines of 'I set my video to record the football last night, but because Thatcher resigned the news over-ran and it didn't record it. She's no longer the Prime Minister, but she's still messing my life up.'

I had arranged for an old Pontin's Bluecoat friend of mine to visit me in London, Dave 'The Rave'. Dave's nickname implied he was a party animal, or a hedonistic pill-popping clubber. But in fact he was called Dave 'The Rave' for no other reason than it rhymed. He could have quite easily been called Dave

'The Shave'. Or Dave 'The Cave', but in the end I suspect he felt 'Rave' was a little more rock and roll. I took him to the West End and we went on a pub crawl. I got a bit drunk and have no conscious memory of deciding to go to a comedy club that night. Or, indeed, why we thought drinking After Shock was a good idea. It tastes like Listerine mixed with shoe polish. And I was once a student, so I know what that tastes like.

I certainly wasn't going to 'discover' myself, or find out how to finally crack the world of comedy. Because I didn't even know what the world of comedy was. Yes, I'd seen it on *Saturday Live*, but I wasn't aware of the notion of a circuit of live comedy clubs where people honed material. I don't think I even knew what 'material' was. I assumed people just turned up at the TV studio and casually started talking about the week they'd had, without any particular thought about writing or rehearsing. You know, like watching *Hollyoaks*.

Looking back I'm gobsmacked at how naive I was. Like the time I heard Ben Elton's comedy album *Motormouth*. I couldn't believe he was doing the same stuff that I'd heard him do on the telly. I don't mean I was outraged, I loved it, and was more than happy to hear it again. I was just surprised that this was actually a 'routine' and not the casual thoughts of a man who'd noticed things the day before. It might sound strange that I thought this way, but remember in the mid-eighties 'alternative' comedy was still relatively new, certainly to the wider non-London audience like me. I hadn't really heard observational material like this before. And it sounded exactly that, an observation, not a joke. OK, I had heard Billy Connolly and Jasper Carrott doing what you could class as observational stuff, but that was way before my love of comedy had been ignited so I wasn't really paying much attention. I was too busy thinking things like 'If we had a colour telly then Billy Connolly's banana feet would be yellow and not grey. I might sack my parents.'

I didn't think of what Ben Elton was doing as 'gags' (cue his critics saying 'I still don't'). I thought of it as somebody's random funny thoughts and observations. I didn't think they worked on their jokes because I didn't see what they did as 'work' or a 'job'. It was just the natural ramblings of talented people. A talent that they just 'magically' had. Like Paul Daniels's ability to cop off with Debbie McGee, it was just 'mystical'.

Although naive, it demonstrates how much I thought comedy was for 'special' people, for people with uniquely amazing minds, for people different to me. I knew nothing about this world. I certainly didn't know about The Comedy Store – I hadn't even heard of it. But why would I have? I'd never been to a comedy club in my life. To be honest, when I was twenty I'd hardly been anywhere. I used to think of Wimpy as a decent night out. Actually, I still do (he says, not even knowing if Wimpy still exists).

We'd stumbled across The Comedy Store because we were looking for another place to go drinking that night. I was in no rush to go back to the flatmates from hell (the ones that weren't perfect like me).

We saw a queue of people and wondered if it was somewhere we could go for another drink. I walked to the front of the queue and stopped at the doorman. If I'd known then what I know now I'd have probably said 'We're the comedians', and walked straight past him without paying. But instead I asked him what the people were queuing for. I have always had this mentality. If people are queuing, I want to know what I'm missing out on.

He told me this was a comedy club and pointed to a load of photographs on the wall. I immediately recognized some of the faces from *Saturday Live*, even though I couldn't remember their actual names. I couldn't believe that they performed here in this tiny club. Surely they performed in . . . well, I didn't know where they performed. I hadn't really thought about it. Somewhere in showbiz-land, I guess. Certainly not here, to a queue full of kebab-holding drunks like me.

I immediately joined the queue. Not the back obviously, about halfway. There's always a way. My favourite is to start ranting to someone in the queue about the price of petrol (or whatever). They always assume you're mad and so ignore you, and the people behind assume you must be with them and that they were saving your place. As long as you keep throwing in the odd line to the confused person you've joined – 'Pigeons are getting bigger, aren't they?'

Twenty minutes later we were sat in our seats and the house lights went out. I remember thinking how glad I was that we were now sat in the dark, as the atmosphere was so electric that I assumed everyone there came every week, and me and Dave were the only new people there. The anonymity of the darkness made me feel like we fitted in more. Plus I assumed, like every audience member that has ever existed, that I would be picked on if the comedian saw me making eye contact with them, so I was glad to disappear into the blackness. If you don't want to be picked on, by the way, go cross-eyed and stick your tongue out a bit – you will definitely be left alone.

I would like to pretend that I remembered all the acts from that night, but through a combination of being quite drunk and the fact that it was well over twenty-one years ago, I can only remember three: Eddie Izzard, Steve Coogan and Jeff Green. Bearing in mind I had never heard of anyone on the circuit at that time, a few things happened which helped those three names and faces lodge in my head.

Firstly Jeff Green did a brilliant routine about a pilot almost being killed when he was sucked out of an aeroplane. The story he was referring to had been in the news very recently, and so this added to my sense that these people were just 'chatting' about stuff they'd seen, which in turn made me, again, think these people were different to me. I could never think of stuff that funny, line after line, so they must be 'special'. If only I'd known then they were gags. Brilliant, honed gags, but gags nevertheless.

I remember Eddie Izzard because the next day, and by

sheer coincidence, I saw him having a heated debate with a drunken tramp whilst I was walking through Covent Garden. This may have been due to the fact that Eddie was a street performer early on in his career, so may have been interrupted by the tramp. It meant I was able to remember him years later when I saw him on telly, especially as during the tramp row I was now sober. Or maybe my memory is playing tricks on me, maybe *I* was the tramp.

The thing I remember about Steve Coogan was his introduction, as he was brought on as 'one of the voices of *Spitting Image*'.* I loved *Spitting Image*, and suddenly to have a guy a few yards from me who provided some of the voices of the puppets was the most exciting thing imaginable. Actually performing myself should have been the most exciting thing imaginable, but I couldn't imagine that.

All three were brilliant. The whole night was. It was like I'd stumbled across a secret basement where loads of other like-minded people had got together to laugh at the kind of stuff only we thought was funny. Like a bunch of weirdo fetish freaks who'd spent their lives thinking they were odd, only to find there were other people with the same weird desire for a sadomasochistic Jimmy Krankie sex party.† Obviously 'alternative'

* The purpose of this footnote was to explain what *Spitting Image* was to the younger reader, then I realized that the younger reader is so used to Googling everything now that no explanation is needed for anything any more.
† Buy my follow-on book for more details.

comedy was starting to appear more and more on TV, so it might seem odd to suggest that I'd stumbled across a 'secret gang' of like-minded folk. But what you've got to remember is that I'd only ever seen this on the telly, and that was something you watched mostly on your own. OK, you might talk about it with your mates afterwards, but it was still a solitary viewing event. Again, a bit like *Hollyoaks* (only without having to close the curtains first). Now I was in a group of people, and I was totally swept up by the occasion.

As each act came on I was genuinely mesmerized. Even the people that were introduced as the new open spots were brilliant. To be honest, I think I was so caught up in it all I would have been in awe if an Alsatian had walked on stage, stood on his hind legs, and done a massive crap. Which isn't a million miles away from what that dog did on *X-Factor* (or whatever show it was on).

What is most memorable for me about the night was just how intimate it all felt. It was so relaxed, and not like a 'show' in the traditional sense. Certainly not like the shows they put on at Pontin's, where the comedians opened with a song, and the band backed them in their sparkly suits. This was all so much more casual. I remember Eddie Izzard walking on in clothes that looked like he'd just pulled them out of a wash bag, and one that didn't even belong to him, which all added to the idea that he was making everything up as he went along. It was shambolically brilliant. I genuinely remember thinking that I too was going to buy a green jumper that didn't quite fit me, then I might be that funny as well. Then I remembered I *was* wearing clothes that didn't quite fit me, and I *wasn't* that funny.

I stood at the bar in the interval and some of the acts that we'd seen were also there. Again I couldn't believe that they were just 'hanging out'. Surely they didn't just stand at the bar and get pissed. That's what I did.

I desperately wanted to talk to one of them. Ask them how you get involved, how you get started, where they get their ideas from. Basically every question that I have subsequently been asked myself a thousand times. But I didn't. I just stood there hoping that one of them might come over and say 'I've just overheard your witty banter to your mate Dave the Rave. I liked what I heard. Well done, you're in.'

Despite none of the comedians introducing themselves to me and offering me a life-changing career, I still remember coming away having had the best night's entertainment I'd ever had.

And more importantly I'd found out what it actually meant to be a comedian. I now knew this was a real tangible world, and not just an abstract, unattainable thing in the mystical world of TV. It was an actual real thing that I had just been part of, albeit just as an audience member.

This was a world that totally made sense to me, and I would give anything to be part of it.

But the problem for me, and the reason that I was still four years away from doing my first proper gig (I don't count Pontin's, the bit of my brain that does 'dignity' won't allow it) was that I still had this notion that these comedians were 'special' people. I remember sitting there watching one of the comedians doing jokes about Thatcher's resignation, and I pictured them all backstage after the show in deep political discussion about the rights and wrongs of Thatcher's legacy (as opposed to the reality which was probably that they talked about whether the gags got a laugh or not).

I thought to get up on that stage you have to have many attributes. You need to be worldly-wise, intelligent, educated, informed, articulate and more importantly über-confident in yourself. There's no way you could get on that stage if you felt even the slightest bit insecure. These people must be the most mentally sorted, grounded, 'together' people in the world.

If I knew then what I know now about comedians I would have got on that stage there and then, instead of waiting another four years to actually do it.

PSYCHIATRIST'S OFFICE

BRIAN: So why do you go on stage as Lee
          Mack and not your real name of Lee
          McKillop?

LEE: Oh yes, it's back to these self-
          defence mechanisms, isn't it.
          Sorry, you're not keen on me using
          the phrase 'self-defence
          mechanism', are you?

          Lee has just said the phrase
          'self-defence mechanism' twice, so
          knows that when he transcribes the
          recording of the session he will
          have got two more mentions of it
          in his book. Brian thinks Lee
          should use the phrase less, yet
          here he is childishly finding more
          ways of getting it in. It's a bit
          like when people tell Lee not to
          swear on stage, which to him is
          like a red rag to a bull. It's the
          reason he swore so much at a
          corporate gig years ago for
          Waitrose and died on his arse,
          vowing never to do corporates
          again.

BRIAN: Well, like I say, I'm more
          interested to know what's behind
          the self-defence mechanisms.

          There's another one. Result.

LEE: Not going on stage as Lee McKillop
            is a way of not going on stage as
            myself.

            There is a pause. Lee knows that's
            not enough of an answer as
            that's pretty much what he wrote
            at the beginning of the book.
            Brian clearly wants more.

BRIAN: Is it a fear of being judged? I
            don't understand.

            Lee doesn't really understand
            either. He was hoping she would
            tell him. Lee feels like seeing a
            psychiatrist is a bit like going
            to the doctor's, and the doctor
            saying 'What the hell is that
            rash?'

LEE: Look, when I first went to watch
            comedy I thought stand-up comedians
            were a special breed. Different to
            me. I felt this was something that
            they were born to do, and
            certainly nothing I could ever
            achieve. Like I say in the book, I
            thought they were 'special'. I now
            know that is absolutely *not* true.
            It's about working hard and
            putting in the hours. But I can't
            lie, me thinking they were special
            probably helped me enjoy the
            night. Because I felt I was then
            watching people that were amazing,
            different . . . special. So I know
            that if the audience think that,

it helps the night, it makes my
life easier. They're already
impressed before you walk on. Now
in my home town people know me on
a personal level, so they
absolutely know I am not
different, or special, because I'm
not, and so in my head it makes
the night harder.

BRIAN: So you want to be thought of as
special.

*Lee is mortified. Does she mean in
real life? Because that is not
what he said. It comes in handy a
bit on stage and makes the gig
easier, but that's it. The idea of
him needing to be thought of as
special makes his flesh crawl, as
he sees that in other comedians,
especially the mad ones. He
doesn't want to be one of the mad
ones.*

LEE: Not at all. I don't want to be
thought of as special, but from my
own experience as an audience
member I am acutely aware that it
massively helps the gig. If they
think you are naturally funny, and
that it all comes easy to you,
then they will laugh more. If they
know that you spend hours working
on it, like my mates and relatives
back home, it shatters the
illusion and so might make the gig
tougher. Comedy is a lot about

smoke and mirrors. If someone was doing magic on stage and some people in the audience thought the performer really did have magic powers, which, let's face it, some do . . .

What Lee meant was that some audience members think that magicians really do have magic powers. But he realizes this could be interpreted as Lee saying he thinks some magicians really do have magic powers. This would make him sound like a complete and utter idiot, but he is so trying to get the message across that he's not interested in looking special that he presses on without explaining. Basically he would rather look like an idiot than look like he's trying to be special.

LEE: . . . then it makes the show easier for the magician. Even though it's clearly not true that they can do magic. Because they can't. None of them can.

Lee says the last bit to clarify he's not an idiot.

BRIAN: So you want to be seen as unique?

LEE: No!

Lee doesn't understand why she

isn't getting what he's trying to say. It's only when he listens back to the tape later that he realizes that actually Lee has made this more confusing than necessary, and it's actually he that is to blame. All he needed to have said was:

   'Only on stage, not in real life. And even then just to make the gig easier.'

   But he doesn't say that. Instead he confuses the issue even more by going into some long-winded history of theatre, something which he knows nothing about.

LEE: You see people have always wanted their performers to appear special. That's why performers are literally put on a pedestal . . . a stage.

          Lee suddenly realizes that a stage isn't literally a pedestal. That's a pedestal.

LEE: They do this because they want to 'look up' to the performer.

          Lee suddenly realizes that actually it's more to do with sight lines, but carries on anyway.

LEE: Because they really need to feel that the performer is 'above them'.

          Lee suddenly realizes that actually

>   *many stages are at ground level*
>   *and the audience are looking down*
>   *at the performer.*

LEE: Apart from the stages that are at
                ground level. But these are only
                the modern ones, and are
                relatively new.

>   *Lee suddenly realizes that may*
>   *actually not be true.*

LEE: Apart from Shakespearian times.
                When they were at ground level. I
                think. But the traditional way of
                performing stand-up comedy,
                certainly in the Victorian music
                halls and theatres, is to put the
                performer on a stage and literally
                'look up' to them.

>   *Lee feels that he may have just*
>   *snatched victory from the jaws of*
>   *defeat. Then suddenly remembers.*

LEE: Apart from the audience members
                who are sat in the circle.

>   *Lee realizes that there is*
>   *absolutely no danger of Brian*
>   *thinking Lee is 'special'. Well,*
>   *not in the traditional sense of*
>   *the word anyway.*

CHAPTER TEN

(Im)mature student

So finally, after years of having a sense, a sort of vague notion, of wanting to be a comedian, I now had a more definite focus on what that meant. If only I too could be like the 'special' people at The Comedy Store that night who did this for a living. But the thought of doing it scared me so much that instead of just getting up and having a go, I looked for an excuse to avoid it, a way of not motivating myself to just do it, a way of lying in bed dreaming of it and not actually being bothered to do anything about it. Hang on; 'excuses', 'not being motivated', 'lying in bed'. It was obvious. I'll become a student.

Stand-up comedy wasn't something in 1993 you could really train for. Nowadays it's slightly different as there are many stand-up comedy courses available, and I believe that some universities actually do it as part of their drama degrees. Don't get me wrong, there were *some* comedy courses available back then, but I certainly hadn't been told about them, and why would I have? I hadn't told anyone I wanted to be a comedian, so someone suddenly bringing it up would have been odd, unless I'd been talking to David Blaine or Derren Brown, or anyone else that can't actually really read minds.*

I felt that if there was just some way of cushioning the blow of having to do stand-up for the first time it would really help, even though I suspect deep down I knew I was just putting off the inevitable of just having to get on with it and do it. The nearest thing I could think of was becoming a student and studying some sort of performing arts course. I didn't like this idea at first because it all felt so very . . . and I've spent the last five minutes trying to think of a better word but can't . . . 'wanky'. Even now, seventeen years after leaving that university course, I still struggle saying the word 'drama', which is actually what the degree was. Instead I will often mention, especially in interviews, just the minor part of the degree: 'Film and Television'. My theory is that if you say you're a film student, you sound like Quentin Tarantino, but if you say drama student you sound like . . . er . . . well, a wanker.

* I've always had an aversion to anything 'mystical' that presents itself as 'real', particularly the nonsense that is stage hypnotism. I once shared the bill with a man who got his dog to do the hypnotism, which made me even more cynical. Although I have to say my wife Tara went to see Derren Brown live and said it was one of the best shows she'd ever seen. Or maybe he 'made' her think that (cue spooky music and large cape over face).

The audition to get into Brunel University* was traumatic. I had to do a five-minute 'piece' in front of all the other wannabe students who were auditioning. Now bearing in mind the only other 'piece' I'd ever performed in my life at this point was to tell loads of holiday-makers they were cunts, this was, to say the least, nerve-racking. The only thing I had on my side was years of experience getting up in front of people, from the bingo days, to the Bluecoat days, to the much more recent DJing days. But these other kids all had at least two years of A-level drama behind them. In fact they'd probably all been doing this sort of stuff for years, whereas I'd never been in a drama club, or an amateur dramatic performance of anything. I'd never acted, because I didn't want to be an actor. I wanted to be a comedian, and that was different. Even now, after six years of doing *Not Going Out*, I still find it odd if I'm described as 'comedian and *actor*'. The course I ended up doing was very much theoretical, so I'm not an actor, I'm not trained (cue some critics saying 'We know, Lee, you don't need to convince us').

The reason I baulk at this description is probably two-fold. Part of me probably, even after all these years of working in entertainment, still sees 'acting' as just a

* It was actually called the West London Institute of Higher Education when I first started there, but thankfully during the three years I was there it became part of Brunel University and changed its name accordingly. I say thankfully as the previous name made it sound like a learning centre for illiterate adults, whereas Brunel suggests I could now build an internal combustion engine.

little bit 'poncey'. I say this not aimed at the world of acting itself, but aimed more at myself, the kid who grew up in a working-class environment in the north-west of England who thinks of the world of acting as just a little too . . . I'm thinking again . . . er . . . no, it's no good, I'm afraid it's still 'wanky'. I'm not proud of feeling like that (well, maybe a little bit) and totally get that it probably says more about my working-class chip on the shoulder mentality than any negative aspects of the acting community.* The other reason I'm not comfortable with the description of 'actor' is that, like stand-up, it takes years of working and training to become any good at it, and I simply haven't done that work. Occasionally on the stand-up circuit an actor type will have a go, and it looks awful. I've been at the back of the room with comedians slating the poor bloke because it's clearly an actor 'pretending' to be a stand-up, and not actually being one. Likewise, I have no illusions that real actors would look at what I do and probably have similar derogatory comments about my acting abilities. They are two different worlds. Basically the difference between an actor and a comedian is that an actor goes on stage and pretends to be someone else, whereas a stand-up comedian gets up on stage and pretends to be himself.

In the end, I decided my audition piece for Brunel University was going to be a five-minute extract from

---

* Having said that the world of acting is very wanky, and loads of actors I've met are wankers.

the monologue 'A Chip in the Sugar' performed by Alan Bennett in his *Talking Heads* series. Because that's a good idea, isn't it? If you've never acted before in your life, what easier way to start than playing a repressed homosexual with a history of mental health problems. To be honest, if I'd known that's what the monologue was about I'd have probably not chosen it out of fear of not being able to take on such a weighty role. But the truth is I'd never seen or read this monologue in my life, and I'd taken a random bit from the middle of it not bothering to read the whole thing (not exactly what you'd call 'method', is it?). The only reason I had chosen it in the first place was that I was a massive fan of *Spitting Image* and I really liked the Alan Bennett puppet. I used to do a fairly decent impression of him to my mates (copied from the puppet rather than Alan Bennett himself) so my theory was 'I may not be able to act, but I can just about do a passable impression of someone who *can* act, so I'll get the audiotape of him performing it, learn it, and mimic him.' And that's what I did. I sat there in front of about fifty other students who were auditioning, stared at the ceiling for fear of making eye contact, and suddenly started doing a strange sort of *Spitting Image* impression of Alan Bennett. Albeit an impression of Alan Bennett getting his lines wrong.

To this day I have absolutely no idea how I got in to university. Maybe it was my geography O-level that swung it. Nice one, Mum. The university was in St Margarets near Twickenham and the first thing I needed to do was to find a place to stay. I was twenty-five and classed a 'mature' student, so I wasn't allowed to live on campus. I guess this was for fear that the 'mature' students might get excited by the young girls and attack them. 'Mature' was a label that I wore with pride, as to this day I have never had that adjective bestowed upon me by anyone. But then again, if I think it's funny to write jokes about young girls being attacked on campus, I suppose I've only got myself to blame. I shared a house with two girls, also both mature students, who likewise were not allowed on campus as they were obviously a threat to young boys. One girl was called Becky, and the other Tara. I had met Tara briefly at the freshers' ball* but our first proper meeting was with a mutual friend at the Cabbage Patch Comedy Club in Twickenham. We started going regularly to that club before I did stand-up, and despite the fact that it was a small room above a pub with a tiny stage, getting to play there when I finally started doing stand-up was a genuine thrill and quite nerve-racking, as I'd spent so much time there as an audience member thinking 'That's what I want to do.'

Tara, Becky and I shared a three-bedroom house in Hounslow: 2 Howard Road, which coincidentally is the same address Sid James lived at in *Bless This House*. (If you don't know what *Bless This House* is, look it up. If

---

* I always think 'freshers' ball' sounds like a competition for men to show who's got the cleanest undercarriage. Actually I don't 'always' think that, I just thought of it now, but in comedy 'I always think' is better than 'I just thought' because it sounds more passionate and thus more personal.

you don't know who Sid James is, then this book probably isn't for you.*) One of the bedrooms was massive, one was medium-sized, and one was tiny. We drew straws to decide who got what room. Becky drew her straw and got the biggest. Tara got the medium bedroom. I'm not telling you who got the smallest room, you can work out the rest yourself.

The day we moved in Becky immediately left to go on holiday and so Tara and I were left on our own for two weeks, during which time we started having a fling, a fling which I am delighted to say is still going on nineteen years later (having said that, I am only on page 169, so if anything changes I'll keep you informed).

Within days we were sharing Tara's room and using my room as storage. The only problem was that we now had to inform Becky that things had changed. She was now sharing a house with a 'couple', which is understandably hard to hear when you think you're going to live with two single people. On Becky's return, Tara decided it was best if she disappeared for a few hours so I could be the mug who broke the news. This way of leaving me to face the music seemed to work for Tara, and she decided to adopt this philosophy on an ongoing basis, which I'm pleased to inform you is still working out for her today.

So Becky returned. The conversation went *exactly* like this:

* Which I appreciate is a bit late to be telling you, given that this is page 169.

Me: You know you won the draw and got the biggest room, Tara got the medium and I got the smallest?

Beck: Yeah.

Me: Well, things have changed.

Pause.

Becky: I'm not swapping rooms.

Me: I know you're not. The thing is . . . I'm now in the middle room.

Pause.

Becky: Tara's agreed to take the little room?

Me: No.

Pause.

Me: We're both in the middle room.

Pause.

Becky (confused): You're going to *share* the middle room?

Me: Yes.

Becky: That's odd.

Me: Not really.

Long pause of realization.

Becky: Oh fucking hell.

It all worked out fine in the end, and we kept the public displays of affection down to a minimum, which, as a Lancastrian, I considered the norm anyway.

One night I made the big decision to tell Tara I wanted to be a comedian. That might not sound like a big decision, but up until that point I'd never told a living soul. It was a dirty secret. Like wanting to be a porn star, or a serial killer, or a judge on *Britain's Got Talent*. (I think Britain genuinely *does* have talent, so it never ceases to amaze me that the one show that calls itself that is also the one show that seems to demonstrate the opposite.)

Tara's reaction couldn't have been any more laid-back. She didn't bat an eyelid (or maybe she wasn't listening). I may as well have said doctor, or binman, or shelf stacker, or lawyer. She made me feel like it was a completely normal thing to want to do, and because of her own love of watching live comedy we started going to a few gigs with one eye on me finally getting up and having a go. It still took a year before I did, but I was now at least heading in the right direction to that all-important first gig.

And it really is all-important if you want to be a comedian. Without doing that first gig, you're not a comic, you're just the funny bloke in the pub. I would like to point out that the use of the word 'just' in that previous sentence is only aimed at those who, like me at the time, really, *really* want to be comedians. Because if you don't want to be a comedian, then 'just' being the funny bloke in the pub is more than enough. In fact, I would strongly recommend it. That way you don't risk turning into a self-obsessed, fragile loony. Stay in the pub and turn into an alcoholic instead.

But if you do want to be, or at least try and be, a comedian then at some point you've got to just get up and have a go. No amount of watching comedy, or doing comedy courses, or university degrees, or whatever other bullshit you've convinced yourself will help, is going to prepare you to do it. You've got to just jump in at the deep end and hope for the best. And from a man who took about ten years to jump in, trust me, I'm speaking from experience. It took me about nine and a half years before I even put my trunks on.

You see, by getting on stage for the first time you immediately go into the top one per cent of the UK population in terms of being the best stand-up comedian in the country. You've actually had a go, whereas most others haven't. Other people, perhaps even much more 'naturally' funny people than you, simply won't take that leap in terms of the first gig. So, if you genuinely want to be a professional comedian, then you're better off being the unfunniest man* in the world who's had a go, than the funniest man in the world who hasn't. Actually the best scenario is probably being the funniest man in the world who doesn't actually want to be a comedian at all, but who wants to be one of those serene, happy in their own skin, laid-back losers.

---

* Or woman, of course. I don't want to upset any female comedians, and would like to state publicly that I am well aware that women can be extremely unfunny too.

PSYCHIATRIST'S OFFICE

BRIAN: Is joking around important to you?

LEE: Yeah. Certainly with friends and family. I love it when I make one of my children laugh so much they wet themselves. My dad was the same.

Lee decides he'd better clarify that his dad was a joker, rather than someone who wet himself.

LEE: Both my parents would be people you would class as 'jokers'.

Lee realizes he has just told a psychiatrist how she would class somebody, when in fact she is probably in a better position to know how they should be classed. Maybe she would class them as 'showing symptoms of attention deficit hyperactivity disorder eased by self-administered Cognitive Behavioural Therapy which, although effective, is still bringing out a maternal protective instinct in those around them'. But Lee thinks 'joker' is more catchy. Certainly if you were describing yourself on a dating website.

BRIAN: Joking certainly seems the way you

communicate with people.

LEE: I don't do it consciously. It's just the way it's always been. I was brought up like that, and I'm in a job surrounded by comedians who talk to each other like that. To me it's a normal way of speaking.

BRIAN: But it is clearly important to you when you are communicating with friends to get a laugh.

Lee doesn't like this. He sees other comedians who are always cracking gags as a bit tiresome at times. Like children who are lacking attention. He thinks of himself as different to these people. So to be told by a professional that this is clearly a part of his make-up slightly annoys him.

LEE: Not really.

Lee decides that's a good counter-argument and leaves it at that. The silent pause by Brian suggests that she is expecting more, so Lee wonders if 'not really' was actually enough of an argument to convince her, and so decides to say something else.

LEE: I think 'getting a laugh' is much less important to me than most of

the comedians I know. It's
probably the reason I get less of
a thrill on stage when I do stand-
up than other comics. In fact, if
I was so bothered about 'getting a
laugh' I wouldn't be here, because
there is an argument that
psychotherapy can ruin a comedian.

BRIAN: Why?

LEE: Well, Freud said there was no such
           thing as jokes . . .

           *Lee suddenly realizes that not
           only does she know this, it was
           actually Brian that told him this
           in the first place. Lee has a
           habit of doing this. If someone
           tells him some interesting fact,
           Lee will forget who told him and
           find himself telling it back to
           the person who told him in the
           first place. When Lee is told by
           the person it was actually them
           that told Lee, Lee will often save
           face by saying 'No you didn't',
           with such extreme confidence he
           makes the other person question
           their own sanity. He can make
           people crack. Which Lee sees as a
           small price to pay for being seen
           to be in the right.*

LEE: . . . and that the joke only
           represents something else. A
           release valve, or a way of covering
           up a deep-rooted sadness . . .

Lee realizes that he doesn't know what he's talking about. He is talking about Freud even though he knows virtually nothing about the subject, and what's worse is that he's saying it to a psychiatrist. Lee knows he can either bail out now and admit defeat, or talk with even more confidence, and slightly more loudly, in the hope that he will get away with it. Due to his vast experience with this technique, he opts for the latter.

LEE: (slightly more loudly) . . . or issues that were created during childhood . . . (even louder) . . . and stuff.

Brian doesn't pull him up on it. Once again Lee has got away with it.

LEE: Anyway, if I was bothered about 'getting a laugh' I wouldn't have seen a psychiatrist because these 'issues' that the joke represents might be cured, for want of a better word . . .

Lee really did want a better word.

LEE: . . . and so although 'cured', I wouldn't be 'funny'. The fact that I'm here proves that getting a laugh is less important to me than most of my piers.

Lee realizes that in transcribing the session with his psychiatrist for the book, he has just spelt 'peers' wrong, so has in fact just compared himself to a large wooden structure that juts out over the sea. Lee decides to keep the error, on the basis that the explanation of the mistake will hopefully get a laugh.

CHAPTER ELEVEN

Bun Shops and balloons

I often get asked what was my big 'break' in comedy. Despite the fact that, like most slightly neurotic comedians, I don't have a sense of having 'arrived' so therefore don't then have a sense of having 'broken', I always say 'Doing that first gig.' It was on 20 September 1994 in Surbiton, at a place called the Bun Shop, which has subsequently been renamed Brave New World, perhaps in recognition of that historic performance, as they realized something changed that day that was to shape the world for ever. Or maybe The Chancer Who Told Knob Gags doesn't sound like a good name for a pub.

I had spent that first year at university realizing that the Film and Television degree (OK . . . Drama) wasn't going to make me a stand-up. The main problem was the hours I did. I thought I would be doing forty hours a week at university, that it would be all-consuming, that lunchtimes would be about hanging around the café as one of the students played piano and we all joined in with a song and dance routine, which spilled out on to the street as we jumped on taxis. But it was only nine hours a week, and I spent most of my time working in William Hill the bookmakers next to Hounslow bus station. I had started a brand-new life as an arty student that was hopefully going to encourage me to start stand-up, and yet I was spending most of the week taking two-pound bets on the greyhounds from old men with roll-ups. Also, I realized that most of what we were doing was theoretical and not really performance-based, which I felt wasn't really going to help my comedy career. The few classes we did do seemed to be about dressing in black and rubbing walls, in what is described by the arts world as 'physical theatre' but what I would describe as 'fucking embarrassing'. This just wasn't going to make me a stand-up comedian. However, what I didn't appreciate at the time about this university degree was that it *was* giving me other things that would prove vital in the long run. To start with it was making me write essays, and hand them in on time. That might not sound much, but for someone who hadn't done A-levels, or barely bothered to do his O-levels for that matter, this was new. Sitting down and writing with a deadline is probably the thing I do now most in my job. The course also allowed me to run my own comedy nights and count them towards my degree, and these nights were invaluable in giving me stage time when no one else was booking me. If you can't get a gig, create one. It's probably the reason I now don't trust chefs who've had to buy their own restaurant.

But this was all *after* I'd done my first gig, I still had that to get through, and suddenly I had an opportunity.

The Bun Shop's comedy night was called the Gong Show, and because of its proximity to the university, Tara and I had been to a couple of nights out there, when I wasn't performing my own comedy routine in the middle-sized room (this is a 'I am bad at sex joke', and not to be taken at face value. I would genuinely rather you think of me as being bad at sex than think of me practising comedy to my girlfriend in the bedroom). It was called the Gong Show because in the middle of it, in between the paid performers, amateurs were allowed to get up and have a go (the comedy night, not sex with my girlfriend). When the audience had had enough they would shout 'gong' and a man, who for some inexplicable reason was dressed as a gimp, would hit a big brass gong and the unfortunate act would have to leave the stage. It was pretty brutal, because the audience often wanted to shout 'gong' even before the poor newbie had reached the microphone. The few new acts I'd seen there had all been pretty bad, and I thought if I'm terrible surely I can't be much worse. Could I? So, after days of weighing it up and trying to pluck up the confidence, I decided I would have a go. I had finally, after ten years, made my decision to actually make a start.

Although, thinking about it, that's not strictly true. I'd sort of tried to make a start about a month before, but it hadn't quite worked out.

I had been reading in the newspaper about a

competition that was happening at the Edinburgh Festival that week called 'So You Think You're Funny', which was aimed at people who wanted to make it in stand-up. I remember thinking it was quite a brutal name for a competition, like a dancing competition being called 'So You Reckon You Can Foxtrot Do You, Knob Head?' They printed a joke from one of the contestants, called Martin Trenaman. I can't remember the joke, but I remember thinking it was funny, and being slightly surprised that a sort of silly one-liner, which is what it was, was 'allowed'. When I say 'allowed' I don't mean within the rules of the competition, I mean allowed by the world of comedy. Although 'gag' men were starting to appear on the circuit a bit more often, the general rule, or certainly from what I could see, was that comedians were quite observational and, to a degree, still slightly political, although this was starting to fade, thank God. I say 'thank God' as any attempts I've ever done at proper political comedy have failed dramatically, and so if politics had stayed as the main agenda for comics I wouldn't have lasted five minutes in this job. Possibly not good for society, I agree, but if things hadn't changed I might never have ended up playing Idle Jack in the ITV Christmas panto, so in terms of the wider good it did for the nation, it's swings and roundabouts.

I still hadn't been to many comedy clubs at this point so maybe I just hadn't seen a big enough variety of acts, but as far as I was concerned traditional one-liners were out of vogue. To read about someone in a comedy competition and their funny one-liner was a bit of an eye-opener. It's not that I was a gag teller as such with my mates, but my theory was that if I could get together enough one-liner-type ideas, then it might be easier for me to do my first gig. I felt it would be easier than me actually baring my comedy soul by saying stuff like, 'Hey, guess what I've noticed', or 'Guess what gets me angry.' I suppose in my mind it was a way of saying 'If you're not laughing that's fine because it's not me you find unfunny, it's these jokes.' A way of hiding behind the gags. A weird statement, I grant you, but one that I genuinely felt was true. I think, looking back, I performed with this in mind for the first few years of my act, and to a degree still slightly do today.

I rang the offices of the Gilded Balloon theatre, who ran the competition, and told them I would like to enter, and what day did I need to arrive? They laughed in my face (which was a good start) and told me that you couldn't just turn up, you had to audition and do heats. The thing in the paper was referring to the final (like the Alan Bennett monologue I'd only scan-read it). I was shocked. I couldn't believe that so many people wanted to be a comedian. I thought it was just me and Martin Trenaman (who I'd only just read about). Surely there weren't that many other deluded people (because that's what I still felt at this point) in the world? I was told to start doing some gigs and contact them in a year's time for the next competition. 'What? You mean there's enough deluded people to warrant a competition *every* year?' Blimey, you'll be telling me next that they could turn this talent contest-type format into an (inexplicably) successful series of television shows.

But luckily, a month later, I had found a place that *would* have me, the Gong Show. I phoned up and booked myself in for the new-act section. It was going to be in a few weeks. All I needed now was an act.

PSYCHIATRIST'S OFFICE

BRIAN: The fact that you decided to 'hide behind' your gags when you started out is another example of you using CBT. You were protecting yourself. You were dividing up and saying it's the jokes that would be the problem if the audience didn't laugh, not you. It's a coping strategy, and it was actually a healthy thing.

Although Lee agrees with her, as this got him on stage in the first place, he is also aware that this sort of protection for yourself means you are not always 'being yourself', which is limiting in terms of how far you can go. But Lee is happy that she thinks of it as a healthy thing, as he doesn't want her to think of him as just the bloke with the ADHD, he wants her to think of him as 'the king of the coping strategies'. Lee's mind wanders, and he wonders if 'king of the coping stategies' is a good name for his next tour, or whether it sounds too negative, like the best he will achieve on the night is 'coping'. He decides against it, and wonders if 'Lee Mack on Tour' is more likely to sell tickets.

BRIAN: CBT can be used for all sorts of things. Like we get you to challenge your notions about flying, which you write about later in your book. Does worrying really keep the plane up?

LEE: Yes.

Lee knows this question was rhetorical, and he was clearly joking in his response. He knows that worrying doesn't keep the plane up really. But to him it's like knowing that the sun doesn't really move in the sky; it's one thing knowing it, but another thing feeling it. Despite the fact that every person in the world knows that it's actually the earth moving, we all still think of it as the sun that is moving in the sky. Lee's mind wanders and imagines a great scientist like Stephen Hawking sat in his garden in the sun not enjoying the heat, and thinking 'I'm looking forward to the sun moving over there', even though he knows that it's the earth that is moving really. In his imagination Lee moves Stephen to the shade. Lee is very kind like that and deserves some sort of OBE.

LEE: Do you think me changing my name from Lee McKillop to Lee Mack was a form of CBT?

BRIAN: Yes, I do. And again I think it was healthy.

Lee has always worried that changing his name, and doing 'gags' as opposed to talking about himself, was, to some degree, a bit of a cop-out in comedy, as it was a way of not being totally himself. But here is a professional psychiatrist telling him that actually it is a healthy way to be. Lee starts to reconsider his long-held belief and wonders if he might change his name to Frankie Marrow and tell knock knock jokes. Lee's mind wanders and he starts to think about the real Frankie Marrow, a comedian that never turned up at one of Lee's early gigs. Lee has always wondered what happened to him. Lee then daydreams that Frankie is also sat in a wheelchair wanting to be moved into the shade. Lee moves Frankie under a tree and decides that actually a knighthood would be more appropriate.

CHAPTER TWELVE

Gags, mags and slags*

'Where do you get your ideas from?' is the question that I, and I guess most other comedians, get asked more than any other. And despite the fact that I should now have a stock response for that question, I still don't really know how to answer it. Imagine if someone said to you 'You know those thoughts you have in the day-time about stuff, where do they come from?' 'Er . . . My head?' 'Yeah, but how do they get in your head?' 'I dunno. Sorry, have we met?'

This isn't really the book to be analysing too deeply how comedians come up with ideas because A: it could go on for ever and fill a book itself, and B: I don't really know what I'm talking about and I might struggle to fill a page.

But what I do know is that it takes for ever, it's a right

* Actually there aren't any mentions of 'slags' in this chapter, I just needed something that rhymed with gags and mags.

pain in the arse, and I often hate doing it. Writing is God's way of punishing comedians for having one of the best jobs in the world. If I ever find the magic person that can write all my gags for me, I'll commit bigamy and marry them, regardless of age or sex (as long as they're over eighteen. And female. In fact, if you're thinking of applying you don't even need to be able to write jokes).

Sitting at a computer all day wasn't always the way though. For the first few years my act consisted of randomly generated thoughts, gags and observations. A lot of these would happen just before I would fall asleep. This is quite common, and it's why a lot of comedians sleep with a note pad or some sort of voice-recording device next to their bed. There are basically two types of comedians, the ones that think of good ideas when they are in bed and bother to get up and write them down, and the ones that can't be bothered to get up, fall asleep, then completely forget what the idea was. I used to be the former, now I'm the latter.

I'm not saying I'm lazy, far from it, but nowadays writing is a job. I sit at my desk and write for a set amount of hours.* After that the workday is over, and if a nun walked into my house and fell in a giant bowl of custard, I wouldn't bat an eyelid. I certainly wouldn't

* From about eight o'clock up until about eleven in the morning if I'm writing stand-up, and until about two in the afternoon if I'm writing my sitcom, or this book. Oh hang on, is that the time? Right, I'm off.

make a note of it, because I'd have finished for the day. Obviously I'm not saying I *never* just casually notice something which then makes it into my act or sitcom, but I very rarely write it down any more because I don't want to be on a state of high alert twenty-four hours a day looking for material (and, trust me, some comedians are). I know comedians who deliberately pick odd days out, like a visit to the sex shop, just to generate material. Well, that's what they tell their wives anyway.

The idea of casually noticing stuff and putting it in my act was fine when I started out because I only needed a very small amount of material. For the first few years on the circuit I never needed more than twenty minutes so random thoughts got me through. In fact for some comedians this is how they *always* produce new stuff, even when doing big tours. I've heard many a comic say the phrase 'I've never actually *written* anything in my life.' I'm often left with either the feeling of 'You lucky sod' or 'Yeah, it shows.'

For me I soon realized that if I was going to generate enough material to do longer sets or telly shows then this process of randomly thinking of stuff simply wasn't going to be enough. Living your everyday life and hoping that eventually you will notice enough funny things to fill a whole TV series, or stand-up tour, simply doesn't happen. Unless you're an extremely lucky person, or shit. I used to get paranoid that I simply wasn't 'noticing' enough funny things in everyday life, and that this would hold me back. Then I realized it's the same for most comics. Comedians don't go round seeing funny things, they see things that they can make funny. There is an important difference. In fact, some comedians do the almost impossible and see funny things that they then make unfunny, but enough of _ _ _ _ _ _ _ (fill in your own name according to who you dislike. And if you're thinking of putting my name in there, count the dashes. I'm ahead of you).

Coming up with new ideas from scratch is hard, especially early on in your career when you're not used to doing it. The problem with writing from a blank piece of paper is that you can write about literally anything. That might sound liberating, but it's not. Given the choice it's much easier to write about something specific. I find it a lot easier if someone says 'Write a joke about a tortoise on an escalator'* than if they say 'Write a joke about anything you want.'

That's why, a few years after I started stand-up, I started to develop a technique for writing that forced me to write about something specific. And no, it's not just a system for writing jokes about tortoises on escalators.

I developed the technique when I was working on one of my early TV shows, *The Sketch Show* on ITV. I was suddenly in a position where I could perform as many sketches as I could think of in front of millions of people. But I didn't have enough. So I went off with my old college mate Neil Webster, and we locked ourselves away in a cottage for three days. After a day of achieving

* Having said that I've just spent the last five minutes trying to think of one and can't.

nothing I decided that I'd had enough of staring at the fireplace not knowing what to write about, so out of frustration I picked up a magazine and told him to pick a random page number. There were loads of different little articles on the page, so I asked him to narrow it down to a corner. He said top left. It was an article about fishing. I told him that we would both sit and write a sketch with a ten-minute deadline about fishing. So we did. Afterwards we read our sketches to each other, and obviously given the fact that we only had ten minutes, they were a bit crap (or 'carp' as I punned at the time, as Neil wept, knowing he had three days of this). Then we did it again, a new page, a new random corner. We found that about every one in four mini-sketches had just about a funny enough premise, or key joke, that it was worth exploring a bit more. We'd then spend the next hour or two extending it and working on it together. The only rule is that you *have* to write something. Even if it's the silliest, most groan-inducing, childish, want-to-stab-yourself-in-the-eyes-with-a-fork nonsense (I sell those ones to Tim Vine).

It's a technique that also seemed to work for stand-up, and that's pretty much how I've written a large part of my stuff for the last ten years. Don't get me wrong, I'm not saying *all* of it. A lot of it does come from every-day observations or thoughts, and I will jot them down, and then expand on them (well, if there's a pen close to hand, otherwise I just fall asleep again). But, like I say, it's never enough for a whole show, and that's when the magazine comes out.

I've never really enjoyed the process of writing. What I enjoy is finishing it. Like exercise. I suppose I am what is classed as a 'hard-working comic', although I reckon that on average, over the course of a year, I still only do about a forty-hour week. When I'm writing and touring at the same time then this can easily be a sixty-hour week, but there are times when I am not touring or writing where I am doing a no-hour week. So all in all, spread out over a year, I do no more hours than anyone else does in a full-time job. Apart from the blokes from the council who had to fix the drain outside my house. They somehow managed to do a six-hour week, which is both frustrating and impressive at the same time.

To be honest, the idea that I am a 'hard-working comic' says as much about the work ethic of an average comic as it does about my capability for hard work. It's a bit like when people use the phrase 'comedy genius' to describe a comedian.* Although the people they are describing are often really great comics, I sometimes think genius might be pushing it. What they mean by comedy genius of course, is that in relation to other comedians they are a genius, which isn't actually the same, is it? Other fields of work don't feel the need to prefix the title genius with the title of the job. Einstein is known as a genius, full stop. Not a 'science genius'.

Nowadays, when I'm writing, I spend about six days

* Not me, I hasten to add. In fact, the most memorable description I've ever had was 'fey'. I wasn't 100 per cent sure what it meant, but someone described it to me as having a 'fairylike quality'.

a week at my computer, getting up at about 7 a.m., sometimes even earlier, and writing until about lunchtime. The reason I do this is two-fold. Firstly I always seem to be more creative at the crack of dawn, before my brain fills up with other things that need doing in life, like paying the gas bill. Actually 'need doing' is sometimes a bit of an exaggeration, as, like many writers, I will find things that need doing just to avoid writing. Many a day has started with me thinking things like 'Actually, I'd better not write today. I really need to wash those conkers.'

Secondly, and more importantly, I want it out of the way.

You see, this was never part of the plan, the sitcom, the book, the TV shows, the tour, and so, to a degree, it still feels odd that it eats into my day. In fact, I didn't really have a plan. All I wanted was to be a regular on the circuit. As jobs go, it doesn't get much better than that. You work three or four days a week, and even then you're only doing twenty minutes a gig, with the rest of the day to yourself. And you don't even need to write, as your act is so short, and so few people know who you are, you can just rely on having a collection of casually generated funny thoughts, rather than continually writing new shows year after year.

Of course it would be a lie to pretend that I am doing all these projects reluctantly as someone who doesn't actually want them or need them, because if that was the case I could easily go back to just doing the circuit. The reason I don't is that I really enjoy the challenge of continually coming up with new ideas. Without the deadlines of new tours or sitcoms, I simply wouldn't do it. That's the problem with the circuit. You don't need to generate as many ideas to stay afloat, and I haven't got the natural instinct to do that without the huge kick up the arse that these deadlines give me. If it wasn't for these other projects I'd be still spouting the same old gags I've been doing for years, and that would eventually send me insane. Instead I spend hours every day trying to come up with new ideas, which will eventually send me insane.

Preparing material for the first gig was difficult. I had no gags and no experience on how to get any.

The first joke I remember coming up with was this:

'A man came up to me in the street the other day and said *"Big Issue"*. I said, "Bless you."'

It was something I used to do to amuse my mates if we went past a *Big Issue* seller. Not in earshot of the seller of course, because I'm not a complete twat (some people who know me will now be tempted to follow that phrase with the old joke 'Why, what bit's missing?'). It would get a little laugh from my mates, and I thought maybe a real audience would laugh too. So it was in.

My second memory is not so much writing a joke but expanding on an already existing one. My dad used to tell a joke, an old shaggy dog story pub gag, about a prawn called Steve who had a friend called Christian, who was a lobster. The crux of the gag is that the prawn is convinced to turn into a lobster (not sure how, but in a world where prawns are called Steve you have to let go of natural history). After trying out being a lobster, he decides to go back to being a prawn, and when asked what had happened he said 'I'm a prawn again Christian.' Which to many is a terrible joke, but it still makes me giggle. I'm not sure if it's because it's good, or because it's so terrible it's good, or because I like prawns. I think it might be all three.

Before I did comedy I was very naive about how it all worked, especially the writing process. I thought it was fine to do jokes people had told me because this first gig wasn't about doing what I thought was funny, or working hard, or being original (basically all the things you have to actually do, and even then that only gives you a fighting chance of being any good), it was just about getting through this gig as painlessly as possible. I had so much riding on it. The point wasn't so much to succeed, it was *not* to fail. And in my (confused) head a pub gag was to some degree 'safe'. This was naive of course, because the audience at a lot of comedy clubs are 'professional audiences' who go to comedy a lot, and they expect more. They weren't born yesterday (or prawn yesterday if you prefer. Eh? You don't. Fair enough, they weren't keen back then either). Plus I was personalizing it, so surely that would make it fine, right?*

I went out to the local fishmonger's and bought a real lobster and a prawn, and turned this otherwise basic

* Wrong.

joke into a mini soap opera and acted it out. I also decided to stretch it out to include lots of other fish. So I expanded the cast list to include a cod, three haddocks and a crab. I recognized that if I was silly enough with the whole thing then maybe the fact that it was just an old gag wouldn't matter.

I have always been a massive fan of Tommy Cooper, and despite the fact that many of his jokes are retold today, and some are classics, people forget that occasionally some of his material wasn't actually that strong, and that it was his sheer funniness in the face of adversity that made it great. In other words, he was sometimes funny *because* the jokes weren't great, not in spite of it.

I thought if I too could make this joke silly, it would be celebrating its averageness instead of being ashamed of it. I sort of knew the joke wasn't that good, and I think that's why I chose it, so I too could have some 'adversity' to face up to, which would then make it funny. Lesson number four: If you're doing your first ever open spot, come up with some good jokes; don't use ones that are deliberately average in the hope that your ability to overcome this hurdle may endear yourself to the audience. It's probably making life unnecessarily hard for yourself.

Most of the gags I used that night fell into the category of 'so bad they're good', but actually, it turned out, 'so bad they're bad'. Although I've still got the set list I took on stage that night, it's hard to remember what all the gags actually were as I didn't get to tell most of them (remember that man with the gong). Some of the others I was planning to do, or did, were:

Picking up a rubber snake and doing a deliberately bad ventriloquist act saying 'One plus one is two, two plus two is four, four plus four is eight.' Then, looking at the audience, I would say 'He's an adder.'

This joke was to stay in my act for a few months as I found the ventriloquist part of the joke worked really well for the sheer stupidity of it. So I dropped the punchline to make it look even more absurd. I even expanded this joke by saying to the audience 'Has anyone got a . . . (mimes cigarette) . . . snake?' This would get a tiny laugh, followed by a bigger one when someone actually did throw a rubber snake from the audience. The person who did this for me was usually a mate, and they would often hate the fact that I had roped them into the act. Friends started to dread answering the phone in case it was me. 'I've got another gig! Can you throw the snake?'

I went to buy my girlfriend some sanitary towels. The bloke said 'What type do you want?' I said 'Any.' He said 'Carefree?' I said 'Yeah, I don't give a fuck.'

Again this stayed for a while as Carefree were advertising heavily at the time so it was on a lot of people's minds (and pants).

A tramp came up to me the other day in the street and said 'Have you got a spare fag?' I said 'I don't smoke.' He said 'Any change?' I said 'No, I still don't smoke.'

Even though I now see the majority of my jokes from this time as bad, or deliberately bad (so as to overcome adversity), I actually think this is quite good. In fact, it's taken writing this book to remember it, and I think I might sneak this one back in my act.

Visual joke: I wore a pair of glasses with no lenses in them so I could put my finger through the 'lens' and scratch my eye.

This was something I used to do with my real glasses. One of the lenses in them was always popping out and so I would do this for a laugh with Tara (well, *I* used to laugh anyway). I think the main reason for me choosing to do this on stage was so I had an excuse to wear glasses, like Eric Morecambe. Glasses on a comedian are handy as you can fiddle with them after a punchline, which somehow always seems to make the joke funnier. I've tried the modern approach of readjusting my contact lenses after jokes, but this never seems as effective. Also the glasses helped me be 'someone else'.

They say laughter is the best medicine, but that's not true. My grandmother got cancer, I pissed myself, and she still died.

Wrong on many levels. Not nice (cancer), not logical (the phrase relates to the person who's ill laughing, not someone else), and also jokes on that particular phrase are well-trodden ground.

> *A copper stopped me and said 'You're swerving all over the road'. I said 'Course I am, I'm pissed.'*

This was a line I'd heard Peter Cook once say. But I thought I'd get away with that as surely the average audience member wasn't as big a fan of comedy as me, and wouldn't know that. Right?*

> *I was at an ice-cream van the other day and asked for an ice cream. He said 'Hundreds and thousands?' I said 'No, just the one.'*

This was a joke my mate had told me. I knew he hadn't written it, but I didn't know (or care) who had. To me it was just a pub gag.

That's the problem with getting other people to give or write jokes for you. Unless you trust them, they might be stolen. Many years later, I had two of my best routines nicked and used on a video by a comedian who has got a bad reputation for stealing gags. At the time I was struggling to make a decent living, and here was a man in the top ten of video sales using my material. It really stuck in my throat. In fact, for a while I hoped

* Wrong.

something would stick in *his* throat. Some people might say a man choking to death is a case of the punishment not fitting the crime, and they are right. He should have been hanged, drawn and quartered as well.

All comedians at some stage have either told a gag that has been written by someone else, which turns out to be nicked, or have at least told a gag that has already been thought of by someone else. It's easily done. But if one person is perpetually doing it then you have to assume that this person is on the take. The 'alternative' comedy scene that was born in the early 1980s has a few aspects to it that I do not particularly like, namely its shunning of anything that came before it and its slightly Oxbridge mafia* mentality that still prevails today. But it also has many, many positives about it, and the biggest is that it encouraged, in fact insisted on, originality of thought. However, I was naive on those first couple of gigs, and didn't know better. More experienced people should. End of rant.

I cannot remember what else I was planning to do that night, but it's fair –

Actually, no, not 'end of rant'. If there's one thing that gets on my tits it's people saying 'imitation is the sincerest form of flattery' when it comes to gag theft. If

---

* It is this mentality that has made me omit the name of the gag thief in question. Although I suspect he is, to some extent anyway, a gag thief, the real reason some comedians criticize him is not to defend the honour of gag ownership (which is morally justified) but actually a way of doing some cultural bullying.

someone broke into your house and stole your clothes and you then saw them in the street wearing them, you wouldn't say 'Look at you, trying to be like me, I'm genuinely flattered. Here, have my shoes as well.' End of rant (promise).

I cannot remember what else I was planning to do that night, but it's fair to say that through a combination of thinking of some one-liners, doing some 'sillies', having some props, nicking a joke from Peter Cook, and using my mate's (nicked it turns out) gag, I now had an 'act'. As far as I was (naively) concerned, that would do, as it wasn't about the material, it was whether I was funny or not.

So I had an act, all I had to do now was do the gig.

PSYCHIATRIST'S OFFICE

BRIAN: I think you have a lot of resilience.

LEE: Thanks.

Lee wonders why he is saying thanks. Maybe it's not a compliment. Maybe she has seen his act and the best word she can come up with as a summary of what she saw was 'resilient'. Lee thinks about including this as a quote on his next tour poster. Maybe he should get rid of 'Excellent – Sunday Times' and replace it with 'Resilient – Brian'.

LEE: Do you mean my childhood?

BRIAN: Well . . . yes . . . but also your job. The comedy.

Although Lee has just been wondering if she was referring to his act, he was actually being light-hearted, knowing that it might look quite amusing in a book to think that a psychiatrist regards his act as 'resilient'. He actually really thought she meant in his childhood. But now he genuinely thinks she might be referring to his act.

BRIAN: You talk about the fact that most
          of what you write is never heard,
          it doesn't make the grade, and so
          is thrown away and never used.

LEE: Yeah but I don't see that as
          resilient. I see it as the job.
          When people are mining for
          diamonds they don't get annoyed
          that they are hitting the pick axe
          against the wall of the cave a
          thousand times in the hope of one
          lucky strike, they see it as part
          of the job.

          *Lee is pleased with this analogy
          for about two seconds then
          worries. Firstly he knows nothing
          about diamond mining and has no
          idea if this is how they are
          mined. Secondly he doesn't know if
          they are found in caves and so
          might have just looked really
          ignorant. And worst of all he is
          comparing his jokes to diamonds,
          which might appear conceited. He
          perhaps should have said another
          precious stone. Maybe something
          less known for its value and more
          known for its resilience. Lee
          can't think for a moment which
          stone fits this description, so
          decides that if he ever uses this
          analogy again he will say 'Writing
          is like mining for steel.'*

BRIAN: But earlier on in your comedy
          career you didn't know this was

part of the job. In fact you thought stand-up comedians were 'special' people, and so the fact that you didn't feel like one of them meant that you probably thought you had to compensate by working hard. And that shows resilience, which is a good thing. The ability to be resilient may be something you developed in childhood after the break-up of your parents.

Lee isn't listening properly. He has just remembered that you don't mine steel, you make it from iron and something else, like glue or something.

BRIAN: By the way, I saw your appearance on *Live at the Apollo* on TV the other night.

Lee decides to put to rest once and for all his doubts about whether she thinks his act is 'excellent' or just 'resilient'.

LEE: What did you think?

BRIAN: I really liked your introduction.

Lee wonders how easy it is to become a coal miner.

CHAPTER THIRTEEN

The gimp and the gong

I cannot properly describe to you the nerves I had from the time of booking in that first gig to actually doing it. Suffice to say, it was the scariest thing I've experienced, and I've experienced the sight of three human beings coming out of my wife's body.* It got worse as the gig got closer.

I didn't actually refer to it as a 'gig' at the time, as it took me quite a while to adopt this phrase. I used to think 'gig' sounded just a little too affected, and something that was more relevant to music. I always felt as though comedians were perhaps trying to sound more rock and roll than they actually were when they used the word, and comedians acting rock and roll has always slightly put my back up. That's why I've never actually

* If you're wondering what seeing someone give birth is like, ladies, imagine giving birth, but ten times as bad. (All letters to be sent via my management company, Avalon.)

felt comfortable with the often-used phrase 'comedy is the new rock and roll'. I think comedy perhaps should be taking the piss out of the nonsense and vanity of 'rock and roll', not embracing it. Actually comedy being the new rock and roll is the least of my worries now, because it's become much worse. Comedy is now the new pop.

But, like any word, if you hear it enough you inure yourself to it and forget how you felt about it when you first heard it (like 'sat nav' or 'banoffee' or 'Clarkson'). So 'gig' it became.

The two or three days leading up to the gig are a bit of a haze to be honest, because I was so nervous I was drunk for a lot of it, mainly on Taboo, which I'd developed a taste for at Pontin's. Taboo was an alcoholic drink that was first marketed (i.e. pushed, like any other drug) in 1988, the year I first became a Bluecoat at Pontin's. I suspect that they had some sort of deal with Pontin's because part of our job was to constantly give out (push) small miniature bottles of the stuff to the customers (potential addicts). Most of it ended up in my and Saul's chalet, hence it being the drink of choice that year. They also brought out Mirage at the same time, the sister drink to Taboo, and the advertisement campaign asked the question 'Which one are you? Taboo or Mirage?' Not drinking at all wasn't one of the options, and so we had to make a choice. And Taboo won. It says a lot about the amount of alcohol me and Saul consumed that year that Mirage soon disappeared from the shelves, and Taboo went from strength to strength.

If I wasn't drinking, I was learning my act in the tiny bedsit I was now sharing with Tara. She found my rehearsals amusing, but not necessarily in a good way, and videoed me doing it using the huge camera that we had that I had borrowed from university as part of my Film and Television degree (as I was very much a Quentin Tarantino and not a wanker). At first I objected to this, then realized that if I couldn't over-come the nerves of being filmed, then getting up in front of a crowd would be non-starter. I also managed to film Tara doing my act for a laugh, a video which she made me swear would never be shown to another human being, hence me suspecting she has at some point in the last eighteen years thrown it away (I have spent the last two days trying to find this video in my attic so I can write about it in this book, but to no avail. She denies any foul play, I am suspicious).

Friends visited me to see how I was doing. It was like I was about to have a huge operation or something, and they were worried that they might never see me again. If it was a very close friend I would even run through the 'act' with them to get some feedback. This was, looking back, desperate. But that's what I was ... desperate. One of these visits almost changed the course of my early career, drastically.

My close friend Terry turned up on the afternoon of the actual gig to help steady my nerves, and had also come to watch the show itself. I asked if I could show him my 'act' to see what he thought. He agreed, but just for a laugh I decided to do a wind-up on him and do an act that was deliberately terrible to see his face. I told him to play some music and introduce me, as I quickly prepared in the bathroom. As soon as the music started I came running out of the bathroom, bollock naked, wearing a rubber Arnold Schwarzenegger mask, and proceeded to dance around the bedsit, waving my tackle around, until the music stopped. When the song ended, I took the mask off hoping to see Terry in a state of shock at how terrible my act was. How days and days of work had culminated in this sorry performance. But he wasn't shocked, or disappointed, or bemused. He was absolutely wetting himself laughing and thought it was the funniest thing he'd ever seen. I told him that this was just a wind-up and it wasn't what I actually intended doing that night. He asked me what I *did* intend doing, and so I got dressed and showed him. He smiled politely for five minutes, then told me in no uncertain terms that it was not as funny as the 'naked Arnie' routine. I was already full of self-doubt, I didn't need to hear this. I'd spent days preparing my material, and learning it, and I was now being told that some quick ad hoc lunacy was funnier. Maybe he had a point, maybe it was so 'crazeeeeee!' it was hilarious. After all, the number one rule in comedy is do what you find funny. This was confusing, because what I found funny about it was the fact that it *wasn't* funny. That was the wind-up. Maybe the audience that night would do the same as Terry though, and find it hilarious. Maybe it was hilarious because it was *not* funny. Did that count? I was now in a real dilemma, I was on in four hours and now I was considering a brand-new act. What should I do? I know, I thought, I'll drink some more Taboo. After a few more shots of the silly sauce, I had made my mind up. I was going to be bold and do 'Naked Arnie'. Maybe, just maybe, it would be the thing that made me stand out from the crowd. I think, for a brief moment, I may have done what they do in films and imagined my name in lights a few years from now: 'Tonight, fresh from Broadway, Naked Arnie'.

An hour or so later my other mate, Tim Healy, turned up, or as I now call him, Tim 'The-sensible-fucker-who-thankfully-turned-up-that-day-otherwise-I'd-now-be-living-under-a-bridge-drinking-meths-mumbling-some-incoherent-nonsense-about-listening-to-Terry-whilst-burning-the-box-set-of-*Terminator*-film' Healy.*

Terry got the music ready, informed Tim he was going to love this, and pressed play. I exited the bathroom and did exactly the same act. When the song ended I removed Arnie's face and waited for the applause. Nothing. Not even a polite grin. There is only one thing worse than trying and failing to make someone laugh, and that's trying and failing to make someone laugh whilst being stood naked and holding a rubber mask of Arnold Schwarzenegger. Tim told me it was terrible and that I couldn't go on stage and do it. I told him that was the point I was trying to make earlier, but Terry had swayed me. Tim asked to see the other act. I did it, and

* Not to be confused with Tim 'I-played-Dennis-in-*Auf-Wiedersehen-Pet*-and-was-married-to-Denise-Welch-off-of-that-*Loose-Women*-show' Healy, who is someone else.

although I didn't exactly take the roof off, he smiled a few times, maybe even the odd titter. And more importantly, as far as he was concerned, at no point did I get my penis out. It was a done deal as far as he was concerned, and it didn't take much for him to convince me to revert to the original act.

I turned up at the gig just before show time and was quickly shown into the 'dressing room', which, like a lot of circuit gigs, was the beer cellar/kitchen. I was introduced to the four or five other Gong Show participants, and one of them very quickly asked 'How many have you done?' I didn't really understand this question for a moment, as I assumed that all of us were brand new to this. In fact, I assumed that was the point of the Gong Show, complete novices. Maybe he meant something else? Maybe 'How many have you done' meant 'How many drugs have you done?' to steady your nerves. Maybe I should say 'None, just Taboo. You?' Maybe he's a psychopath and 'How many have you done?' means killings. Maybe I'm next. Maybe I should say 'A couple. You?' so as to look like I'm not judging him, so he doesn't kill me. Or maybe I should stop pretending I thought all of these things and just answer him. 'It's my first time,' I replied. His face lit up and he immediately announced to the group 'We've got a first timer!' I asked him how many he'd done and he said sixty. Bloody sixty! What the hell was he talking about?! How could he have done sixty?! Surely that made him a professional (unless he *was* a psychopath?). That wasn't fair. He told me that he'd been doing it for a year or so and that he and the others were regulars on the open-spot circuit, where they went round and did unpaid gigs for club promoters with the hope of getting paid work. This was all news to me. 'Open-spot *circuit*?' I'd been to a few comedy nights at this point, so I knew the concept of 'open spot', and that, sometimes, newer people would get up and have a go, but I'd always assumed that you did this once, or maybe twice at most, then got booked. Or they realized they were terrible and stopped doing it. Sixty? What was he waiting for? Surely he should know by now if he was good enough to do this job. If he hadn't been actually booked by now, surely the answer was clear.

Again, my naivety about how the circuit, and comedy in general, worked is startling when I look back now. People often say 'You have no idea if you're funny or not until you've done a hundred gigs.' That is not only true, it's also massively underestimated. If I'd known this before that first gig, I honestly don't think I'd have had the bottle to do it. I had put so much time and effort into thinking about (and putting off) this first and only gig, that the thought of a hundred would have cracked me. It would be like being told you had to take a hundred driving tests. As opposed to just the two that all the best drivers have. First-time passers are worse drivers. Fact.*

I was also told that night, by another one of the Gong Show contestants, to wake up the next morning and immediately book in loads more open spots regardless

---

* Actually, sort of a hopeful guess.

of how this one went. She told me to buy *Time Out* magazine and look in the comedy listings, where I would find dozens and dozens of clubs with open-spot sections. She said it was important that I didn't do just one gig at a time, otherwise the waiting round between gigs was too big and I would forget what I'd learned. What the hell was this woman talking about? I wasn't going to 'learn' anything. There was nothing to learn! (I had a lot to learn.) I would go out there tonight and find out immediately if I had a future in comedy. If so, great, they will book me, and word will spread very quickly that a new comedian has arrived and he was great, and you should all see him. Or (more likely) I would find out I was terrible, and give it up, but at least I'd have tried and wouldn't regret it later in life. So it's fair to say that, in my head, there was a lot riding on it. Maybe far too much. Was it too late to back out? Maybe I could come back next week when I was less nervous and more sober. Maybe with the Arnie mask.

To add to the pressure of the night, I had about eight friends sitting in the front row. To this day I am still not sure why I allowed this to happen. Nowadays if I have friends in a huge three-thousand-seat theatre, I will still make them sit at least halfway back for fear that I will catch their eye whilst on stage and it will put me off. It's back to this notion of 'it's slightly someone else who's on stage', so seeing people you know is a bit of a clash of two worlds. It's like when one of your close friends meets another of your close friends for the first time, and you suddenly realize you've spent the last twenty years acting slightly differently to both, and now you've got to own up that the whole thing has been a lie and the pressure gets to you and you scream into their face 'It's no good, I can't continue with this false persona any more, it's got to end now!' Actually, what you really say is 'Dave, Pete. Pete, Dave.'*

So how or why I had a group of mates all on the front row is a mystery. Maybe I felt that I wasn't ever going to do this again, so I wanted as many of my mates as possible to at least witness it. Like I'd been asked to play in the Premier League against Man Utd at Old Trafford; I knew I would be terrible and mess it up, and be the worst player on the pitch, but you'd still want your mates to witness such a big event, wouldn't you?†

Finally the gong master was in place, and it was time to start the gladiatorial executions masquerading as a talent show. A couple of Christians had already been gobbled up by the lions (I'm keeping the gladiator thing going, that wasn't their act) and now it was my turn. I stood by the side of the stage with my suitcase and prop glasses. I was so nervous I actually double-checked to make sure there weren't any lenses in the glasses by poking my finger in my eye, as the prop ones were very similar to my real ones and I was worried I'd mixed them up. Someone in the audience saw me doing this, and I saw them laugh to their mate. I panicked. Were

* Only say this if that's what they're called.
† I recently played in front of 35,000 people at Old Trafford in a charity match and missed a penalty. I really wish I hadn't invited my mates.

they laughing *with* me or *at* me? Looking back it must have been the latter, because never in the eighteen years of me doing stand-up has anyone in the audience pointed whilst laughing.

The regular host at the club was an Irish comedian by the name of Jack Russell.* I'm not quite sure why, but some people refer to this job as 'host', some as 'MC' and some as 'compère'. I tend to say 'host' as 'MC' sounds just a little too American and 'compère' a little too French. 'MC' always feels like we're about to have some sort of 'rap-off', like in that Eminem film.† If someone says 'compère', I always feel like there's a floating apostrophe left hanging in the air like an annoying bad smell (you know like garlic or cheese).

I had seen Jack hosting this show before on previous visits, and was always very impressed with the way he would talk to the crowd instead of doing material. He just seemed to be making stuff up, and I thought this was amazing. For the first few years of doing stand-up I would watch other comedians doing this. The host's job was often to be the 'chatty link' person rather than the 'material' person. I was often in awe of their abilities to just make stuff up. It took me years before I volunteered for the role of host, as I was so used to

---

* Not his real name. It was actually Fred Basset, but he felt that was a little too canine.

† I know it's probably not called a 'rap-off' and that might make me sound like a granddad, but there's a part of me that actually likes that. It's probably the same part of me that says 'that Eminem film', when I know damn well it's called *8 Mile*.

'hiding' behind the jokes. It's only when I started letting go of the gags and actually started talking to the audience that I realized it was something I really liked doing, and was (hopefully) quite good at.

It made sense of course, because the number one rule you learn in this job is 'be yourself' and 'do what *you* find funny'. When I was making my mates laugh in the pub I didn't do 'material'. It wasn't stuff I'd prepared, it was just chat. So it made sense to have an element of that in my act. Of course, you can't *only* do that because it's not foolproof enough. When you're making your mates laugh in the pub it isn't an hour and a half of laughs, it's a few sporadic bursts of laughs, followed by long periods of normal chat. Unlike your mates in the pub, the audience can't nip off to play the *Who Wants to be a Millionaire?* quiz machine when they get bored with you.

I was about to be introduced. This was it. Ten years of wanting to be a comedian had now come to this. 'Please welcome Lee Mack'.

As I said at the beginning of the book Lee Mack isn't actually my real name, it's Lee McKillop. I hadn't had to make any big decisions about this before this first gig. That decision had been made many years earlier when I was DJing at Pontin's. I had applied to be a DJ on a cruise liner* and had to send in a publicity photo to

---

* I never got the job. Thank God as well. It turns out if you're a performer on a ship you're classed as 'crew' and therefore the last to get in the lifeboats. No chance.

accompany the application. I had arranged for four of the Bluecoat girls to put on their can-can costumes from the 'Naughty But Nice' show and fan out loads of records whilst I stood in the middle of them smiling like a professional (i.e. grinning like a sexual predator). It was the single cheesiest photograph I have ever had done and I would like to pretend it was laced with irony, but it wasn't. It was so 'showbizzy' that using my real name felt really odd because I felt very 'un-showbizzy'. I don't mean that in a 'I'm so down to earth you wouldn't believe it' kind of way. I mean it in a 'I didn't have any discernible performing skills, so who the hell was I to think I was Mr Entertainer' kind of way. So using a pretend name made sense. What better name than that of my great-granddad Billy Mac. After that it was always going to be the case that if I ever did do comedy, then 'Lee Mack' would be the name I would perform under. Actually I contemplated Lee Savage for a short while, because that's my wife's maiden name and I thought it would make me sound a bit like the kind of bloke you'd see in an action movie. Then I realized it sounded a bit like 'Lily Savage', which is an altogether different image.

As Jack Russell announced my name at the Gong Show I immediately stepped on to the stage. I think I went on the 'Lee' rather than the 'Mack' for fear that if I waited for the 'Mack' I might have a chance to talk my way out of it and run away. I stepped on to the stage and my immediate thought was just how blue everything was. When you're in the audience you don't actually appreciate just how bright the lights shining on the stage are. It is extremely rare to see anything past the first few rows because all you experience is the sensation of a very bright light being shone in your eyes. This particular stage had quite a lot of blue lights for some reason. So, as I started telling my jokes to the crowd, all I could think about was how blurry and blue everything was. It was like chatting up a Smurf without your glasses on.

My second thought, before I'd even reached the microphone, was that this was actually all going to be fine.

I had spent so long building up to this performance, so many years of wanting to do it but not having the guts, that I'd heaped so much on to it, it was ridiculous. I was so fearful about what might happen, how much of an idiot I might make of myself, that I had had to drink loads of alcohol just to get me to turn up. I had built and built it up in my head as this huge monumental thing in my life, and the thought of actually doing it consumed me. I honestly think it's because of all that that I felt OK. Because when anything gets so built up in your head, the reality is never quite as bad as how you'd imagined it. In fact it was a relief, because it really wasn't as scary as I thought it would be. But then again how could it have been, because I'd turned it into such a huge thing.

It might sound like a convenient soundbite phrase that is written in a book but didn't actually exist in reality, but it really is the truth when I say that even before I'd got to the microphone I was so relieved at how calm I felt that I knew there and then that I was going to be a professional comedian. Admittedly I spent the next eighteen years wondering if I'd be able to remain as one, but at least it was a decent start.

I remember very early on doing the Peter Cook gag. It got a half-laugh and then someone shouted out 'Peter Cook.' How the hell did they know that? I thought my love for comedy put me streets ahead of these people in terms of knowledge. Who was this weirdo who, like me, knew stuff like this? Maybe I would get away with it because they hadn't said 'That's a Peter Cook joke', they'd only said 'Peter Cook.' Maybe the audience would think this person was a strange heckler who only shouted out the names of comedians. In a minute I might get lucky, he might shout 'Bob Hope' and they'll all think he really *does* have the problem, not me.

Looking back with experience I probably should have vocalized that last sentence at the time, as it might have got a bit of a laugh, and at least I'd have dealt with it. Actually, that's not true, looking back now what I should have actually done is not nick a Peter Cook gag in the first place, but given that I had, then that's what I should have done.

The other reason I didn't deal with it, apart from the obvious, which was lack of ability, was that I wasn't actually that fazed. I wasn't stood there trembling thinking 'Oh my God I've been found out and now I'm going to die on my arse.' Quite the opposite. Like I say, I was amazed at how calm I felt. This ten-year build-up to wanting to be a comedian was actually nowhere as scary as I'd made it in my head, so one person shouting out 'Peter Cook' wasn't really a massive concern to me. All that concerned me was that I felt really fine, and I knew I was going to be a comedian. Actually, I should have vocalized *that*. That kind of cocky talk would have turned the audience against me and given me the uphill struggle I was obviously looking for. Who needs crap jokes as adversity when you've got bottles hitting you.

I did a few jokes that were met with a combination of titters and bemused looks, and it would be fair to say that the audience sensed my inexperience. The fact that I looked fairly calm probably made the audience tolerate me a little longer, as the number one enemy of the new act is fear. In fact, not just new acts, all acts. Like I say, I think the number one rule in comedy is do what you think is funny. If you look nervous, the audience will assume you doubt whether you actually think it's funny, and if you doubt it, they will too. Don't get me wrong, when I say I wasn't nervous or scared at that first gig, I mean in relation to what I was expecting. I thought it was going to be so utterly terrifying that I would faint. The audience watching that night probably saw a nervous new act, hence the fact I didn't last that long. However, in relation to what they were expecting, a brand-new physically shaking wreck, which is what a lot of new acts are, they saw someone who was, at the very least, fairly controlled (but maybe not funny), so gave me a little bit more time. Or maybe my memory is playing tricks on me and they were just a bunch of sadistic bastards who were enjoying it for all the wrong reasons.

I glanced at my list of jokes and decided to do the ice-cream gag. This set list was stuck on the inside of a suitcase I'd carried on stage, which contained the stinky fish. This fear of forgetting the act has never properly left me, and for years I would think of elaborate ways to disguise my set list on stage. My best disguise was a Budweiser bottle I used to carry in my hand throughout the act. The label on the bottle had been removed, and in its place another identical-looking label had been stuck on. This label looked just like the original label, but actually on closer inspection each word was replaced with a gag heading. So the big 'Budweiser' slogan was actually *'Big Issue'* but written in the same colour and font. The 'King of Beers' wording changed to 'Ring and Ears'. The problem was, after each joke I was staring at the bottle like some sort of melancholy alcoholic who was cursing his addiction.

The ice-cream gag got a good laugh, and so it should. It's a good joke. Then someone shouted out 'Tim Vine!' Was this the same person who'd shouted 'Peter Cook'? I wasn't sure. Who the hell was Tim Vine anyway? 'What?' I replied, which isn't the wittiest reply I've ever said to a heckler. 'That's Tim Vine's joke.' Shit. Why did I say 'What?' I may as well have said 'There's a person at the back who didn't quite hear your accusatory remark, so for goodness sake speak up, man.' Anyway, he was wrong, it wasn't Jim Vine's joke, or whoever the heckler had just said, it was my mate's joke. Well, all right, I knew he probably (definitely) hadn't written it, so it wasn't actually *his* but that didn't mean it was this Tim Wine's joke, or whoever the heckler had just said. The audience didn't actually care whose joke it was (they rarely do), but they did care that there had been another heckle and I hadn't dealt with it. So, the atmosphere at the Gong Show was becoming a little 'gongy'.

Again, I didn't massively care. As far as I was concerned this was becoming a runaway success. I had done it, I had got on stage and I had done my first gig. It was like I had finally plucked up the courage, after ten years, to do a parachute jump, only to be told halfway down that I was slightly drifting to the right and I was going to miss the big cross I was supposed to land on. Who cares? The fact that I'd jumped at all was the big deal. Although once I had got used to the feeling of jumping after doing it a few times, missing that cross started to feel like I was landing on the blades of a helicopter.

I tried a few more gags from the list, but after the Tim Lime thing it was over, and there wasn't really any way I was going to win them round properly. Had I not been so elated at just being on the stage I may have been gonged off earlier, as I may have started to show what I now call 'the boxer that's not coming back' look.

The comedian/promoter/charlatan Ivor Dembina told me this phrase. He said that there is a point in a boxing match when a boxer gets hit really hard with a big punch. He doesn't go down, and the fight isn't stopped. In fact, he can often carry on for a few more rounds. But after that big punch something happens to his eyes and the crowd knows that, despite the fact that he might carry on a little longer, he's definitely not going to win the fight, and it's only a matter of time before it's over. That's what a comedian having a bad gig does on stage. There's one defining moment where you're never going to win them back.

Gong.

An interval was called and my mates were all coming up to me telling me I was 'robbed' and 'hard luck', like it had been a bad night for me. I can see why they thought that. I'd only done about two minutes on stage (at most) and I'd been gonged off. But I didn't care. All that mattered was that I'd done it, I'd finally got on stage and done stand-up, and so for me that was massive.

The headline act that night was a comedian called Matt Welcome (to this day I'm still unsure whether it's his real name, or a comedy stage name, i.e. 'welcome mat'). Matt had stormed it and after the show I got chatting to him in the gents. First of all I wanted to know who Tim Tine was, and why they had heckled me. He explained that Tim *Vine* was a comedian on the circuit, and that one of the jokes I'd told was his. He told me that that was not the 'done thing', not in a way that made me feel told off, but in a way that made it clear I would be making life hard for myself if I didn't write my own material. I told him that I'd been told the joke by someone else, and that I hadn't nicked it, but he told me that was irrelevant. He made me feel like I was still handling dodgy goods. He was right. And no one likes to stand next to another man at a urinal to be accused of handling dodgy goods.

He also told me that he'd been to another gig that night and this was his second one, and that sometimes he would do three or four in a night. I couldn't believe it. How cool was that? Darting from one pub gig to the next, storming it and getting paid. I decided there and then that's what I wanted to do, and for many years after that my only ambition was to be a regular on the London comedy circuit. Even now, after doing all the telly stuff and the tours, the single greatest thing I've achieved is cracking all the clubs and getting paid as a regular at virtually all of them at some point. The one-man tours are great to do, but nothing ever quite beats those first few years on the circuit, seeing the same old comedy faces at all the clubs, and generally feeling that you're part of it.

The next morning I woke up with a Taboo hangover (i.e. the drink, I don't mean I woke up in bed with a cousin) and decided to get straight back on the horse, which was the opposite to my stable boy days, when I vowed *never* to get back on a horse. I remembered the advice of the previous evening and immediately went out and bought *Time Out* magazine and booked loads and loads of open spots.

This was great. I was a comedian.

Albeit a pretty new, pretty naive, and pretty crap one (nowadays it sometimes seems that being pretty crap is fine, as long as you're pretty). But so what? I could get better. After all, you were looking at a man who could have made it as a professional darts player/golfer/ caddie/astronaut. Being a comedian would be much easier, surely. I mean, how hard could it be?

PSYCHIATRIST'S OFFICE

Lee and Brian are mid-conversation on the subject of alcohol, and why Lee drank so much before his first ever gig. The chat then leads on to a wider one about alcohol sponsorship in comedy. Lee is clearly anti this and the conversation, although not an argument, is definitely 'lively'.

BRIAN: You've very briefly touched on the subject of alcohol in the book, and clearly there's some family history of it, so I understand where your objections come from.

Lee has heard this argument many times before as he has spent many years arguing the case against alcohol sponsorship. Well, with friends anyway. He hasn't actually campaigned or anything, as that would involve getting off his arse.

LEE: There's no history of heroin addiction in my family. But if a Colombian drugs cartel wanted to sponsor my show I would still object. Some things are just common sense and have nothing to do with family history.

Lee is pleased, in his head it's

> *one-nil to him. Not that it's a*
> *competition or anything, it's just*
> *a healthy debate (but if it was*
> *he'd be one-nil up).*

BRIAN: But do viewers really care who
sponsors these shows?

LEE: No, of course not. But it clearly
works. The only statistic you need
to look at to prove it works is
the fact that the alcohol
companies do it. And if alcohol
sponsorship results in more people
drinking alcohol then surely it's
morally suspect.

> *Two-nil (not that it's a*
> *competition).*

BRIAN: But you drink in *Not Going Out*.
Loads of scenes are you sat at the
bar.

> *Two-one.*

LEE: But that's not me, that's a
fictional character.

> *Lee spends a lot of time in*
> *interviews, and indeed this book,*
> *saying he is not an actor and just*
> *plays himself, and so realizes*
> *this is a bit of a dodgy argument.*
> *But he hopes the* ~~referee~~
> *psychiatrist hasn't spotted this.*

LEE: I am an idiot in the show. I spend

time drinking in the pub when I should be making something of my life. Surely I can show me doing that and yet in real life still object to booze sponsorship of the show.

If this was a competition, which it isn't, Lee would think about calling that three-one, but then realizes he referred to himself as 'I' rather than 'Lee', admitting he is playing himself and therefore negating his previous argument that he's playing someone else. So Lee decides that if he was having a competition, which he's not, then he would keep it as two-one (which means he would still be winning).

LEE: Look, I'm not anti-booze as such. I drink myself. But I do think it's odd how much it's allowed to be 'pushed' in adverts considering it is, after all, an addictive drug.

BRIAN: But loads of things are addictive. You could say the same about chocolate.

Again, Lee has heard this argument before and so has an argument ready. It's lucky this isn't a competition, otherwise Brian would be about to go three-one down.

LEE: But you don't hear about marriages
            being wrecked because of chocolate.

BRIAN: I do. I see people who break doors
            down to get to a bar of chocolate.

            *Damn. Lee has used this argument
            countless times and it never
            fails. No normal person has ever
            met anyone whose marriage has been
            affected by addiction to chocolate.
            But this isn't a normal person,
            it's a psychiatrist. It's now two-
            all in this competition that
            they're not actually having.*

LEE: OK, due to your job maybe *you*
            have. But personally I have never
            met anyone who has messed up his
            life because of one too many
            Yorkies. The bottom line is that
            alcohol is addictive. Much more
            addictive than chocolate. Fact.

            *Lee has no actual evidence to prove
            this, apart from common sense, and
            so to play safe he adds the word
            'fact' on to the end of the sentence
            to signify that anyone who doesn't
            agree hasn't done as much research
            as Lee. Even though he hasn't
            actually done any research himself.
            But that doesn't matter as it is
            clear that alcohol is worse because
            . . . Well, it just is. Fact.*

BRIAN: Well, I drink, and you drink. And
            we're not addicted to it.

LEE: Well actually I don't agree. I
           think anyone who drinks is
           addicted. If you smoke three
           cigarettes a day, it means you're
           addicted, albeit only very
           slightly, to fags. If you smoke
           forty a day it means you're *very*
           addicted. Likewise if you drink
           one glass of wine or three bottles
           a day, they are both forms of
           addiction, just to different
           degrees.

           *Three-two. Lee's victory (which
           isn't a victory because it's not a
           competition) is now complete. Lee
           then suddenly realizes that he has
           told a professional psychiatrist
           that she is an addict.*

LEE: (light-heartedly) Obviously I've
           not come here to tell you that
           you're an addict.

           Beat.

LEE: But you are.

           *Lee puts on his best psychiatrist
           voice.*

LEE: So tell me, why do you think
           you're an addict?

           *If Lee were in a competition
           (which he is not) he would have
           felt that this jokey remark would
           give him one extra injury time*

goal, and thus the final result would have been four-two to Lee. But when he gets home and listens back to the tape he actually thinks it makes him sound like a bit of an argumentative prick. So if it **was** a competition it would have actually been an own-goal.

Three-all.

CHAPTER FOURTEEN

The good, the bad and the mad

The next eight months, from September 1994 to June 1995, involved me doing many lots of open spots on the London circuit.*

The open spot circuit is tough. Before I started doing comedy I thought I was the only person crazy enough to want to try it – apart from those 'special' people who were born to do it (who I was now starting to realize weren't so special after all). But I was not the only crazy person wanting to do it, in fact there were hundreds. And many lots were much crazier than me was.

When I was doing the open spot circuit, there were basically three types of people doing it: the good, the

* 'Many lots' is an error I made when I first wrote this, and missed when checking back the first time. The fact that it could have gone to print like this really made me giggle as it would make me look like an absolute idiot, and so I decided to keep it in. If the secret to stand-up is to do what you find funny, then I don't see why that shouldn't apply to a book.

bad and the mad. Which one was I? Sometimes the good, sometimes the bad, never the mad (the maddest I ever saw was a man who just threw porridge at people and shouted 'I am Jesus!').

When I say 'sometimes the good', what I actually mean is relative to the other open spots at my level. In relation to the other more experienced, professional acts I was often the bad, as virtually all open spots are not very good when they start out (it takes at least a hundred gigs, remember?).

I would often do competition nights where the whole bill was new acts, and occasionally I would win. One of these clubs was the Comedy Café in Old Street, run by Noel Faulkner, or Jack Nicholson with Tourette's as I like to think of him. Why? Because he does a great impression of Jack Nicholson and he's got Tourette's. That's not a joke. He actually performs a one-man show about his condition in what must be one of the greatest names for any stand-up show ever: 'Shake, Rattle and Noel'. He's also one of the few people I have seen perform who uniquely fit into all three categories. He's good, bad *and* mad (and before anyone complains, I'm not saying he's mad because he's got Tourette's, I'm saying he's mad because he's mad). I really like Noel. He's the kind of person that I like seeing in the world of comedy and wish there were more of; people who seem to have spent their lives on the fringe of society looking in, not the other way round.

If you won the Wednesday night new-act night at the Comedy Café your prize was twenty-five quid, and the chance to perform ten minutes the following night with the professionals. That's when it used to show that you were new, as, on the couple of occasions I won, the following nights were distinctly trickier when I wasn't surrounded by other open spots.

My newness was very evident on one particular night.

When you start out it is very tempting to use 'stock' heckle put-downs. These are lines that have been done by so many comedians for so long that they no longer seem to belong to any particular comedian (which is a shame, as they probably once did). For example, 'Don't teach me how to do my job, mate, it's not like I come round to where you work and tell you how to flip hamburgers'* or 'Save your breath, you'll need it to inflate your girlfriend', or the very common 'The idea of heckling is to make *me* look stupid, not the other way round.' These lines tend to show a lack of originality, but they always seem to work in getting the comedian 'off the hook' when faced with a mouthy heckler. Unless they are used like I used them on this particular occasion.

I asked someone in the front row where they were from. They replied Sheffield. I realized that due to me being a very new comedian I couldn't think of anything to say. There was a few seconds' silence followed by me saying 'The idea of heckling is to make *me* look stupid, not the other way round.' The man calmly said 'I'm not

* There's a great story on the circuit about a comedian doing this line forgetting that he was doing a corporate for McDonald's. So instead of a put-down, it just felt like a statement of fact.

heckling, you asked me a question.' I said 'Oh yeah.'

At this point my act was still lots of one-liners, but I had slightly started to get more absurd. I would start stories with things like: 'So there I was, in the bath, with my mum . . .' Not as a way of shocking, but more a way of confusing. I told stories about meeting Snoop Doggy Dogg, but mixing him up with Scooby-Doo and interviewing him accordingly.

Although I genuinely thought these stories were funny at the time, looking back I think part of the reason I was doing this kind of stuff was a sort of defence mechanism. On the first few gigs I had decided to tell gags as a way of hiding behind the jokes. Now I was starting to hide behind absurdity. Instead of saying 'If you don't find me funny don't worry, it's the jokes you don't find funny, not me', I was now saying 'Don't worry if you don't find me funny, it's because you don't understand me.'

It's a defence mechanism I often recognize in other performers, even some that have been around for a while.

If it's a choice between the audience not laughing at them or not understanding them they will often choose the latter, because that way they've always got the get-out clause of 'I wasn't trying to make you laugh anyway, I was trying to confuse you.' Which is a lot nicer than standing there like a twat because a joke has just failed.

The first proper paid gig I got was at the King's Head in Crouch End on 3 June 1995. I know this because I was so proud that I could finally call myself a professional comedian (only thirty-five quid, but it still meant I was 'professional'), I kept the promotional leaflet from that night. I had done their new-act night on a Thursday night and the promoter, Pete Graham, a man who has probably had more famous comedians play his gig than any other, offered me an actual paid gig. I genuinely couldn't believe it. In fact, for those first few years I was so amazed that I was actually doing stand-up I kept loads of things: press clippings, posters, videos of performances. They all went in my scrapbook or on the shelf. I think, looking back, that maybe it was my subconscious saying 'This will all go tits up soon, so keep a record to prove you did it.' Nowadays, I don't really like seeing any evidence of work in the house because it reminds me of exactly that: work. When the front door closes I just want to spend time with my wife and children watching some nice family telly shows, like *Would I Lie to You?* or *Not Going Out*. ('Stop talking! You're missing the best bit!')

One of my favourite keepsakes from that time is a leaflet from a new-act night called 'Upstairs at the Redan'. I like it for many reasons. To start with it was the first time I had ever had my name on a poster or leaflet. I felt I'd arrived. I look back at my naivety with pride. I also like it because it was the first time I had ever been phoned by a promoter, not the other way round. It was an unpaid gig, but it still made me feel like I wasn't wasting my time pursuing this mad new vocation of mine. The other thing that always appealed to me about this leaflet is the names on the bill. Not only is there a 'Bert Satsuma', there's also a 'Frankie Marrow'. Here I was, pinning my first 'billed' appearance on to my toilet door, thinking it looked great, and not actually caring that I wasn't paid or that I was sharing the bill with two men named after fruit and veg.

Frankie Marrow never turned up that night, and I sometimes wonder what happened to him. Maybe that was his first gig and he bottled it, and now he spends his life wondering what could have been. Or maybe it was supposed to be his 101st gig, but he realized after his magic hundredth that, despite rumours to the contrary, it takes a lot more than a hundred to become any good and he'd had enough. Or maybe he was so happy in his own skin making his mates laugh that he realized he didn't need the acceptance of strangers to make him feel like he was doing something with his life. Or maybe he realized the name was holding him back, changed it to Michael McIntyre, and has gone from strength to strength.

PSYCHIATRIST'S OFFICE

BRIAN: It's interesting that you categorized the comedians you did the early shows with as 'the good, the mad and the bad'. When I was first learning psychiatry I used to do a similar thing and categorized patients into four: the mad, the bad, the glad and the sad.

LEE: What would I be?

BRIAN: Hard to say after just a few sessions with you.

LEE: Go on, just for a laugh, what am I?

Although Lee is pretending this is now a parlour game, he actually feels there is a lot riding on it. Lee thinks that there are basically three results that are good, and one not so good. The three good ones are 'glad', 'mad' and 'bad', and the not so good one is 'sad'. Lee thinks that if you're 'glad', then surely it means you're happy, which is a decent result. If you're 'mad', it means either you've got a certain off-beat way of viewing the world, or that you kill people and eat them. So assuming she doesn't

*think he's a psychopath, he will
take 'mad' as a positive. The
'bad' does of course suggest Lee
is not a nice person, but with a
bit of a positive spin Lee can use
this to make him sound like a bit
of a rogue, like the 'bad' cop in
a drama who drinks too much whisky
and has lost his family, but
actually has a change of heart and
becomes good, and always ends up
shagging the dolly bird. The only
one that isn't a good result is
'sad', as that word suggests he is
at best a miserable person, and at
worst a loser.*

BRIAN: I honestly would need a lot more
          sessions with you to determine
          that.

*Lee isn't letting this go. Lee
thinks that despite her protests
she probably **can** make an educated
guess, even after just a few
sessions.*

LEE: Come on, if you had to stake your
          mortgage on it now, what would I
          be? The 'mad', the 'bad', the
          'glad' or the 'sad'?

Brian thinks long and hard.

BRIAN: I suppose somewhere between 'glad'
          and 'sad'.

Lee decides that Brian has rushed

this answer and should have waited
a few more sessions. It's far too
early to say.

LEE: Oh. Well, at least you didn't say
'mad'.

At first Lee would have actually
quite liked 'mad', but he is sort
of glad she didn't say it, because
he now doubts the system, and she
might have meant the psycho
version of 'mad' rather than the
zany maverick version he was
hoping for.

BRIAN: Oh I don't know, the mad ones can
be very entertaining!

Lee wants to be the mad one again.
And the fact that he isn't makes
him feel less glad. In fact he's
now somewhere between glad and
sad, so maybe she's right in her
assessment. This worries Lee at
first, but then he realizes that
being described as 'being somewhere
between glad and sad' is pretty
much every human being he's ever
met. So basically he's run of the
mill. This pleases Lee for a
moment, then makes him feel
boring. Which in turn makes him
mad. Which means he's entertaining.
Result.

CHAPTER FIFTEEN

Coming out of the closet (well, wardrobe)

One way of establishing yourself on the comedy circuit when you start out is to enter a competition.

The big three when I was starting out were the Hackney Empire New Act of the Year (previous winners include Ronni Ancona), the Open Mic Award (previous winners include Frankie Boyle) and the much more prestigious, much more important, much more difficult to win so you really had to be brilliant, So You Think You're Funny Award (previous winners include Lee Mack). I entered all three in that first year of doing comedy and was lucky* enough to reach the final of all of them.

The first one was the Hackney Empire. This was

---

* I obviously mean 'good enough' but don't want to appear conceited. But, honestly, luck didn't come into it. Apart from when I lost two of them, then bad luck played a part.

terrifying because it was on an actual stage, in an actual theatre, and it was packed to the rafters. Before this I had only ever done small clubs, and bearing in mind these were often on new act nights, small clubs that were sparsely populated. Even for some of the more established acts on the circuit at the time, playing a theatre was unusual, and only for that handful of acts that were big enough to tour.

I realized that there were about sixteen acts in the final and decided I needed to find a way to stand out. I was going to open with a magic trick.

The idea was that right at the start of the act a wardrobe would be carried on stage with me hidden in it (honestly) and after getting out of it I would ask a member of the audience to get in. Then magically this audience member would appear at the other side of the stage in a basket. This was to be achieved by the 'random' audience member actually being a mate of mine, Will, who had an identical twin brother called Robert, who was already hiding in the basket.

Hopefully the trick itself would impress the audience, but the real reason for it was that halfway through the act, with the wardrobe still on stage and with Will still in it, he was going to bang on the wardrobe door as if he was panicking. I was going to pretend to be surprised, get in the wardrobe and ask Will what the hell he was playing at. We would then proceed to have some scripted banter about how he was 'getting hot and claustrophobic' etc. Well, that was the plan anyway.

I opened with the 'trick' and the audience seemed

genuinely surprised and it got a round of applause. They had expected a gag, but I had done it straight, and this was the first bit of non-comedy they had seen all night. So far so good. I did my act, and I was heading for a 'score draw'. I hadn't got the biggest laughs of the night, but nor had I died on my arse. It was fair to say though, at this stage, I wasn't going to win the competition. So there was a lot riding on the ending.

Right on cue the banging on the cupboard started. The audience laughed as the great magic opening was now going 'wrong' – which was obviously the intention. I did my best 'what the hell is going on?' face, which again got a small laugh. I was delighted. Wait until I got inside and did the scripted banter, this was going to kill. I walked towards the wardrobe and was about three paces away from it when suddenly I was stopped from moving any closer. The microphone lead had reached its maximum length and was stopping me getting any further. I wondered what the hell to do next. I couldn't drop the microphone because we needed this for the scripted banter once I got in the wardrobe. There were thousands of people looking at me and I was stuck. There was only one thing to do. You know you hear these stories where a mum has somehow magically gained superhero strength to rip off car doors to rescue her child? I reached down and grabbed the bottom of the wardrobe, and somehow managed, with one hand, to drag the wardrobe and the man inside it, towards me. To this day I don't know how I got the strength, and, more importantly, why I bothered. I stepped inside the cupboard and started the scripted banter that was pinned on the inside of the door. Will stood there, mini-torch in hand and shone it on the script:

Me (reading): What the hell are you doing? Why are you knocking? You're ruining the trick.

Will was now supposed to read out a rather humorous monologue I had written about how he was getting claustrophobic. Instead he improvised, which was a bold move for a man who had never been on stage in his life.

Will (improvising): Get me out of here. It stinks. It's my own fault, I had a curry last night.

I looked at the script. My response about claustrophobia being a learned condition, probably brought on by a childhood incident, would now not make sense.

Me (improvising): What?

Will (not expecting the question): Hey?

Me: What the hell are you doing?

This was me both trying to get back to the script, but was also me genuinely wanting to know what the hell he was doing.

Will: I've had a curry, it stinks in here.

Oh God, he was back to the curry improv. It wasn't getting laughs. Even when you're in a wardrobe you can hear the sound of silence.

Lee: What the hell are you doing?

Will: Hey?

Why the hell did he keep saying 'Hey?' There was a script on the bloody door. With an answer to the question 'What the hell are you doing?' And it was quite a funny answer. I can't remember what, but trust me it was funny. All right, maybe just 'amusing', but definitely funnier than 'Hey?' I grabbed the torch from him and shone it on the script to remind him that we had a script to stick to.

Lee: What the hell [the fuck] are you [fucking] doing [you fuck]?

Long pause.

Will: Hey?

I now just wanted this to end. I moved the microphone away from my mouth, and told him to get out. This was both a mini-tantrum but also what was planned for the end. Luckily he didn't say 'Hey?', he just exited the wardrobe with the microphone and said 'Ladies and gentlemen, Lee Mack!' The lights went to black, as planned, and I got out of the wardrobe and ran off. The host, Mark Lamarr, came back on, looked baffled and said 'Well, there you go, that was a bloke in a wardrobe.'* Which was a fair reflection of what had just happened.

I didn't win, and later Will told me he had panicked and had said the first thing that came into his head. I learnt an important lesson that night. Don't lock identical twins in cupboards, just do gags.

Comedians love horror stories. If there's one definite way to lose the interest of another comedian it's to tell them how great a recent gig has been. They don't care. If you're a new act and you want to ingratiate yourself

---

* Well, that's what I'm told he said. I'd run off.

backstage to the more established comics, tell them how bad a recent gig went. If you haven't got a story, make one up that involves dying on your arse and making an utter twat of yourself. Or even better make the victim another comic altogether, preferably a more successful one than them, they'll love you for ever.

You see, comedians aren't 'special' like I used to think, they're not full of self-confidence and they are not self-assured. They are often neurotic, bumbling, paranoid wrecks that fear the worst. They also like nothing better than to hear the worst is happening to someone else, not themselves. Not me of course, I'm much nicer than that. I'm like some kind of messiah. The others of course are deluded and mad.

Don't get me wrong, I'm not saying *all* comedians are like this. What I *am* saying is that they are not the grounded, mentally well-adjusted, worldly-wise 'special' people I assumed they were before I started doing it. It probably says as much about my expectations as it does about comedians themselves.

And it's not just comedians, it's performers in general. What I find is that in 'real' life, away from television and comedy, about nine out of ten people are usually nice people of sound mind. In the world of showbiz it tends to be about fifty-fifty. What I'm also saying is that if, like me, you've always wanted to try stand-up and the only thing stopping you is that you don't feel you are that 'type', then you're wrong. There's no such thing.

It's hardly surprising that comedians are often slightly

neurotic. People are expecting you to be great, and if you're not, you've let them down. Like I did in 1996 when I was booked to do Stoke University with Al Murray's Pub Landlord, and *The Mighty Boosh*'s Julian Barratt.

In the old days, before my wife selfishly decided that our babies were more important than jokes, Tara would come with me to a lot of the gigs. On this occasion she was keener than ever because her sister Caragh* was also in Stoke visiting her boyfriend Igor,† who went to the same university where I was performing. We decided to stay in the student house that night with Igor and his gang of student mates. When we arrived the house seemed pretty full and these other students were delighted to see us. They'd never met us and they certainly had never seen me doing comedy, but they loved the regular comedy night at the university, and there was definitely a sense from them that they were pleased to meet someone who was actually going to be performing that night. So far that comedy season they had seen nothing but brilliant acts, and so in their heads there was no reason to doubt that tonight would be any different. You live and learn. And a few hours later they *had* lived and *had* learned.

We walked to the gig, and on the way they were

* Yes, my wife Tara has a sister called Caragh. The fact that these names rhyme always seems amusing to people, which always bemuses us. It's equally bemusing to her other sister Clara, her brother Dara, her mum Zara, and her father, Brian Lara.
† Please trust me, I am not making these names up.

firing questions at me: how did I get involved in comedy, did I know so and so who had performed the previous week and was 'amazing', was it a brilliant job etc. This was probably the first time they'd met a comedian and they seemed to be enjoying the encounter.

I got to the gig late. This is not uncommon for me, and although I try my best to leave in good time, I still, even after twenty years of living here, make the mistake of forgetting it takes a good couple of days to just get out of London. Being late meant that Julian had to go on first. This was a disaster for me. I'd never 'headlined', that was far too much expectation. I didn't feel ready. It didn't help as well that Julian was great that night, the audience absolutely loved him. Julian was a great stand-up, and I always wondered why he stopped doing it (although I can't lie, that night I wish he'd never started). An interval was called, then soon after Al was back on stage doing what he always did, and still does, which is taking the fucking roof off. Usually I would mean 'fucking' as an expletive to emphasize what a great comic he is, but in this case it's a way of demonstrating what was going through my mind at the time.

I was finally introduced and my new 'posse' waited with baited breath for me, their new best mate, to be amazing.

But I wasn't amazing. I was terrible.

A combination of nerves, not being ready to headline, and following acts that were far more sure of themselves at that time meant I was slow handclapped off after about five minutes. Al had to come back on and pick up the pieces.

Don't get me wrong, I had had other bad gigs early on in my then short comedy life. This wasn't the only time it had gone really, really badly. But this was different. I had 'family' in. Not only that, but a group of students who I now had to go back and share a house with for the night, who now thought of me as a conman. They literally didn't come near me after the gig. Caragh and Igor were fine, because they had seen me before so didn't have any deluded thoughts that I was going to be 'amazing', but these new people had been expecting it to be brilliant.

And it hadn't been, far from it.

On the way to the gig they had been swarming around me like a load of bees meeting a comedian for the first time.* Now, after the gig, they weren't coming near me, in case whatever I had was contagious.

That first year of me doing stand-up culminated in me going to the Edinburgh Festival in 1995 to do the final of the Open Mic Award and the other far more prestigious, much more widely regarded, for the better-looking (etc.) So You Think You're Funny Award. The Open Mic Award was a big deal. Actually it *wasn't* a big deal. These competitions never are in the long run, they just give a tiny step on the comedy ladder (apart from So You Think You're Funny, which is a true barometer

---

* I've never been good at analogies. I use them like a wolf uses a boat.

of genius). What I mean is it *felt* like a big deal, which, let's face it, means it then is a big deal. It's hardly surprising it felt big, it was to be filmed for BBC One and shown after *Match of the Day*.

This stand-up malarkey was now starting to get surreal. I'd only started out ten months or so earlier, and now I was going to be broadcast to the nation. In my head I convinced myself I was now like the comedians I'd seen on *Saturday Live*, but in reality this was of course different. They were booked as professional comedians who knew what they were doing. I was in a competition for new acts, and part of the appeal as a viewer was the fact that actually we didn't know what we were doing. They were selling the 'newness'.

Although I was obviously nervous about the actual gig, I was surprisingly calm about the idea that it was going to be on TV, mainly because I knew that by the time the thing was actually broadcast a few months later, then the event would be long since over in terms of my involvement. I've always had this attitude towards telly. For a control freak like me, there's something quite relaxing about the idea that the end result of what you're doing, the actual TV broadcast of your show, means it's too late to do anything about it. Also, unlike stand-up, which all culminates in that one performance, TV is a series of events, from writing, to filming, to editing – there's not one moment where it all hinges on one thing, so in some ways TV is a lot less stressful. Apart from the writing. Oh yeah, and having to deal with too many people who want an artistic input. Then there's the censorship. Oh, and the overly sensitive actors. Actually I take it back, TV's more stressful.

Although being on TV for the first time was very thrilling, it also had its downside. A few weeks after the broadcast of the Open Mic Award I was best man at my old school mate's wedding. John Clegg, 'Cleggy', was getting married and part of my job as best man, as is always the case, was to do a speech and make them laugh. Now for many people this is an extremely stressful proposition, and I guess the assumption is that for a stand-up comedian it's a walk in the park, as that's what you do as a job. But it's not true – it is just as stressful for that very reason. People are not only assuming you'll be funny, they are expecting it. Plus for someone like me, who sees their on-stage persona as being a slightly different person, it's the clashing of two worlds that you'd rather keep separate. It's all very good me saying that I would never do stand-up in my hometown for fear that people I know would be in the audience, but when my old school mates are at a wedding I can't avoid it. Much more importantly, I wasn't actually that good at this point, I was still very, very new with probably about sixty gigs under my belt. Of course, if I hadn't just been on telly, no one would have even known I was actually a stand-up. Even then, I probably would have got away with it if it wasn't for the fact that Cleggy's mum kept introducing me to people as a 'comedian'. The first introduction went something like this:

Cleggy's mum: This is the best man, Lee.

Them: Hello.

Me: Hello.

Cleggy's mum: Lee's a comedian.

Them: Really?

Me: Yeah . . . sort of.

Them: I'm looking forward to the best-man speech then.

Me (panicking): Well, I've only been doing it for about a year.

Cleggy's mum: Yeah, but he's just been on telly.

Them: Oh, you must be pretty good then.

Me: Well . . . it was actually a competition for new acts. I'm very new.

Them (not listening): Mick, come over here, meet Lee. He's the best man and he's a professional comedian who's won a big competition on TV.

Me: Hang on . . . I didn't win.

Mick: So you're the funny man, hey?

Me: Well . . .

Mick: I'm looking forward to the best-man speech then. I bet it's going to be brilliant.

Me (modestly): Oh please . . . [fuck off]

Mick (shouting): Steve! Come here. Meet Lee, he's got his own TV series.

By the time I did my speech, word had got out that a huge Hollywood star with a big career in comedy movies was going to be doing an hour of blistering stand-up (or at least that's what I heard from Peter Paranoia who lived in my head). All I had was a few half-arsed anecdotes and a few stock best-man lines about Cleggy's lack of abilities in the honeymoon suite. If I'd been a milkman it would have been considered a success. As a professional stand-up comedian it was probably considered passable, at best. The annoying thing was that I had only been doing stand-up for twelve months, and so in reality my abilities were closer to the milkman's than the stand-up comedian's, so it should have actually been judged as a success. Next time I'm dressing as a milkman.

The Open Mic Award went fairly well, and although I didn't win, it was a great experience. The best bit for me was that I met Barry Cryer who was one of the judges. He's a legend in the world of comedy who's written jokes for them all, including Cleopatra. Barry's the kind of person I look at and hope that when I'm his age I'll be like him. He's totally on the ball, sharp as a tack, and genuinely likes the newer comics, which is not that common with older performers. Most of all he's bloody hilarious, especially with that comedy haircut he has, which should only be seen on the top of a Mr Whippy cone.

The other thing that made an impression on me was meeting the comedian Daniel Kitson, who was also a contestant in that final. There are many people in Britain who may never have heard of Daniel, as he tries only to play to fairly small rooms, and basically rejects all forms of TV. Some comics refuse to go on things like panel games on the pretence that they see them as artistically bereft, but actually it's because they know they wouldn't cut the mustard. But Daniel's one of the few who *would* cut the mustard. In fact, he'd not only cut it, he'd spread it all over his baguette, add some cheesy squares and shove it in his big fat face. Daniel is one of the few who have rejected TV purely for artistic reasons, and would more than shine on it if he wanted, because he's a brilliant comic.

That's not what I remember about him from that night though, because I didn't actually get to see his act; we were all locked away backstage awaiting our turns. What I remember about him was meeting him backstage just before the night started. He was about sixteen or seventeen years old at the time, and I felt a bit sorry for the 'little kid', who I assumed would surely be a bit rubbish because he was so young. I asked if he was OK, and was he feeling nervous. Now what I didn't know about Daniel at the time is that he has a stammer.* It's hard to actually write down in words his reply, because the first bit wasn't actually a sound. It was more like a man trying to answer you with a frog in his mouth and he didn't want to open his gob in case it jumped out. Then after what seemed like an eternity he swallowed the frog and said very calmly 'Yeah, I'm fine.' Now, bearing in mind at the time I still felt that stand-up was for the 'special' people, the worldly-wise people with the self-assured personas, it's fair to say that a young kid

* Or is it a 'stutter' – I always mix these two up. What I should do is go on Google and find out the difference, but surely it's better to admit my lack of knowledge on the subject than pretend I know, otherwise we're papering over the cracks of society's ignorance. All right, I admit it, my internet's down.

with a stammer as thick as the lenses in his glasses was not what I called textbook comedian. Far from it. In fact, Daniel was so far from what I considered a stand-up should be that I genuinely assumed he was a character act. The transition between the 'nervousness' of the stammer, with his eyes tight shut, desperate to get the words out but unable to, and then the sudden, genuinely calm, 'Yeah, I'm fine' was so extreme that I assumed it was an act. Why was he doing this back-stage? I assumed he was getting into character and, to be honest, slightly taking the piss out of me. I was literally on the verge of saying 'All right, mate, cut out the bullshit and talk to me normally.' Now I have subsequently got to know Daniel a lot better, I would give my right arm to go back in time and actually say it.

If I was running a stand-up comedy course for beginners I would start by showing a video of Bill Hicks next to a video of Daniel Kitson and tell them that proves beyond doubt there isn't a 'type' that does stand-up; you can be any 'type' and still end up brilliant.

A week later I was in the final of the other competition, the Channel Four-sponsored So You Think You're Funny. This was the competition I had thought I could just phone up and enter the year before, thinking there were only a few deluded people like me in the world who wanted to become a comedian. But, like the previous year, there were actually loads of wannabes. I had had to do a showcase and a semi-final, and now finally it was the grand final, with Eddie Izzard as the host, Reeves and Mortimer as two of the judges and, more importantly as a skint student, fifteen hundred quid as the prize for winning. Just think how many Pot Noodles I could buy with that.*

First up that year was a very new comedian by the name of Johnny Vegas. I met Johnny backstage, and I would like to recount how I immediately knew this bloke was a natural-born, gifted comedian, who one day I would watch do a show that I still consider the best ever performance of stand-up I've ever seen. That's what I'd like to say, because it would make me look like I was a visionary in recognizing really talented people. But the truth is, all I remember thinking was that he was an absolute loony. I think that was an opinion shared by most of the audience that night. A few months later I saw Johnny doing an open spot and I can't lie, I thought 'Has this nutter not given up yet?'

The rules to the final of So You Think You're Funny were that you had to perform ten minutes of material, but five minutes of the material had to be different from the semi-final. So, in other words, you needed fifteen minutes of stuff. This was a problem as I only had ten. It's all I had ever needed, as I was an open spot, and open spots only did ten minutes. And that's only if they didn't get booed off. I've done open spots where just 'Hello' was enough material.

So I needed a new five, and quickly. The final was just a few days away.

* Asda are currently selling a four-pack of Pot Noodles for £3.60, which means they are 90p each. So the answer is 1,666.

I locked myself away in my Edinburgh flat and decided I would write. But I couldn't think of anything, and panicked. I decided I needed a little help with my creativity; I smoked some weed.

This was not a good idea, not least because I wasn't used to it. I'd done it, on very rare occasions, but I certainly wasn't what you'd call a smoker. I can't remember now where I got it from (probably one of the other finalists, who realized it was a terrible idea), but before I knew it I was sat in my Edinburgh flat, off my face, writing drivel, and thinking it was hilarious.

I'm not sure why I thought it would help, but I guessed I'd fallen for the oldest mistake in the world and believed stories about how most of the great artistic masterpieces of our time are created by people who are off their faces on some sort of hallucinogenic drug, when in fact the boring truth is that most are created by somebody locking themselves away and just doing the hours, which is never quite as glamorous. Despite the generally held opinion, 'Lucy in the Sky with Diamonds' was not a song about LSD, but was in fact a song about John Lennon's attitude to having to write songs, which he always found was a Long, Solitary Drudge. And that is a fact.*

I ended up writing really stupid, incoherent nonsense about offering people cups of tea, then pouring it all over the floor. Then, offering them toast, and that also going all over the floor. It's extremely hard to describe it on paper

---

* Well, a sort of fact. That's what someone told me, anyway. Well, not told me as such just . . . all right, I just made it up.

as it involves a fair bit of mime, and, like I say, it was slightly nonsensical. When I was off my face I genuinely thought I'd written something as funny as anything that had ever been written by anyone in the history of comedy.

The next day, when clarity hit, it was no longer the funniest thing that had ever been written in the history of comedy, it was the funniest thing that had ever been written in the history of yesterday afternoon by me. Well, the *only* thing to be more accurate. So it was staying in the act. It had to, I had no choice.

That night I opened with my best 'old' bits and it went well for the first half of the act. Because I was on a roll, the new bits also went fairly well as the audience had bought in to what I was doing, and luckily didn't stop to consider that actually what I was saying was perhaps incoherent nonsense. I think the last minute or so might have confused them, but I'd just about bought enough goodwill to see me through, and I won the competition.

As I received the winner's cheque I remember thinking how close I had been to ballsing it up with the new material, and I made a mental note to myself: 'Never, *ever*, write anything again unless you're 100 per cent of sober mind.' I've totally stuck to that for the last eighteen years. If I can now just apply those rules to other things than writing, like living, I might have an outside chance of making it to fifty.

In the bar afterwards Seamus Cassidy, the then head of comedy at Channel Four, and one of the judges that night, said we should meet up for a chat when we got back to London.

This should have been exciting, and in some respects it was. But I'd already experienced a TV 'chat', and it had been odd.

It had happened after I had performed an open spot at a comedy club in Hampton Court called Screaming Blue Murder. It's funny, you get so used to the strange names of comedy clubs in this job, such as Screaming Blue Murder, Ha Bloody Ha, The Chuckle Club, that you end up saying it in conversations outside the world of comedy not realizing how mad you sound. I have had many a bemused look over the years after saying such things as 'I won't be joining you for dinner tonight, I'm opening The Banana'.

In the audience that night were a group of TV bods and after the gig, which had gone well, one of them approached me and told me he was head of comedy for something or other. I say 'something or other' because, in the world of TV, people swap jobs with each other so much it gets confusing. There aren't that many people in TV comedy, and there aren't really that many jobs, but they seem to spend about a year in each one, so it's confusing about exactly who does what. It's a bit like watching *Match of the Day* when you think 'Oh, he plays for them now does he?'* He said he'd enjoyed my

* I appreciate that my use of football to show examples and analogies in this book is not abating, and I think it's fair to say that, had I been good enough, that would have been a preferred occupation. I was never good enough though, so it wasn't even a consideration. Which, when you consider how much astronaut and golfer was a consideration, shows you how very average indeed I was at football.

gig and would I like to meet up the next day for lunch and a chat. I couldn't believe it. I, a relatively new act, was being asked to 'chat' with the head of comedy for ITV, or was he the comedy developer for Thames TV, or did he play for Bolton Wanderers? Whatever it was it didn't matter, he was a bigwig.

I immediately went home and told Tara what had happened and we both got very excited about what was going to happen. Was he going to offer me my own TV series? Or perhaps he wanted me to host a TV show? Whatever it was, he clearly had big plans for me, otherwise why would he have invited me for lunch to 'chat'. Don't get me wrong, it's not like I had any ambitions at this point to be on telly, my aim was still to try and just become a regular on the circuit. Likewise, I wasn't *against* the idea of doing telly either, far from it. It just felt so far removed from being a realistic goal at this point that I hadn't even entertained the notion properly. OK, I'd been in the Open Mic awards on BBC One, but even I knew that wasn't 'proper' telly. It was a talent contest, and like all talent contests, particularly Simon Cowell's lot, part of the fun isn't to find the talented, it's to find the deluded. If I were a *proper* comedian doing a *proper* show that would be different. But what could I do on TV? I didn't know, but surely this man knew because he was Head of Talent Development at ITV Thames Talkback Hat-Trick Tiger Aspects Incorporated, or whatever it was he did.

I turned up the next day with my freshly ironed shirt and my freshly ironed Tara. I'd brought her along thinking it was best if he got to know my girlfriend as well, because if he was planning a long-term career plan for me, it was best he got to know the missus. When we arrived at the lunch we saw that there were about three or four other TV people he'd brought with him. This was getting better. He'd brought his 'team'; he was clearly serious. We started making small talk about where I was from, how long I'd been doing comedy etc., and the excitement was building in me, waiting for the 'anyway' moment. That moment in any important meeting when the small talk ends, and there are a few moments of silence, then the person who's called the meeting says 'Anyway . . .', which means 'And now down to business.' After about an hour we reached the 'anyway' moment. 'This is it,' I thought. The next few words could send my life spiralling in all sorts of directions. What he actually said, though, was 'Anyway . . . we've got to get going, it was nice meeting you.' Then they went.

Tara and I were left utterly confused.* It wasn't like an interview, we hadn't blown it. It had actually gone very well and we'd had a really good time. In fact, he'd done exactly what he'd promised the previous day, he'd taken me for lunch (they paid) and we 'chatted'. And

* The reason for this footnote is that the word 'confused' is exactly the point where I have reached sixty thousand words in this book. I often give myself little landmarks when I'm writing so I feel I'm getting somewhere. At the end of writing a series of *Not Going Out* I always have a cigar and champagne, but it's nine thirty in the morning as I write this so I think I'll just have a Wagon Wheel.

that was it. No offer of anything. Nothing. So why the chat? To be honest, having had about five hundred of these 'chats' over the last eighteen years, I'm no clearer now than I was back then. I am often left at the end of a meeting or chat with the feeling of 'What was that about?' Now also the novelty of a free lunch has worn off, it's a question that I wish I knew the answer to. If I had to hazard a guess I would say that the reason is . . . . The purpose of those dots is to represent the passage of time of about ten minutes as this is what it has just taken me to try and eloquently explain my theory as to why TV people endlessly meet about stuff to 'chat', but I genuinely, hand on heart, realize I still don't have a clue. I suppose I should just ask one of them, but I suspect they don't really know either.

So when the meeting with Seamus Cassidy at Channel Four was arranged many months later, because he wanted a 'chat', I took it with a pinch of salt.

I got to the meeting and he said that since seeing me in the So You Think You're Funny competition the previous year he had been thinking of me for various shows that had been pitched to him. This was news to me, and was obviously very exciting, if somewhat surreal. It was just over two years since I had finally plucked up the courage to do my first gig, and here I was, sat with the comedy commissioner at Channel Four and him telling me he had been 'thinking of me'. I couldn't wait to hear what he had to say next, and prayed that it wasn't just 'Let's chat over lunch.'

He told me he was going to do a stand-up show on the channel with the specific aim of putting new comedians on it. I couldn't believe it, I was being asked to perform a stand-up slot on a TV show as an actual proper act, as opposed to the freak show that is a talent competition. What's more, on Channel Four, the channel that used to show *Saturday Live*, the thing that got me wanting to do stand-up in the first place. I was utterly gob-smacked.

So you can imagine how shocking the next sentence was.

'Oh no, I don't want you to do a slot on it, I want you to host it.'

PSYCHIATRIST'S OFFICE

BRIAN: You seem naturally protective of those close to you in this book. You do briefly mention your children, but not that much.

LEE: It's a book predominantly about me getting into comedy. The decision to do that was when I was at school and I didn't have children then . . .

Lee is tempted to do a gag about northerners like himself usually having kids when they are fourteen years old, but then decides against it owing to the fact that it's well-worn ground with comedians. Basically the rules you learn on day one of comedy school is that if you're from the north you are involved in teenage pregnancies, if you are from the south you are a Cockney and therefore a criminal, and if you are from the east or west you sleep with your own sister. If you are from anywhere else you are a combination of all of the above, depending on the ferociousness of the heckle.

LEE: . . . and when I finally started doing comedy they weren't even born yet. Basically my children had nothing to do with my desire to do comedy. In fact, if anything, they are more connected to my desire to maybe want to get out of it.

BRIAN: Yet you mention your dad. Was *he* connected to you going into comedy?

LEE: He sort of was actually. I remember sitting with him years ago, well before I did my first gig, and he said that he would have liked to have pursued a life in entertainment, but didn't. I remember thinking 'I don't want to get to his age and regret not having done it.' I think that was my main motivation, to be honest. Not actually doing it, just not regretting not having done it.

Lee is tempted to tell Brian the story about his dad and EastEnders. When the character of Dirty Den first left the soap, Lee's dad had written to the BBC applying for the job as replacement landlord of the Queen Vic pub. Apart from his amateur acting days, he had very little acting experience, but he did have many years' experience running a pub, which he mentioned in his letter. Lee's reluctance to mention this to Brian is because when he has told people this before it

*makes his dad sound a little bit
deluded and a dreamer. Yet Lee has
always respected his dad for doing
this as he took his chances of
getting the part from 'impossible'
to 'very unlikely', which in Lee's
opinion is a good enough shift in
odds to warrant doing it.
Basically his dad had always had
an attitude of 'You can't win the
lottery if you don't buy a
ticket.' This attitude was passed
on to Lee, and for this Lee will
always be grateful, as, in some
respects, Lee **did** win the lottery.
Albeit it sometimes felt like he
only got three numbers, like when
he did the Stoke University gig.*

CHAPTER SIXTEEN

The gasman cometh

The next day I went for lunch with Tara. For a chat. This was perfectly acceptable, as I too was now a TV person. I was half tempted to make small talk, then say 'Anyway . . .', and then just walk off, but I'm not sure she would have laughed. And as any comedian will tell you, without the laugh everything is pointless.

We sat outside. Al fresco, I believe, is the right phrase, but I think it should be against the law to use Italian words if there's an English equivalent (can someone tell Starbucks 'medium' and 'large' was a system that was working fine). There were many people passing us in the street. I told Tara that very soon this would all change and that it would be hard to eat without people recognizing me.

This is utterly laughable for two reasons.

Firstly it is a terrible thing to say. It sounds like the egotistical ramblings of a self-obsessed lunatic. But in my head it was just a fact that needed to be addressed.

I genuinely thought it was about to have a major impact on our lives. I remember sitting there in the bright sunshine at this fairly average café thinking that with fame comes money, which meant that although I wouldn't be able to eat out any more, the restaurants I wasn't able to go to would be a lot nicer, and so the food I wasn't going to be able to eat would taste much nicer.

Don't get me wrong, I wasn't massively concerned about the concept of being recognized; in fact, it excited me. How could it not? Especially if you'd never experienced it.

And I wasn't about to experience it either.

That's the second laughable thing about me saying what I said.

Doing that TV show didn't make a jot of difference, as I was not going to be recognized anyway. In fact, six months after this meal, and way after the TV show in question had been broadcast, I was to perform my first solo stand-up show at the Edinburgh Festival, on the back of this new-found 'fame', to an audience of just four people. More of that nightmare in a moment, but suffice to say it was *un incubo completo e assoluto*.

Basically what I didn't realize is that far from TV being the pinnacle of success that says you've 'made it', you're simply starting again on the bottom rung of a new ladder. I was finally starting to establish myself on the comedy circuit, the thing I actually always wanted, and I was now becoming an 'open spot' of television.

Looking back it's totally understandable that I would think it would be life-changing. After all, I knew nothing about the TV industry. When I used to watch the comedians on *Saturday Live* I assumed that the fact that they were appearing on it meant they had 'made it'. To me they clearly were taking a break from their other world, which was being well-established comedians who'd 'arrived'. The reality was that some of them were probably still trying to actually make what would be considered a living doing what they did, certainly in the 1980s when comedy was a lot more alternative and fringy. But how was I supposed to know that? All I could see was that they were on the telly, and so assumed they lived in mansions, went everywhere by limo, owned a pet monkey, enjoyed parties with Shakin' Stevens, wore diamond-encrusted undies, slept in oxygen tents, owned a Corby trouser press, married *Blue Peter* presenters, and ate swan. Because that's what TV people did, right?

A few months after that meal with Tara, I was in a TV production office getting ready to host *Gas* on Channel Four. The name had been chosen because it was a stand-up show and of course 'gas' can mean 'to talk'. I don't think that anyone ever really got that, and assumed it to be called *Gas* because there was loads of steam coming out of the stage floor. Which must have seemed an odd way round, making the show, then saying what it looks like in your title. Of course, it's much worse when it's the other way round, when you suspect a show has been made just because someone has thought of a good title. Like *Desperate Scousewives* (which is real) or *Wife's Too Short* (which I just made up). Or *You Ain't Half*

Hot Mum (which not only have I just made up, I now genuinely want to make. TV people love family sitcoms and they love sexual tension, why not combine the two?). The best thing about the title *Gas* was that when I introduced the person making the show, a lovely lady by the name of Sandie Kirk (who saw sense and got out of the madness of television to become a reflexologist), I was able to say 'This is Sandie, she produces *Gas*.'

The idea was that each week I was to introduce two or three very new stand-up acts, most of which were making their first TV appearance. This was an odd concept for me, as here I was introducing new people, when I was new myself. In many cases newer than the people I was introducing. Which brings me on to the biggest problem: I didn't have enough jokes.

I was supposed to come on at the start and do about three or four minutes. Then I had to come back after the break and do another few minutes. On some episodes we had three guests, so the problem became even worse as there were then even more links for me to do.

At this point, although I was just starting to establish myself on the circuit, I still only had about a twenty-minute act. Well, twenty that I felt was any good anyway, as the thing about writing new material is that you get better the more you do it, so you soon see your old stuff as being a bit pants (or diamond-encrusted pants, as I used to think TV people wore).

I simply didn't have enough stuff. My jokes were like

the loaves and fishes but sadly I wasn't Jesus. And, trust me, it is panic stations when a comedian starts thinking he's *not* like Jesus.

Sandie, the producer of *Gas* (see, it's funny, isn't it?), decided I needed help and brought in some writers – Ivor Baddiel (brother of . . . well, work it out), Ashley Baroda and Dominic Holland. Dominic was basically doing what I wanted to be doing: he was a circuit regular, playing all the clubs, well regarded, and more importantly he was good. Really good. Certainly much better than me, and it must have been odd for him to be writing jokes for a newer act. I was just starting to break through on the circuit, but there were still many, many people who didn't know who I was. Dominic was one of them. It was agreed that I would give him a video of my act, and then he could see my style and work out what needed to be done to make this show happen. I gave him the video tape, and the next day I waited with baited breath at what this more experienced comic would think of my act. He entered the room, and I said 'Well?' He replied 'We've got a lot of work on, haven't we?' Which was probably a fair assessment.

You see, I'd only been going for just over two years. I simply wasn't ready for this. More importantly I hadn't chased it. It was handed to me on a plate. And when people hand me stuff on a plate, if it's free, I eat it. I sometimes even nick the plate.

Most comedians spend years, sometimes decades, trying to establish themselves on the circuit with the hope of getting a TV show, yet here I was sort of doing it the other way round. I wanted to do the TV show to help establish myself on the circuit. I am under no illusions that my name must have been mud for a while in comedy club dressing rooms. Although there is a general camaraderie amongst comedians, there is also a very competitive edge that brings out the worst. Even in those who seem to be doing OK, and therefore you would assume don't need to bitch.

This is particularly prevalent when it comes to taste and language. If someone like Ricky Gervais or Frankie Boyle says a joke which is considered unacceptable, some comedians will very quickly join the debate and immediately slag them off. Basically there are two types that do this. There is someone like the comedian Richard Herring who will vocalize his unhappiness at what's been said because he is genuinely displeased about it. His work with charities such as Scope means he has a personal interest in the subject of disability. So, if a comedian is doing 'mong' jokes, or jokes about Katie Price's son, then you end up trusting Richard's opposition to the comment or gag; you know it's coming from the right place.

Then there's the other type who don't really care what's been said, they just want to appear morally superior. Basically, they are *glad* it's been said, so they can now prove that they are a better person. Or, more importantly to them, a better comedian. Of course, the press do this all the time, but I always naively thought that comedians would know better. Then again, I always thought comedians were 'special'. The bottom line is that the latter types are glad it was said in the first place, and if they could go back in time and get the comedian to *not* say the joke about Katie Price's son, or the 'mong' joke, they wouldn't bother. They'd much prefer it if the comedian said it in the first place so they can look superior, even if it was at the expense of the victim of the joke they claim to be protecting. End of rant.

Doing *Gas* was very exciting. Not least my first experience of how you're treated in telly land. When I first walked into my dressing room I saw there was a wrapped gift awaiting me. It was a CD Walkman that the production company had bought me as a thank-you for doing the series. A thank-you?! For God's sake, I was being asked to host a Channel Four stand-up show, the same way Ben Elton had hosted *Friday Night Live*, the show I loved. I was being taken to work in a chauffeur-driven Mercedes, and I was being bought very expensive new clothes by the costume department. On top of all that they were paying me loads of money. Why were *they* thanking *me*?

The next day I went round telling the production team how much I really appreciated the really nice gift of the Walkman and the fruit. They didn't know what I was talking about, as they hadn't bought me any fruit. I explained that there had been a fruit basket in the room with cling-film on and, assuming it to be a gift, I took it home. They explained that this wasn't a gift, it was something that the TV studios put in every dressing room and wasn't really to be taken home. It's a good job I never mentioned the iron.*

Looking back, *Gas* was a decent enough show that gave names like Noel Fielding, Julian Barratt, Tommy Tiernan, Mackenzie Crook† and Peter Kay their first bit of proper TV exposure. One of my favourites was a comedian and poet called Hovis Presley. Some of his lines were absolute classics, and we still say them in our house all these years later. Like 'Wherever I lay my hat, that's my hat.' That still makes me laugh, even writing it now. His most well-known poem, 'I Rely on You', was read out at our wedding (mine and Tara's wedding, not mine and Hovis's). Sadly Hovis died far too young, so you may not have heard of him, but if you're looking for a good book recommendation, then try his *Poetic Off Licence*. I think it's fair to say that he was a top bloke.

There are some clips of *Gas* on YouTube and it amazes me how skinny I used to be. When I started out in comedy I was about ten stone. I recently reached fourteen and a half. I'm almost 50 per cent more of a human being than I was back then, and sadly I don't mean spiritually. An extra four and a half stone! That's like eating a seven-year-old. The Atkins diet helped me lose a bit since then, which is very bad for you, but

---

* Although that is obviously a joke, I was once told by someone very high up at the BBC that there is a well-known TV presenter who nicks the iron from her dressing room every week.

† Although you might not have recognized Mackenzie in those days, as before he was in *The Office* and *Pirates of the Caribbean*, he used to do a character called Charlie Cheese, a game show host who used to spin a wheel of cheese. Honest. It was very funny actually.

mince for breakfast, what's there not to like? In fact, I think you *can* eat seven-year-olds on the Atkins diet. If, like me, you've got a seven-year-old, you'll know how tempting that is.

For me the best thing about *Gas* was that it helped me cement myself as a circuit regular, which was great, because, after all, that is what I really wanted. Bookers who maybe hadn't seen me before, or who wouldn't book me, suddenly started showing interest as I was the 'bloke from the telly'. Despite what some comedy promoters would like to believe, they *are* swayed by this. I had finally done what I set out to do when I started doing stand-up. I was now a circuit regular.

Gas also gave me my first bit of proper money. I was not long out of university and I left with the usual overdraft. I was starting to earn a bit from the circuit, but not enough for you to say I was a full-time professional. Now suddenly I was paid a wad of cash. Not much by TV standards, but more money than I'd ever earned in such a short time. I was paid about £9,000 for doing that TV series, and going to the cash machine and seeing my balance go from the usual fifty quid or so to such a large amount overnight blew me away. This was the best thing that had happened to me since NatWest had given me that free porcelain pig.

I was able to spend some of the money I earned from *Gas* on going out to fancy restaurants with Tara and sitting outside. Despite my earlier concerns, my life didn't really change, and I was hardly ever recognized. I can't lie; when I did get recognized it felt great. If someone came up to me and said 'Hey, are you that bloke from the telly?' I liked it for the simple reason that I assumed it meant they must like me as a comedian. I was making the mistake of mixing up being recognized with recognition. There is a key difference.

When people ask me what it's like to be recognized, I tell them they already know, because it happens to everyone at some point. When someone comes up to you and says, for example, 'Aren't you Sheila, Tommy's mum from school?' that's an example of being recognized (unless you're not of course, in which case it's an example of blindness). How does that make you feel? I'm guessing not much. It makes you think 'Er . . . yeah . . . I am.' That's about it. Well, that's what it's like when someone says 'Are you that bloke from the telly?' or 'Are you Lee Mack?' or the always odd 'You are Lee Mack' (I know). It doesn't really feel like anything. It doesn't bother me, nor does it excite me. It's just a statement of fact.

However, if they say 'I really like *Not Going Out*' then that's recognition. Like 'Hey, you're Sheila, Tommy's mum from school. I just wanted to say I think he's a great kid.' You think 'Oh, that's nice.'

But you have to keep a check on reality. People are almost always nice about what you do, as we are a nation of polite people, despite what the *Daily Mail* will have you believe. So only the people who like you are the ones who comment. If a hundred people out of a hundred tell you they like your show, it's easy to start believing 100 per cent of *all* people like your show. But it simply isn't true. A hundred people out of a hundred will tell you that little Tommy is a lovely kid, but you have to accept that there are some that are saying nothing to you, because they think he's a right little shit.

The lack of impact that *Gas* had on my recognition factor was made extremely clear when I did my first solo stand-up show at the Edinburgh Festival in 1998.

At this point I had done a second series of *Gas* and although I had realized that it was not having any major impact on my day-to-day life walking down the street, I *did* think that it would make a massive difference to my ticket sales at Edinburgh. I thought Edinburgh would be full of hardened comedy fans and surely they would all have seen *Gas*, wouldn't they?

Doing your first solo stand-up show is a daunting task. I would say the second-hardest hurdle to jump in comedy (the first being the first ever gig). Suddenly the whole night is about you, and you have to be ready. This is particularly daunting when you consider that there is very realistic possibility that only a handful of people will be turning up to watch.

This is always a bad atmosphere for a stand-up show. In my stand-up career I have performed in front of four people, and I have also performed in front of fifteen thousand people, and, trust me, four people is far more terrifying. You can hear them breathing between jokes.

Luckily things were going to be different for me. I'd been on the telly. It was going to be packed, surely (have I milked this set-up enough yet?).

Before the first show, I paced up and down behind the

curtain, gearing myself up for what was to be the start of a month's run. I had absolutely no idea how many people were going to be coming to see this opening night, because I'd avoided finding out advanced ticket sales in case they were not what I was hoping for. It was also impossible to see people coming in because the curtain I was hiding behind was directly in front of them and even the tiniest peek would have meant everyone would have seen me. Added to the fact that the house music was blasting,* I literally didn't have a clue how many people were out there waiting for the show to start. I did one last mantra to myself to gear myself up, telling myself that this was 'my year'. The year when I would take the Edinburgh Festival by storm. My intro music started and I leaped out on stage, all guns a-blazing. I ran straight to the front of the stage as the intro music thumped round the room and stretched my arms out as if I'd just run on at Wembley Stadium. The lights were so bright I couldn't see a thing. I was still no wiser to how many were out there. The music was so deafening it was clearly covering the wild applause (I hoped). My eyes adjusted to the lights, and I could see that the back row was empty. I immediately went to the next, and then the next, my head frantically moving from left to right searching for a human being. It was

---

* I have always liked the house music to be loud, thinking that if The Jam are blasting really loudly round an auditorium the audience will laugh more when the show starts. I know, it makes no sense whatsoever, but like I said to my road manager on my last tour, 'Just bloody do it.'

like someone scan-reading a death certificate. I couldn't see anybody. I then felt something on my leg. I realized that I had run with such gusto to the front of the performance area that my legs were touching the knees of someone in the front row. I looked down and saw my audience. It was four people. Not only that, two couples. This meant there was a chance that only two people actually wanted to be there, and the other two had been dragged along. Before my Edinburgh had even started, it had gone wrong.

I spent the next month slowly spiralling downwards and hating every moment of it. The numbers got a little better, but not significantly, which led to the ultimate no-no at the Edinburgh Festival. I cancelled a show.

The Edinburgh Festival is a very small place packed with the whole of the comedy industry, and bad news travels quick. There are basically two types of comedian that go there. The ones who understand the concept of playing the 'game', of bigging themselves up and getting the message out that they are having a great time, and that theirs is the show to see that year. That they should be winning awards. Then there's the other type. Me. Happy to whinge in the bar that it's all gone wrong and 'What's the point?' If you think I'm being self-deprecating by saying that, you're wrong. I would rather be the type that acknowledges defeat when things aren't going to plan, than start putting on a glassy-eyed smile and saying that life is great, when it's not. Those people are called 'deluded'. Or PR people.

The problem with the show I did that year was that it

simply wasn't good enough. I had gone to Edinburgh having not worked hard on it. Instead I had decided to do all my best bits of the last two series of *Gas*. The problem with that was that it was lots of little segments squashed together to make a show. More importantly it wasn't new to me, I wasn't excited about saying the words. I wasn't passionate about it, and this meant I hadn't done enough previews of the show, assuming I knew all these jokes anyway. Basically, I didn't care. And the worst thing to be is a comedian that doesn't care. (The second worst is if you use props. Even worse is a comedian that uses props and doesn't care.*)

Another problem which didn't help was the poster. It had been suggested by someone that I call the show 'Return of the Mack'. The Mark Morrison song of the same title had recently been in the hit parade† and, I thought 'Yeah, all right, whatever' (because I didn't care). The name itself would have been just about passable, but what wasn't was the image. Somebody in my promotions team suggested it might be funny if I

* Comedians are very sensitive, so I would like to take this opportunity to state, on record, that this is just a joke. Some comedians that use props are actually very good. Having said that, the ones that use musical instruments want shooting.

† I am obviously using the word 'hit parade' to suggest I am an old fogey, but this is clearly very disingenuous of me as 'hit parade' is such an old reference in popular culture I am far too young to remember it being common parlance. In fact, if anything, by using it ironically I am actually trying to be 'hip', which is actually a much bigger crime than acting like an old fogey.

dressed like Mark Morrison, the joke of course being a northern, skinny, pasty lad trying to act like a tough gangsta rapper. But this joke only works if people know who you are, otherwise you just look like a twat.

That's a perfect example of losing track of reality in this job. You do a TV show and you get so wrapped up in what you're doing you assume that everyone knows who you are. So much so that you think you can play with the notion of how you're perceived and make a joke about it. The truth was most people, in fact virtually everyone, didn't even know who the hell I was, and the few who did now couldn't even recognize me because I was dressed like a gangsta rapper. It was a huge mistake, but at least I learned a very important lesson. Never listen to the money people when it comes to artistic decisions. In fact, I've subsequently taken that one step further: never listen to anyone but yourself. My next step is to go the whole way and actually not even listen to myself. Then finally I will be the ultimate control freak.

I stood on stage one night during that Edinburgh '98 run, performing to about twelve people, and, like every night, I wasn't enjoying it. It was mid-show and my latest gag had just fallen on twenty-four indifferent ears. I then made a decision that would indirectly lead to most of the TV work I did over the next ten years, and in particular *Not Going Out*.

I decided that if I came back to the Edinburgh Festival the following year I would share the stage with other people. The theory was that if it wasn't going to plan, I could look to my left and right, see other performers, and laugh in the knowledge that we were all drowning together.

So that was the inception of *Not Going Out*. Not a desire to make a sitcom, not a burning ambition to become a television star. Just the idea that if it all goes tits up again, I'm taking some other poor buggers down with me.

PSYCHIATRIST'S OFFICE

LEE: Did you get my email?

BRIAN: Yes. You want to discuss being a
          'control freak'.

LEE: Yes, I do. But just to be clear, I
          actually don't think I am one.

          *Lee realizes that by sending an
          email saying how he would like the
          session to pan out could in itself
          prove he is a control freak, but
          hopefully she won't pick him up on
          that.*

BRIAN: You refer to yourself in the book
          as one.

LEE: Yeah but I use the phrase so much
          nowadays that I now say it as a
          joke. I actually use it in a self-
          deprecating way, especially when
          working in television. You see, if
          I tell an actor that I don't know
          very well I want things doing a
          certain way, I worry that it will
          cause tension. So I pretend that
          I'm a really bad control freak.
          That way they think the problem
          lies with me and not them, when in
          fact I actually think the problem
          is the way they are delivering the
          line. There are hundreds of ways
          of delivering a straight line, but

often only one way of delivering a
joke. Unfortunately a lot of
people don't realize that, so I
pretend the problem lies with me.
When really I think the problem
lies with them.

*Lee worries that if he includes
this information in his book his
secret is out. Then remembers that
actors won't be buying an
autobiography as that would involve
having an interest in someone
else's life, and that's not really
an interest for actors.*

BRIAN: It's just another form of CBT.
          You're doing it as a disarming
          technique to get your own way.

LEE: Is that a good or bad thing?

BRIAN: It can be both.

          *Lee wanted her to say it's a good
          thing, and she didn't. In fact, by
          saying 'good or bad' what Lee was
          actually doing was giving her a
          fifty-fifty chance of getting the
          right answer, but she failed the
          test. If this carries on he might
          just have to leave her to think
          for herself and see how she likes
          it then.*

BRIAN: 'Control freak' usually carries a
          pejorative meaning. Whereas what
          you are doing is actually being

self-effacing to ease any tensions, and so I actually don't think you are a control freak. In fact, I would say the reason you're saying it is for the right reasons, and I think you should carry on the way you are. It's a really great way to be. Well done you on being a really wonderful human being.

Lee is delighted that she has said this as it is what he has always felt, and he vows to include it in the book so those idiots who keep thinking he really is a control freak will read it and learn something from a qualified professional. Lee realizes that perhaps Brian hasn't worded her last speech exactly how she perhaps should have and so he decides to edit it in a way that says exactly what Brian probably meant to say in the first place.

CHAPTER SEVENTEEN

Bits and bobs

So my decision was made; next time I would appear at the Edinburgh Festival I would be standing on stage with other people. The question was how? And with who?* The answer was a sketch show called *Bits*. And with a bloke called Bob.

Actually, that's not true. I just needed to make sense of the chapter title. It was actually Catherine Tate.

Catherine had just started doing stand-up and I had first seen her the previous year when I was asked to judge a heat of the So You Think You're Funny Award. As a previous winner I was now classed as an expert with the ability to judge others. This is obviously dubious in one respect as how can anybody judge somebody's 'art' as being more worthy than someone else's, but also quite enjoyable as it gives you power to rid the

---

* Some people may think that should say 'whom'. Likewise, some people need to look at themselves.

world of the crap ones. In the middle of Catherine's act she did an impression of an old woman. Although her stand-up was really good, this is when her act really came to life.

I'd like to tell you that I recognized in that small moment a talent so amazing that she would soon be acknowledged as one of Britain's leading funny women, and as a result I wanted her to be part of my future plans for world domination. The truth is I found out she was doing another show at the Edinburgh Festival that following year, so I figured if I asked her to be in my show I wouldn't need to pay for her accommodation. Plus, as a bonus, she was quite good.

I also managed to find another person who was already going up that year and thus would save me money . . . sorry, I mean I also managed to find another person who was clearly an extremely talented performer, stand-up comedian Dan Antopolski. A man who, unlike my own personal decision to change my name from McKillop, is obviously not as bothered about people spelling his name incorrectly.

So I had the cast, I just needed the show.

Within weeks of returning from my disastrous 1998 Edinburgh festival show, I started working on the next one. This was ridiculously early as it was only September and the festival wasn't until next August. Most comedians weren't going to be even thinking of getting their shows together until the following February or March, if not later.

But this time I wanted to be ready. (I've just read that

back and it sounds like a line Chuck Norris would say. But I'm keeping it in. And if any of you mothas have a problem with that I'm taking you down.)

Although there is some truth in the last line of the previous chapter, about sinking together with other people and laughing about it, this was obviously only the worst-case scenario. What I actually wanted was for it to be good, really good. What I learned from that previous Edinburgh, and what has stuck with me since, is that for it to be good, and to really enjoy the on-stage performance, you have to have done the work (oh yeah, and don't disguise yourself as a gangsta rapper, especially if people don't know who you are anyway).

So I set about writing sketches. This wasn't easy. I'd had a brief fling with sketch writing whilst at college a few years earlier with a show called *Gagging for It*. It was performed by me and some student mates and we'd taken it to the Edinburgh Festival. How good it was is hard to say, especially when you look at the two reviews we got for it (see second picture section).

But whichever review was right (it was Danny Wallace's that was right) it was fair to say my experience in writing sketches up to this point was a bit limited.

Unlike my stand-up gags where I often take an idea and distil it to the fewest words possible,* this was

* I often take a long-winded idea, and after months and months of trying it out I'm left with a one-liner gag. This seems the opposite of most comedians, who take a single idea and slowly expand on it, to the point where they have a ten-minute routine. This is probably the single reason why it takes me so bloody long to write a new tour.

about taking a small idea and stretching it out.* Although I didn't have much experience in doing this kind of writing, I was lucky in that a lot of what I was saying in my stand-up was 'I said then she said'-type material, which was sort of like a sketch anyway, but with me playing both parts. In fact, I'm such a control freak, there have been times over the years, including my sitcom, when I've thought it might be easier if I *did* play both parts. After all, wigs and false boobs are quite realistic nowadays. Well, they certainly look real on the bloke who plays Lucy in *Not Going Out*.

To be honest, in comparison to stand-up anyway, I found the whole process of sketch writing a lot easier, as suddenly I could bring stuff to life. For example, if, like me, you suddenly notice that the first few bars of 'With or Without You' by U2 sound like an ice-cream van's musical chimes, then in stand-up that isn't going to work, unless you're going to suddenly have a sound cue to prove it. And people who use sound cues are almost as bad as the prop comics.†

In a sketch show, however, if you think that the first few bars of 'With or Without You' by U2 sound like an ice-cream van's musical chimes, you can prove it. You can build an ice-cream van out of wood. You can dress up like Bono and drive it across the stage. Then you can find out after all that hard work that it's not funny, because, despite your original observation, the first few

* 70,000 words. Jaffa cake.
† See footnote on p. 279.

bars of 'With or Without You' by U2 actually *don't* sound like an ice-cream van's musical chimes after all. If you don't believe me, have a listen. It actually doesn't really sound much like it at all. Actually, that's a great idea for an act, an observational comedian who notices what things *aren't* like. Writing it would be so easy: 'Have you ever noticed that English people using chop sticks look nothing like Keith Moon when he's playing drums in "My Generation"?'

One of the more successful sketches that did make the grade was Neil Armstrong landing on the moon and forgetting his 'one small step' speech. This was based on the idea that Armstrong had genuinely got the speech wrong in reality, as 'One small step for man, one giant leap for mankind' doesn't actually make sense, 'man' and 'mankind' being the same thing. He was supposed to have said 'one small step for *a* man, one giant leap for mankind' (I've been known to get my words wrong at fairly important times, as any audience member at the recording of *Not Going Out* will tell you, but Armstrong's really was the king of all bloopers).

It was an odd sketch to perform, as it was all pre-recorded on mini-disc (remember those? They made Betamax look like it had a shelf-life) because I wanted to edit the sound to make it sound real, like someone on a NASA satellite connection. So all there was left for me to do was stand on the steps of the spaceship, with my face obscured by the astronaut's helmet. Actually, this was a fringe Edinburgh show, so when I say 'spaceship' I mean a barstool, and when I say 'astronaut's helmet' I mean a big white Ikea paper lampshade with a hole cut out and cling film used as a visor.

One of my favourite sketches that year was Catherine's old woman character. I had really liked it when I saw her doing it in her stand-up act and so asked if she would bring it to life in our sketch show. She obviously didn't have the prosthetics that she later had on her telly show; instead she simply donned a head-scarf and an old coat. I played her husband who had dementia and never spoke, and all I had to do was sit there and say nothing for five minutes as she fired a tirade of abuse at me, calling me every name under the sun because I hadn't bought her a jar of piccalilli. I would sit there desperately trying to keep a straight face as this demented old woman continually called me vile names. There are many, many debates about taste and language in comedy, and about the artistic merits of people swearing. But I'm telling you here and now, an old woman calling someone a cunt *is* funny. Full stop. If you don't agree, then you're wrong. There, it's good to have a healthy debate, isn't it?*

On the few times I started cracking up, I knew I was in for it after the show. Catherine's attitude was that this was the one time in the show she had a chance to star and I was messing it up by giggling. She had a point, but

* One of the oldest arguments against bad language in comedy is 'Anyone can get a laugh by swearing.' If that's true, then can I heartily recommend these people give up their day jobs, get on stage and start shouting 'Fuck'. It pays well and you get to travel the world. So what are they waiting for?

I've always had a problem with laughing during performances. The correct term is of course 'corpsing', but again, due to my aversion for anything too theatrical, I have a real problem saying it. Laughing when you shouldn't be laughing is still called 'laughing', surely? When I was being told off by my teacher, and I started giggling, he didn't shout 'Oy, McKillop! Stop corpsing!'

If you watch me in *Not Going Out* you will often see that I don't make eye contact with the other performers, for fear of laughing (again, not exactly method, is it?). Also, one of my hands is sometimes out of view. This is because I am pinching myself on the leg extremely hard, a technique that Sally Bretton (the bloke who plays my landlady 'Lucy') taught me to stop myself laughing during a scene. I am basically what is called 'unprofessional', but for someone who wasn't ever really planning on acting being my profession, I don't actually mind.

The other mistake that I wasn't going to make that year was lack of preview shows. Unlike the previous year, when I'd done about two or three, I was going to do these weekly, for about seven months. We did many, many shows in small fringe theatres, often sharing the night with The Mighty Boosh, who were also getting ready for Edinburgh. It was their second Edinburgh show and they had totally worked out what it was that made them funny. We, on the other hand, were still experimenting and would often be greeted with silence as I drove my ice-cream van across the stage, dressed as Bono.

A lot of these fringe theatres are above pubs.

I find these venues very unusual, as often the all-day drinkers downstairs know nothing about the theatrical world going on above them, and it's a real clash of two worlds. Bearing in mind I grew up in a pub, the all-day drinkers downstairs sometimes feel more like the people from my world than the ones upstairs.

It's always an interesting sight when one of them drifts into the theatre to see what's happening. This happened to us once when there were only two audience members: a good friend of mine plus the local drunk. He watched the show for an hour, perfectly well behaved, then afterwards he came to our dressing room (well, derelict toilet) and banged on the door claiming it was a disgrace and he wanted his money back. I couldn't face having to look him in the eyes knowing I'd wasted an hour of his life, so I sent Catherine out to give him a refund. Which very much *doesn't* sound like a Chuck Norris line.

Looking back, I don't think I've ever worked so hard on trying to make a show as good as I did for that Edinburgh Festival in 1999. I have to be honest and say that the main motivation wasn't to make a successful sketch show, or get some industry recognition, or to try and get a sketch show on TV. It was mainly to not fail and have a miserable time like I did the year before. So it was a surprise that we did make a successful sketch show, and we did get some industry recognition, and I did get a sketch show on TV.

You'll notice 'we' turning to 'I' when it comes to

getting on the telly, but more about that (mistake) in a moment.

We were backstage at the Edinburgh Festival one night ready to go on when someone told me Steve Coogan was in the audience. Like all comedians I was a big fan, and had been since first seeing him in 1990 at The Comedy Store. When I say *all* comedians, I mean *all*. I've never met anyone who doesn't think he's brilliant. I think, like seeing an old woman swearing, it's impossible not to laugh at Alan Partridge. If you don't find him funny, then there's something severely wrong with you (again, it's good to debate, isn't it?). There are just some things in life that I think it's impossible not to like. Any objection to it is usually for effect. A way of bucking the trend and shelving your own real feelings of joy in exchange for a small bit of attention for your contrary opinion. Like Alan Partridge, babies, the Beatles and Pot Noodles.

The show went well enough, and it was a thrill to meet him afterwards in the bar. He said he'd really enjoyed the show, which was nice, but I assumed he was just being polite. After that I didn't really think much more about it.

Many weeks later, well after the Edinburgh Festival had finished, I was told that Steve Coogan's new company, Baby Cow,* were teaming up with my own

* Baby cow, i.e. calf, i.e. Paul Calf, i.e. Steve Coogan's character. I'm worried about my use of 'i.e.' in this book, i.e. that it's becoming too prevalent, i.e. over-used.

management's TV company, Avalon TV, to produce a sketch show pilot for BBC One and did I want to be in it? Did I want to be in it? Of course I wanted to be in it. Why wouldn't I want to be in it?

Looking back now, many years later, I know the answer to that question. The reason I didn't want, or shouldn't have wanted, to be in it was that they didn't want Dan or Catherine. They wanted to put me together with four other performers, but still use a lot of my sketches. Why didn't they want the other two? I have absolutely no idea, but if I had to guess it would be because TV people like to tinker. And I don't mean they go from door to door mending pans and kettles. Although some should.

It was no particular person that wanted this change. In fact that was part of the problem, there were a lot of people making the decisions. In telly there always are. It's extremely rare for anyone, including myself, to be completely honest and say 'I really haven't got a clue what I'm doing here, and have no idea if this will work or not.' Instead, people have to pretend they know the secret recipe. They have to make very assertive changes to things, which helps them ignore the unbearable truth: very often no one has a clue what will make a good show. The industry finds it very hard to admit that to itself. Instead people tend to go the opposite way and make very bullish decisions to cover their own self-doubt. Like thinking a sketch show that is actually doing quite well and finding its feet, slowly building itself up from scratch and performing live to gain both material and experience, should be broken up and messed with.

'And that's why I'm not doing your telly show.'

That's what I should have said, but I didn't. What I actually said was 'Yes.' In fact, I think I even added 'Please.'

I'm not a great believer in regret, but looking back over the last eighteen years of me doing this job, not keeping our sketch show *Bits* together, and jumping at the first offer to put a version of it on telly, without Dan and Catherine, is probably the biggest mistake I've made. Having said that, I was still a relatively new comedian with one pretty forgettable TV show under my belt, who was being asked by Steve Coogan, one of Britian's funniest and most successful comedians, to make a telly show. It's easy to see how tempting it was. Plus, of course, there's a bit of every bloke that fancies Pauline Calf. Eh? You what? Just me? Oh, crap. Where's that delete button?

I'm delighted to report that Dan has subsequently got his own sketch show together, *Jigsaw*, which is currently in development with the BBC, as well as his continuous stand-up shows and tours. Sadly, I don't know what became of the ginger one.

PSYCHIATRIST'S OFFICE

BRIAN: During the last chapter I slightly switched off.

LEE: That's interesting.

> *Lee doesn't really mean 'That's interesting', he means 'What the fuck do you mean you "switched off"? That means the last chapter is no good!' But he says 'That's interesting' instead, because he's been in TV too long, and that's what TV people say when they actually mean 'You know that thing you just said, well, it's bullshit.'*

LEE: Why did you switch off?

BRIAN: You talk about the TV industry, but I'm less interested in that and more interested in you.

> *Lee wants to say 'But I work in television and so my opinions on it **are** about me, because they say what I'm thinking. So again, I ask you, how the hell can you "switch off"? It's bang out of order. Holy fucking shit. What's the point?'*

LEE: Interesting.

BRIAN: It's like the previous chapter . . .

Oh great, there's not just one chapter she hated so much she wanted to pull her own eyes out, there were two. Lee's paranoia about the quality of his book is now so huge he even seriously considers forgetting any thoughts of a Booker Prize. Luckily Lee's ego is there to keep his head level and he soon goes back to mentally writing his acceptance speech.

BRIAN: You wrote about comedians and how some of them act morally superior, but I'm more interested in *your* thoughts than what other comedians are thinking.

LEE: Very interesting. Very interesting.

Lee suddenly remembers that in his book he talks about how TV people are always bullshitting and saying how great you are all the time, and wonders if Brian's blunt assessment of his work is down to the fact that she has digested this information and wants to show that she is not like those people. Lee decides that this is the most likely explanation, as the alternative is that Lee has made a mistake by writing about these things, and obviously it couldn't be that.

BRIAN: I felt it was a bit too 'ranty'.

Lee starts to reassess his opinions of TV people. He thinks maybe he has been too harsh on them. Perhaps they are not bullshitters after all, and perhaps they are right, and that everything Lee does is brilliant, and that this woman has completely got it wrong.

BRIAN: It wasn't my favourite bit of the book. I zoned out.

Lee is looking forward to getting back into the TV world. He used to see it as a world of insincerity and false sentiment, but now realizes that in fact the TV world is a place of wise scholars, who are warm and generous. It is in fact the outside world that has got it wrong. The outside world is a cold place. A heartless place. An illiterate place.

LEE: Interesting.

CHAPTER EIGHTEEN

Yankee Doodle bloody Dandy

So a new 'team' was built: me, Karen Taylor, Ronni Ancona, Jim Tavare and Tim Vine (you remember, the fella whose name was shouted out at me at my first ever gig).

The idea of the show was simple. To present a series of random sketches with no particular theme, and, more importantly, to be joke-driven rather than character-driven. In fact, in most of the sketches we referred to each other by our real names. So in one sketch I was, for example, 'Lee', who was married to 'Karen', and in the next I was 'Lee' who was the brother of 'Karen'. (Some comedians would now do a joke about northerners being inbred, but that's West Country people or people from East Anglia. Northerners are all involved in teenage pregnancies, remember?)

This sounds like it might cause confusion, but it didn't. It was very simple. It was a load of comedians titting around with silly hats on.

All we needed now was an inspiring and clever title. Between us five performers, Steve Coogan, many, many top executives, a producer and a team of writers we came up with the single most inspiring name for a programme in the history of television – *The Sketch Show*. *The* fucking *Sketch Show* (that's obviously me thinking back in disbelief. The name of the show wasn't *The Sketch Show*. *The Fucking Sketch Show*. Although I genuinely would have preferred that). Oh well, it did what it said on the tin, I suppose. But unlike Ronseal Easy To Paint On Fence Varnish, it didn't last very long.

I had a real love/hate relationship with that show. Particularly now when I look back. First the love:

I loved the idea that we could do what we wanted on it.

The rules were simple, if you came up with a sketch, and the majority voted it 'in', then we would film it. Actually there wasn't much of a debate during the voting system as we tried all our material out in front of a live audience to decide what worked and what didn't. So actually the audience were sort of deciding, and they often got it spot on. Apart from when they liked stuff that for my taste was just a bit too 'punny', then they were spot off.

The process of trying out the stuff live was my idea, and it was something I had to really, really push for, as most people simply weren't used to making telly this way.

When I say 'really push for', I don't mean people were actively against the idea, claiming it to be bad; it was more to do with the fact that this was not how things were usually done. That is one of the biggest problems about making telly shows, getting people to think differently. In fact there are times when I wonder if that last sentence would work without the word 'differently'.

I also loved the fact that I was being thrown together with loads of people I didn't really know. Although I'd come across some of the other performers on the circuit, none of them were at the time what you'd call mates, and I certainly hadn't done anything creative with any of them. On the face of it, for a control freak like me, this should have been a concern as I hadn't chosen to work with any of these people. Others had made this decision, and in fact they had actively rejected the people I did want to work with (Catherine and Dan). But, actually, I quite like being forced to let go of things.

Having complete control over a project like *Not Going Out* has many advantages but it also comes at a cost. The biggest advantage is that I honestly believe you then make a better show. Having one person's overall vision on something, particularly comedy, is usually a much better result than seeing lots of different styles and ideas. It's not that my ideas are better than other people's,* it's just that, like stand-up, you have to just do what you think is funny without anyone smoothing the edges of what you do. It goes back to the number one rule of comedy: just be yourself. Having said that,

* But they are.

the number two rule is 'If you're not funny, be someone else.'

The cost of complete control is that you have to be on top of it all. On *Not Going Out* I am asked my opinion on *everything*. The colour of a cardigan, the type of newspaper on the coffee table, the plumpness of the cushions on the sofa, the shoes on the feet, the zip on a tracksuit, the drink in the cup, the meat in the pie . . . everything seems to be run past me. Why? Because that's what I've always insisted on, and I wouldn't want it any other way. But it's also the reason my brain some-times frazzles and I crave lack of choice and to be out of control of a situation, but the problem is I just can't do it. Jack Nicholson once said that when it comes down to his way or the director's way, he will almost always choose the director's way so he can feel out of control. I always choose my way. In fact, I don't even ask what the director's way is in the first place.* I think this attitude makes me then crave lack of control in other areas of my life. It's not a coincidence that since we started *Not Going Out* I now always choose the set menu in a restaurant.

You've got to be careful with having complete control as well. Sometimes what you say will be taken literally. On the pilot of *Not Going Out* there was a scene where some baked beans needed to look over-cooked. I told

* I am trying to be self-deprecating by saying I'm a control freak, but I realize this can read as me saying I'm in total control of the look of *Not Going Out*. That is in fact mainly down to the brilliant director we have, Nick Wood. Is that OK, Nick? Does that footnote cover it?

the props man to do just that, go away and over-cook them. He asked 'How over-cooked?' I replied '*Really* over-cooked. You can't over-cook them.' Well, he proved me wrong. You can over-cook baked beans, even when they're supposed to look over-cooked. How? You stick them in the microwave for forty-five minutes. The end result looked like I'd ordered a very well done orang-utan sirloin at the Chernobyl branch of the Aberdeen Steak House.

I also loved the fact that on *The Sketch Show* we had a proper budget. Unlike my Edinburgh show, where a stool and an Ikea lampshade on my head represented Neil Armstrong on the moon, now we had an actual moon set; a huge, beautifully constructed spaceship, moon-dust, rocks and proper replica NASA space costumes. They'd even provided the infinity of the universe as a backdrop, which is quite an ask when you think about it.

To this day it's still a very surreal thought that because of some tiny little idea I've had, a whole team of people have made such an effort to actually build something so huge.

This was even more surreal for me when watching the German version of *The Sketch Show* a few years later. They had bought all the scripts to the show. Not just the ones we had filmed, but also the ones we had rejected. Like the idea I once had whilst sat on the toilet. I had come up with the idea of a load of professional ice-hockey players doing a pre-match pep talk. They would all be shouting at each other, getting themselves fired up with lines like 'We're going to destroy them! We're going to do this! We're the best!' Then they all go on the ice, but actually they are like little kids who have never ice skated before and start slipping all over the place and falling over (trust me, it's a visual). This idea was rejected on the grounds that the budget wouldn't stretch to any more location shoots, which is telly talk for 'That's a crap idea', and I forgot about it as quickly as I'd thought of it. Then, a few years later I was watching a DVD of the German version when the exact sketch appeared. It suddenly dawned on me that some brief, thirty-second bit of daydreaming I'd had whilst sat on the bog had resulted in a crew of people from another country who I'd never met going to an ice-skating rink in Düsseldorf and bringing the whole thing to life. Weird.

Even now after five series of *Not Going Out* I will sometimes look at all the chaos that is happening around me on a filming day and think 'Bloody hell, this is all my fault.' I don't take *all* the credit of course. If it's going horribly wrong I'm always the first to point out it's a team effort.

Despite my love of some aspects of *The Sketch Show*, there were some bits I really *didn't* like.

The main problem was the attitude towards the material.

The show was to be broadcast on ITV, as the BBC had declined the pilot and so its nearest rival immediately snapped it up. This kind of thing is rare. I suspect many TV execs aren't always 100 per cent sure what it is they actually want, so getting someone to want something that someone else has already rejected doesn't help matters. It's a completely natural concern of course, and probably the reason why my first question when buying a house is 'Why are you selling it?'

It's fair to say that ITV, being a commercial channel, has historically been geared more towards populist television. I felt that this meant that sometimes the gags were just a little on the under-ambitious side. I once asked about a certain joke that I felt was a little too simple, and I was told 'Don't worry about it, Lee, it's a mainstream audience.' Basically they had made the oldest mistake in the book. They had assumed that the majority of the population are thick. In fact, if I was like some of my showbiz peers, I wouldn't have written 'the majority of the population', I would have written 'the general public'.

It's a strange phrase since defining people as the 'general public' means that you yourself aren't a member.

Sadly, that is what a lot of people in my industry do believe, that there are two types of people – the masses and the elite. The masses don't know what's good for them, but the elite do. Referring to a group of people as the 'general public' is like referring to them as 'human beings'; you can only say it if you're an alien. Or a talking dog.

I don't mean that *all* the stuff we did in *The Sketch Show* was overly simple. Far from it. There was a lot of time and effort put in by all of us, particularly the performers, to write as well as we possibly could. It's just that there was just one stinker too many allowed through because it was felt that we were doing a 'mainstream' show and so what the heck. Sadly with comedy it's often your stinkers that you get judged by. Like the comedian whose act is 10 per cent racist or sexist is judged a bigoted comic, a show which has 10 per cent 'stinkers' risks the accusation that it is a puerile show. I felt that sometimes we were treading a fine line.

I appreciate that this may be an odd point of view for someone like me to have, seeing as the show that I am perhaps most well known for is *Not Going Out*, which is in the genre of comedy often classed as 'mainstream' and to some extent 'silly'. But I can promise you hand on heart that every joke I have ever uttered on screen in any show I have ever done is born out of the fact that I think it's funny, rather than giving the audience 'what they want'. How the hell do I know what 'they' want, and, more importantly, 'they' don't exist. We're all 'them'.

As soon as you start trying to work out what people want in this job, you've had it. That's when you go and make a TV talent show.

Having said all that, *The Sketch Show* was a fairly decent success and, dare I say it, slightly ahead of its time (yes, I dared).

For those who remember it, that will be seen as a very bold statement, seeing as it totally embraced what would be considered 'the old school': it had a studio-based audience (never popular with the broadsheet critics), it was brightly lit (never popular with the broadsheet critics) and, more importantly, it was silly (never popular with the broadsheet critics). This was a time when gritty realism was about to take over our TVs (always popular with the broadsheet critics). In fact, one of the occasional gag writers on *The Sketch Show* was Ricky Gervais, who was about to lead the charge in that department. Everything in telly is cyclical, and so what I mean by 'ahead of its time' is that if it was on now it would be embraced a lot more. 'Silly' and 'old school' seem to be making a comeback, as *Miranda* and *Mrs Brown's Boys* are proving. Some would argue that *Not Going Out* proves this also, but who am I to say? Obviously when I say 'some would argue' I mean 'I think'. It just makes it sound more academic and less big-headed. In the same way that some would argue that I'm good in bed. Actually, now I've got three children, my definition of 'good in bed' has changed. I now consider it to mean 'A person stays in their own room, they sleep through the night, and they don't wet the bed.'

We even won a BAFTA for the show, which was as much a surprise to us as it was to the other nominees. In fact, I think some of us were already wearing the 'smile and try to not look bothered face' when they read out the result.

We immediately made another series, but before all the episodes of this second one were shown we were pulled off the air for not getting enough viewers (so much for awards, eh?). At my house there are two episodes of that show that were never broadcast. They are sat gathering dust, right next to my BAFTA. Actually they *were* next to my BAFTA , until my BAFTA fell over and smashed, which was a shock seeing as I thought it was metallic. It turns out getting a copy of a BAFTA for all five performers is expensive, so the makers of the show got the props man to knock up five versions, and he made them from plaster.

The other slightly surprising thing about *The Sketch Show* was that it was remade for the Americans. Not just for some small cable channel either – it was done for Fox TV and shown on prime time television after *The Simpsons*. To add to the slightly surreal feeling that millions of Americans would be watching jokes I'd come up with whilst sat on the bog, Kelsey Grammer aka Frasier was going to be starring in it.

And just when I thought it couldn't get any weirder, it did. They wanted me to actually be in it.

This had all come about after we had been invited over to the States for the annual comedy festival in the skiing town of Aspen, Colorado. It's basically the Americans' version of Edinburgh, but it's a lot smaller, a lot richer, and a lot colder. And if you're colder than Scotland, that's cold.

We had been asked to perform a live version of the show with one eye on selling it to the States. Of course, financially this meant nothing to the performers, as we didn't actually own the show, we'd only been given a small token percentage. We were just happy to be flown out to a ski resort for a few days to get drunk and have a laugh. You see, that's what a lot of performers are like.

They don't really know how to properly exploit their jokes and turn them into cash. And the money men exploit that. That's why they make the money.

It was during this time I realized that owning a show is where you needed to get to. It not only pays better, but it's only then that you get proper creative control. It's all well and good being given artistic freedom to do what you want, like we were on *The Sketch Show*, but unless you've got control over how the money is being spent, your hands, to a degree, will always be tied. I've worked on television shows where it was deemed more important to have decent food in the green room than it was to have a decent amount of supporting artists in the background of the shot. A situation I like to refer to as 'fucking madness'.

By the way, a 'supporting artist' is the relatively new name for an 'extra', as the title 'extra' is deemed to slightly devalue their role in a show. I once asked a supporting artist how they felt about that, and they told me that to feel truly valued, a pay rise would have been handy rather than a new title. Now you know why they aren't allowed to speak.

We'd been received fairly well at the Aspen Festival, but as performers we thought no more about it. People behind the scenes had meetings and eventually the Americans decided to do a remake, and to include one British member in the cast, which was me.

I'm not sure how the other British cast members felt about this because I didn't ask (I was now going to Hollywood, I didn't have time for those losers any more). I have to be honest and say there wasn't even an ounce of me that felt guilty. Mainly because the ITV version had long since been cancelled, so it wasn't like I was breaking up a group. More importantly, I didn't really feel like a 'group' anyway, the same way I was with Catherine and Dan (you remember, those other two I dropped like a stone at the first opportunity).

I'm not sure why I was the one that was chosen to be in the American remake, but a lot of it is to do with my management company, who worked tirelessly to get me in it. Which was good of them considering I genuinely wasn't massively bothered. That might sound like I'm being artificially blasé about the whole thing, but there were so many people in the UK who didn't know who I was, why on earth would I be bothered about chasing after a whole new audience of Americans? To most people America is more glamorous, but I suspect that this is because of the film industry out there, and as someone who had only ever dreamed of being a stand-up comedian I had no aspirations to do that. I would be lying if I didn't say that the idea slightly excited me. Of course it did. It just wasn't something I was actively chasing. I can honestly say that the opportunity to do it here on ITV was far more exciting than doing it in America. After all ITV was the place that gave us *Rising Damp*, *The New Statesman* and *Spitting Image*. America was the place that gave us civil riots, obesity and *Who's the Boss?*

Maybe the other reason I didn't get too excited is that I have always found it easier to get excited about concepts I understand, and I didn't really understand America. Maybe it was just too big a notion. I'm a bit like this when it comes to money; the idea of earning eighty quid for doing twenty minutes of stand-up genuinely excites me more than earning thousands of pounds for doing a corporate gig. My brain understands eighty quid, and what it represents, because before I did stand-up these were typical weekly earnings for me as I had so many low-paid jobs. Yet thousands of pounds, at some level, is just too big a number to understand. My brain's less excited about that amount because it hasn't had the training. It's probably the same reason I like the idea of sex, but not orgies.

What did excite me was the idea of going to America from a travelling perspective. I've always loved to travel, and one of the biggest perks of my job is getting to go to places I may never have been to. So far in my comedy career I've been lucky enough to perform stand-up gigs in Australia, Ireland, France, Italy, New Zealand, Switzerland, Singapore, Thailand, America, China, EuroDisney (that's a country right?), Canada, South Africa and, hardest of all, Germany.

Most of the gigs were performed either in an English-speaking country or to a predominantly expat community, so it meant that the first language of most of the audience was the same as mine. However, in Berlin I performed to an audience of real locals, and I was the only comic on the bill who did their act in English.

The Comedy Store sent a series of comedians out

there to do a club called Quatsch, and suddenly you went from being a circuit regular to the 'new boy' doing just ten minutes, and the act that often got the least laughs. This was obvious, as doing comedy in a language other than the audience's first language is always going to be difficult. They almost all spoke fluent English, as most Germans do, but that's a long way from actually understanding a comedy routine. The reference points were one of the biggest problems. Each night I would open with a routine about gymnastics and what they do when they land on the mat. This was a very visual routine, and one that had worked in loads of other countries and so I felt it should have been an absolute banker. Yet on each of the three nights it really struggled. It was only after the final night that one of the local comics (and surreally the one who played me in the German remake of *The Sketch Show*) told me that what we call gymnastics translates in East Berlin as 'aerobics'. Always good to find out after your final performance, isn't it? No wonder I'd been struggling on stage. Honestly, it was enough to make me want to throw off my comedy Nazi costume and stop goose-stepping.

So the idea of going to the States with Tara genuinely made us very excited. Until they told us it wasn't going to be filmed in the States; they had decided to film it elsewhere as apparently that made it cheaper to make. Excellent, where to then? Mexico? Peru? Argentina? No. Teddington, Middlesex. In exactly the same studio we filmed the British version. We unpacked.

A few months later I was stood next to a hospital bed with Kelsey Grammer, aka that bloke I grew up watching in *Cheers*, doing a sketch about bed baths. I literally had about ten seconds of polite 'hellos' and then I had to pretend to wash his testicles. This job is bloody mental at the best of times. This wasn't helping.

The American version of *The Sketch Show* was probably the least enjoyable period of my comedy career so far. And I've played Stoke University, so that's saying something. It was bad for many reasons.

Firstly, the cast. They simply did not want to be in London. Like me, they had assumed the show was to be filmed in the States. Unlike me, they weren't excited about the concept of travelling, so being told it was going to be done in Teddington Studios didn't exactly thrill them. They didn't even seem to care that this was the same place that *Tiswas* was filmed in. Heathens.

It's also fair to say that there was a slight personality clash. In the eighteen years of me doing comedy there have only been three people who I would say I have not really got on with. They have all been Americans and they have all been actresses.

To be fair, the people in question have all been nice enough, and it's not fair for me to sit here and write a one-sided argument about the problems we encountered (well, actually I did, but my management suggested I delete it). But if I had to say why I think there were problems (which I don't, but I will), I think the key reason is the clash of cultures between the LA mentality and the Lancashire mentality. In LA there seems to be a cloak of success that people feel they need to wear. They have to not only be doing well, but be *seen* to be doing well. In Lancashire it's different. You have to not only be doing badly, but be *seen* to be doing badly. You have to have your feet on the ground at all times, or people will get a hammer and nails and do it for you. If I was diplomatic I would say that both of these mentalities, to a degree, are a form of snobbery – the Lancashire way is no different, it's just a reverse snobbery where you need to know your place. But I'm not diplomatic. The truth is, our way is best, and I'm so glad that a suspicion of success is a motivating factor in the Lancashire psyche.

The second problem was the material for the show – again. *The Sketch Show* had been pitched to the Americans as a huge success. And as any American will tell you, success counts. We'd won a BAFTA, we were a big hit. Well, that's what had been pitched to them anyway. The truth was we had been a decent success that had done quite a good job. That is a long way from being a hit, but it was in everyone's interests to believe it to be a hit. Obviously it's completely understandable to pitch anything you're selling as the best thing since sliced bread, because that's what probably got it on American TV in the first place. What was bizarre was then seeing our own British team starting to believe their own hype and thus being afraid to make any changes. I kept trying to point out that actually we were eventually cancelled by ITV (Yanks: 'You what?') and so maybe it was a good idea to try and improve what we were doing rather than replicate it. People looked at me like I was suggesting we repaint a Ming Dynasty vase in Dulux Neon Lime.

We simply didn't learn from our mistakes, and made almost exactly the same show, shot for shot, word for word, but with different people playing the parts. It was madness. Not least because it now meant that these were predominantly my sketches with the Americans often acting like extras – sorry I mean supporting artists – whilst I stood at the front and did my thing. It's fair to say that this didn't help the 'vibe'.

Kelsey Grammer Presents The Sketch Show went on air in 2005, and surprise, surprise, it was cancelled after four episodes. Who would have thought that the British show that was cancelled, which was remade virtually word for word, would be cancelled again?* Like in the UK, there are two episodes that were never shown and are gathering dust on a shelf in LA somewhere. In fact, being successful is so important in America that I guess they've actually been buried somewhere in the desert.

Still, I had pretty much ended any chance of a career in the States, so I guess it wasn't all bad.

Virtually every one of my sketches from my Edinburgh Festival *Bits* show was remade for *The Sketch Show* and its American counterpart. I say virtually, because thankfully there was one exception. In the middle of the *Bits* show there was a sketch set in a flat, where I would play Catherine Tate's layabout

* Me.

boyfriend and Dan would play the 'mate'. This had come about because I'd had an idea for a joke. A really simple one where a woman walks into her flat and her boyfriend is looking through a telescope. When he realizes she has entered the room he quickly aims the telescope much higher towards the moon, the gag being that he was clearly looking at something he shouldn't have. This was, at best, mildly amusing and definitely couldn't exist on its own with a blackout before and after it. So I didn't bother even trying it out. Then a few days later I thought of another tiny gag set in a flat. Again it couldn't exist on its own, but if I was to put it with the telescope gag, and perhaps a few more I might have a starting point for a sketch that I could build on. That's what happened, and in the end it was one of the strongest sketches in that Edinburgh show.

And that's how *Not Going Out* started. I needed to find a home for a silly gag about a bloke who had been perving at his neighbour through a telescope.

From tiny perverted acorns grow huge . . . perverts.

PSYCHIATRIST'S OFFICE

BRIAN: It comes across in the book that
          you are stoic.

          *Lee wonders if 'stoic' could be
          put next to 'resilient' in his
          tour poster quote.*

BRIAN: It's probably something you
          developed early on in life. But
          the downside to being stoic . . .

          Oh God, here we go.

BRIAN: . . . is that you sometimes then do
          things that you don't really want
          to do.

          *Lee is about to disagree, then
          finds himself daydreaming about
          Stoke University, working with
          Americans and putting the bins
          out.*

BRIAN: You work very hard and take on a
          lot of things. Do you have a
          problem saying no?

          Lee wants to say no, but can't.

LEE: Sometimes.

BRIAN: If you get off the treadmill it
          can be a good thing.

*Lee daydreams about an obese
person with an eating disorder who
has been told to exercise more. In
the daydream Brian is telling this
person to get off the treadmill,
whilst the obese person's mum and
dad are whipping her with a stick
and telling her to get back on it.*

BRIAN: Getting off it gives you more time
for self-reflection.

LEE: I think this job is too self-
obsessive already.

*When Lee first started in comedy
he found all comedians ever did
was talk about themselves, and he
found this surprising. He doesn't
notice it as much nowadays, which
suggests he's either too used to
it to notice, or he's become 'one
of them'. Like a zombie film. But
instead of the zombies eating
human flesh, they just endlessly
talk about their upcoming film
roles, which is worse.*

BRIAN: That's not the same. In fact being
self-obsessed can block out your
ability to self-reflect.

*Lee wonders if this means that
vampires are too self-obsessed.
Which in turn leads to a daydream
about a zombie talking to a
vampire but neither of them
actually listening to the other.*

CHAPTER NINETEEN

Hit the road, Mack

Being someone who was now unemployed TV-wise, you'd have thought, particularly as a father to a new baby, that I would be concerned, but I genuinely wasn't. Not one jot. I wasn't an actor, or a presenter, or a newsreader, or a weatherman. I was, and am, a stand-up comedian. And when you're doing that you genuinely feel that you're never unemployed. That's why I've never stopped doing it. It's both an artistic decision and a necessity. Television is so fickle, and each show you do is constantly in danger of not being re-commissioned, that without this other outlet for comedy I'd go bonkers. It's the only guaranteed part of the job.

A usual year for me goes something like this: I take a large part of January off. I spend February to July writing *Not Going Out*. It then takes September to November to film the show. I then wait until the show is broadcast in January the following year. The BBC then decide if they want another series. If they do, the whole process starts again. If not (and that has happened, but more on that later), I start January with no idea what I'm doing for the rest of that year, because I've had to keep the diary clear in case it does. I obviously do some other TV work, like *Would I Lie to You?*, but this takes up hardly any time at all. Each series of *Not Going Out* takes me roughly ten months to make. Each series of *Would I Lie To You?* takes me eight days to make. They both get roughly the same viewing figures and reaction. I can't work out if that's very frustrating (*Not Going Out*) or a right result (*Would I Lie to You?*).

So, without knowing that whatever happens I can always go back to doing stand-up whenever I want, the pressure to get re-commissioned for TV work would be intolerable. I say 'go back', but actually that's wrong, as I've never felt I've stopped in the first place. I've just had to put a hold on it sometimes to get the TV shows made, and often have done both at the same time. I've never properly understood how I've been capable of doing this, as if you were to ask me to stir some gravy *and* talk on the telephone at the same time, I would struggle (as my wife will attest).

Stand-up is the ultimate self-employed job. *You* decide when it's done, *you* decide how long it's going to be done for, and most importantly *you* decide the content (I don't mean you, obviously, I mean me).

My first stand-up tour happened in 1997. It was shortly after I had done my first proper telly, *Gas*, and came about because Rob, my manager, had said that I

Above: At home rehearsing for my first ever gig (genuinely).

Left: Whatever happened to Frankie Marrow?

The set list for my first ever gig. I can't remember what the 'urine' gag was; perhaps it was a reminder not to wet myself on stage.

GAGGING FOR IT

The Wee Room
Gilded Balloon II
Start: 4.00 pm
9th - 31st August
£6 (£5 conc.)

Live sketch show with film and music

COMEDY REVIEW
★ ★ ★ ★ ★

GAGGING FOR IT

Stumbling blindly across a comic treasure like *Gagging For It* can single-handedly restore all faith in usually tepid Fringe sketch shows. For a healthy, happy start, *Gagging For It* is fantastic.

From the somewhat obligatory opening song to the snippets of characterisations and visual gags displayed proudly on an overhead videoscreen, 1995's *So You Think You're Funny* winner Lee Mack and his three similarly talented pals Geoff Aymer, Kevin Hay and Neil Webster whore their comedy wares with the finest in comic finesse.

A needlessly well hidden secret that deserves to be made public right this moment. (Danny Wallace)
■ **Gagging For It** (Fringe) Gilded Balloon (Venue 38) 226 2151, until 31 Aug, 4pm, £6 (£5).

Lee Mack: you've got to Gag For It

GAGGING FOR IT
Venue 38, Aug 9-31, 1600

I TAKE IT the 'it' in question is a refund. Advertised as 75 minutes of fast paced, irreverent comedy, what you get for your six quid is three-quarters of an hour of turgid, amateurish tripe that would make a hyena yawn. It's a struggle to find anything good to say about it.

The songs aren't terrible, the horny poet isn't dire, and a couple of the video clips that come on after each sketch has died might raise a chuckle, but that's your lot. A spoof TV interview with two ageing punk rockers sets the grim tone. Their band is called the Knob Rifles (like the Sex Pistols, only humourless), and they swear a lot.

Rather than say or do anything funny, people swear a lot in the other sketches too. Appropriately enough it soon had the the audience cursing that they'd ever bought a ticket.
●○○○○   **TG**

'Gagging For It' reviews. Who can you believe?
Danny Wallace, that's who.

Above: My first ever publicity shot. Because we all know the 'man struggling on the toilet' look is a sure-fire way to get a gig, right?

Left: I once had a review from *Viz* magazine that said, 'his gags are as sharp as his ferret-faced features'. Looking at this photo, aged twenty-one, I think they had a point.

Avalon Promotions Presents

LEE MACK

Star of C4's 'GAS'

RETURN OF THE MACK

$

Mack

"Fresh and original. Guaranteed to have you rolling in the aisles"
Melody Maker

August 5th - 31st at 7.35pm (Except 11th & 25th)
PLEASANCE Box Office: 0131 556 6550

For further information call the Lee Mack hotline on 0891 887766 (Calls cost 50p at all times)
http://www.wwcomedy.com

The worst idea for a publicity shot in the history of showbiz.

Above: Me and the wife.

Left: Me and the real wife.

Below: Me and Saul playing the game 'If the Kray Twins Had Been a Bit More Effeminate'.

Above: Meeting a comedy legend at the *Royal Variety Show* (I mean I met one, not Bob).

Below: My fortieth birthday, which had a 'You have to be called David' theme.

Left: The Austrian ventriloquist act didn't take off.

Below: A wrestling outfit from *The Sketch Show*. The six-pack has been drawn on, the man boobs are real.

Left: Me playing that game where you knock on the door and run away. That's not a joke, a few seconds later comedian and Suzie Quatro impersonator Ross Noble, who was taking this photo, did just that.

should now be having a go at touring with my new TV profile (that it turned out didn't really exist).

The thought of it didn't massively appeal to me, as the whole thing felt just a little too scary. In the comedy clubs the whole night is not about you, it's about three or four other comics as well. If you die on your arse it feels terrible, but at least you know there are other acts on the bill to pick up the pieces, as Stoke University had proved. On your own it is only about you, and if it doesn't work you've ruined everyone's night. Actually, maybe orgies aren't such a bad idea after all.

Also my ambition was only ever to be a regular member of the circuit in London, and that was starting to happen, particularly after *Gas*. I was earning about a hundred quid for each gig, and doing quite a few gigs per week. This was more money than I'd ever earned in my life, and I really enjoyed what I was doing, so I didn't feel I needed anything else. Well, maybe a slightly bigger flat would be nice. Oh, and a car would be handy. Actually I quite like going on fancy foreign holidays. 'Rob, ring the Sunderland Empire, I'm going on tour.'

So my first tour was booked, and was to be performed in the spring of 1998. This involves the promoter (Avalon) ringing the theatre, bigging you up ('He's on the telly. Honest') and getting the theatre to give you a guarantee of at least some sort of fee. This last bit is essential when you're new because there's a real danger that the numbers in the audience might be quite low for your first tour (or first *few* tours in my case) and without this guarantee you simply couldn't afford the costs of your publicity, tour manager, travel, hookers, hotels, etc.

I did about forty dates on that tour and it was tough. *Gas* simply hadn't made an impact, and the numbers were low. I'd say on average about twenty to thirty people a night. When you bear in mind that at least half of those were probably taking a punt on someone they'd never even heard of, it shows that very, very few people were actually that bothered about coming to watch me live. Luckily the venues were fairly small: church halls, comedy clubs, small arts centres, so the pain of seeing only thirty people was at least slightly tempered by the fact that they only held about sixty or so anyway. Or, as my PR man told me, 'Well done, it's half full.' PR people's ability to be positive in the face of adversity is heroic or deluded depending on your point of view. Sadly that year my point of view was stood facing the audience and so the reality was clear.

I also had made the decision to take a support act with me, so this also meant I was only just about making enough money to be able to afford to tour. I'd taken a support act for three reasons:

Firstly, without a support act, I would have had to have done two halves, and the thought of that terrified me. Almost all theatres have an interval to make money at the bar, but also because it's what the audience expects. It's all part of the night out, so you have to have one. Which means you have to get up twice, and the thought of that back then sounded awful. What if they didn't like me? I'd have to sit in the dressing room in the interval knowing I'd have to face them again. Part of my brain at that time always went on stage thinking that if worst came to worst and it failed, at least I was safe in the knowledge that I never had to see these people again as long as I lived. It was a self-defence mechanism that kept me going. If I'm going to be totally honest, to some level I still go on stage thinking it.

There was also the issue of material. I was new, and didn't have a bottomless well of gags. If you do two halves you need to do at least two lots of one hour. Whereas if you do one section, then an hour and twenty feels like more than enough. Nowadays I could much more easily generate a show with two halves because I'm a lot more 'trained' in writing material, but I still only do one half because I honestly think that's enough of listening to anybody. Even comedians I absolutely love can only sustain my interest for this amount of time, and it still amazes me that some comedians insist on doing longer. There's a reason why films and sporting events happen over about an hour and a half. The brain can't cope with much longer. I appreciate cricket and snooker are on for much longer, but cricket and snooker are painfully dull. If you don't agree, it means *you* are painfully dull. Again, all letters to be sent to Avalon Management.

The other reason for a support act was, and still is, company. One of the biggest laughs about being a comedian is sharing a dressing room and having a crack. Take that away and all you're left to look forward to after a show is a cold Ginsters pasty at the

Shell service station. I loved being on the circuit with loads of comics, and so to some degree I wanted to take that on tour with me.

Over the years of touring I've had many support acts including Rhod Gilbert, George Egg, Simon Evans, Russell Howard, Rob Deering, Steve Williams, Russell Kane, Steve Hall, Noel Britten and Neil Fitzmaurice. Some of those names you will know, and they now do their own tours, some you won't. The things they have in common, which are vital for a support act, is that they are all a sufficient contrast to me (Rhod Gilbert used to be quite deadpan believe it or not, before things started winding him up, like scones and duvets), they are all a good laugh to travel round with (essential) and, most importantly, they are all really good acts. Well apart from one, but it's not fair to point him out. After all, I don't want him going back to New Zealand and slagging *me* off.*

You'd think that choosing a support act that was really good would be common sense, but actually some comedians deliberately choose 'quite good' rather than 'very good'. The idea of this is that you don't want to risk them being so good that the audience enjoy them more than you. I've never bought in to that, because I like the idea of being on my toes. If the support act is absolutely tearing the roof off, it makes me change gear

* I suddenly got paranoid and thought 'What if one of them has emigrated to New Zealand and I don't know.' So just to be absolutely clear, this is a joke. See, I told you comedians are fragile.

a bit, and it prevents complacency, which is a major risk after a hundred dates. Also, it's not a competition. The audience don't go to a theatre show to say 'Oh the first act was terrible, but I enjoyed Lee Mack.' They will say 'Overall the show was good, but I didn't enjoy the first half as much.' It reflects on the whole show, including you, if the first half isn't up to scratch. Likewise the reverse is true if they're really good. In fact, next time I might get someone so amazing I can actually have the night off.

When I'm gearing up towards a new tour I will spend almost a year turning up at small comedy clubs to try out the new gags, and insisting I don't get paid. The reason I don't want to be paid at most of them is not through some sort of altruistic act of charity towards the poor promoter, it's to do with self-preservation. If you get paid it's only fair that you're advertised on the bill, and then you will get people who have specifically come to see you, and this is bad for many reasons.

Firstly, there's a good chance you're going to be a bit ropey. These are new ideas, often scribbled on bits of old paper. It's not going to be what you'd call 'tight'. You don't want people who really like you becoming people who think you're just OK(ish).

Secondly, audience members don't always know the concept of 'new material' and 'new material nights'. They will come along possibly assuming you're doing forty minutes of pure unadulterated laughs, as opposed to the reality of ten minutes of pure unadulterated mediocrity. That would make me feel like I'm ripping them off. And if I wanted to do that, I'd sell T-shirts and mugs on tours (I'm not exactly the most vocal champion of all the traditional values of alternative comedy, but come on, guys, keyrings? Get a grip).

Thirdly, and to be honest most importantly, there's a danger that if there's a large proportion of the crowd which is 'your' audience, then they just might laugh a little too heartily at jokes that are actually sometimes a bit average. I like the idea of the audience possibly not really being there for you personally, because it then means they're a little bit harder to win over, and therefore the jokes have to be better. I prefer it when I'm slightly up against it. There is an argument that if you go on stage with bits of old paper and look shoddy and underprepared you're not giving the material a fair shot. To a degree that's true. It's also true that for the joke to then work when it's got all these factors against it, it has to be really good. That's why when it does work it's very exciting, because you know that when you then take it on tour to 'your' audience, when you're totally looking prepared and in control and sure of what you're doing, it's going to take the roof off. Or at least hopefully disturb a few slates. I always think it's interesting how comedians' descriptions of doing well involve acts of wanton destruction: 'taking the roof off', 'ripped the room apart', 'killed'. There's a theory that all comedians are frustrated rock stars, but maybe they're actually all frustrated psychopaths.

The second tour I did was in 2002, shortly after the broadcast of the first series of *The Sketch Show*, and this time it had been decided to put me in bigger venues, much bigger. The theory was that I'd now been on the tour already, and combined with the fact I was now on ITV, then surely the time was right to step up a gear. Surely.

Wrong. It turned out that the numbers had approximately doubled, but when you consider that the first tour was to about thirty people, then double this is still quite a small crowd. Especially placed within a thousand-seat setting. At one point I was considering renaming it the 'Close the Balcony Tour' (as opposed to the imaginative 'Lee Mack Live' title I'd given it) because this is what I used to say to the tour manager every single day. I became obsessed with getting the theatres to shut off the balcony, or circle, or anything that made the audience too far away from me. The support act, Noel Britten, was spending a lot of the first half simply getting people to come to the front, hoping that if we could squash them all near the stage there would at least be some sort of atmosphere.

It was a really tough tour, and ever since then I have always been wary of what my manager Rob predicts is the right amount of nights we can do at a theatre, assuming he's over-estimated. To be fair, since that tour he has always managed to get it spot on despite my concerns, and will often convince me to do those extra few nights in a city when I am sceptical, and he's always right. Obviously he's my agent, so it's my job as a self-obsessed neurotic comedian to tell him to his face that everything he is doing is wrong, but in print I'm happy to say he's right. But then again, like any agent justifying their cut of the money, he could argue he only has to be right 15 per cent of the time.

The low numbers on this second tour were put into sharp perspective the day I performed my first Royal Variety Performance, which happened the day after a tour show in Derby. I had to turn up early in the afternoon of the recording for a quick camera rehearsal, and as I did it I realized that there were more people in the orchestra pit than there had been in the audience on my tour the previous night. Usually I never do my material for the crew on the afternoon of a TV show because it's always such a muted atmosphere, but on this occasion I was more than happy because it felt like I was just doing a regular tour gig.

I've been lucky enough to do three Royal Variety Performances to date, and each time it always feels slightly odd. You're surrounded by huge international stars, but also people dressed in ridiculous West End costumes. So one minute you're chatting to Rod Stewart, the next to a six-foot juggling chicken.

The shows themselves are actually a little bit on the tough side, as the audiences are not there to see you specifically. In fact they're not even there to see *comedy* specifically, which is fair enough, because the clue to the nature of the show is in the title.

It's also quite interesting to see comedy treated like it was in the old days, which is 'front of cloth'. The comedians are often asked to stand at the front of the stage so they can lower the curtain and frantically build the next set behind you as you're doing your gags. It's almost like the comedian has been booked to 'kill time', as they get ready for the proper show. Again, this is exactly what it was like in the days of music hall, and actually I quite like it. There's something very reassuringly old-fashioned about comedians being wheeled out front to distract the crowd for a moment. It's like we're suddenly the least important act on the bill, and given there are times when I think comedy has possibly got just a little too big nowadays, then that's not necessarily a bad thing. It feels like we're the outsiders in a world of bigger and better acts, and for some reason I quite like that. I like the feeling that we're the underdogs (as opposed to the dancing dogs behind the curtain*).

My only regret about doing the Royal Variety Performance is that so far I still haven't met the Queen. It's something I've always wanted to do that hasn't yet happened. Each time I've done the show Prince Charles has been the guest, which is very nice, don't get me wrong, but come on, Liz, you can't keep avoiding me. To be fair, Camilla has probably told her to give me a wide berth after the 'incident' in 2006. It wasn't my fault, I was a bit drunk.

There were five comedians on that year: Jason Byrne, Michael McIntyre, Omid Djalili, Ken Dodd and me.

---

* I should clarify that that is a comment about poodles that can dance, not a sexist, derogatory remark about West End backing dancers.

Even sat here now and writing that I was on the *Royal Variety Show* with Ken Dodd makes me chuckle, so you can imagine how odd it felt to actually do it. I was the first comedian up, and I then had a long wait until the line-up when you are introduced to the Royals (Charles again. Come on, Liz, honestly you'll love it. I'm cheeky, never blue). I decided to nip next door in the middle of the show for a quick pint, and was delighted to see Paul O'Grady standing at the bar, who was also on the bill that night. I'd only met Paul briefly once before, so we weren't exactly what you'd call mates. There are some people that you meet who seem to have a slightly cynical tone about them when it comes to showbiz, as if they don't properly trust the world they're involved in, and I'm always drawn to these people, as I feel I'm also one of them myself. He told me he was having a pint 'because it's better than being in there with them lot'. This really made me chuckle, and the brief chat and pint I had with him that night is as fond a memory as any I have of the three *Royal Variety Shows* I've done. Soon Paul had left, and I then found myself having one more with Jason Byrne, who'd also done his set. Two pints became three and before long we found ourselves in the line-up waiting to meet me old mucker Charlie. I wouldn't say I was drunk, that would be unprofessional. But I'm happy to write it. Prince Charles and Camilla walked down the line and me and Jason stood next to each other like a couple of school kids waiting to meet a posh auntie. Eventually the Royals came to us and Camilla asked us 'How come you gentlemen are so funny?' What I should have said was 'Who knows, but that's very nice of you to say so, your Royal Loveliness' (or whatever you're supposed to call her). Basically I should have smiled politely and let her move on. I didn't. I said 'Because we take loads of drugs.' This was neither witty nor appropriate and, more importantly, as a comedian, it made no sense whatsoever as a joke. Being funny and being on drugs doesn't really mean anything. What I was doing was acting like a kid to impress my mate. I may as well have gone cross-eyed and blown a raspberry, that would have been equally clever. She gave me a look as if to say 'OK, that's that over then' and moved on. I hadn't shocked her, or been 'too edgy' for her. She had moved on simply because she knew that she was surrounded by press and cameras etc., and now wasn't the time to be engaging in banter about drugs. Of course not, she was the future Queen (I think, I'm still not 100 per cent sure how that works). I was an idiot. I felt a bit stupid. I won't do it again. I promise. Come on, Liz, just once, please, your Royal Queeniness.

My other recollection of that 2002 tour is waking up every morning in a hotel room with weird writing all over my bedsheets. This had come about because of a routine I used to do.

I was starting to get the taste for breaking up the material and talking to the crowd in the middle of the act. One of the things I used to do to help facilitate that was to ask the audience to guess what I used to do for a living. Various things were shouted, and a combination of stock answers to some things plus genuine improv* would often result in a good bit of the show. One thing that kept cropping up though was that someone would always shout 'Comedian', the heckle implying that I'm not one now. This would always get a round of applause for the heckler and I would always think 'I must think of a clever and witty response to this.' But I never did. In the end I decided it was time for a prop (an obvious sign that a comedian is panicking). I would let the audience member have their moment of glory, then I would turn my back to the audience and 'talk to myself' on the microphone and pretend that I was trying, and failing, to think of a witty response. Whilst doing this I would remove my shirt, on the pretence that I was getting hot and bothered at the situation, and when I turned back to the crowd I was wearing a T-shirt with the words 'one wanker always says comedian' printed on it. This used to absolutely bring the house down (kill, destroy, chop them up, bury them in the garden etc.) as people up until this point genuinely thought I was getting flustered and losing it.

The problem was, I'd already done this on the first tour and one night someone had remembered it. 'Comedian' had been shouted and I did my usual

* 'Improv' is another word I have a problem with. It feels far too prissy and middle class for some reason, like 'workshop', which I think should only ever be used when talking about carpentry or metalwork, and not drama. But the alternative to 'improv' is to write 'making stuff up', which makes you sound like you're an eight-year-old.

pretence of looking like I was in trouble and losing the crowd. Then suddenly, just before the big reveal, someone shouted out 'We know you've got a T-shirt on and it says "one wanker always says comedian."' This was a disaster. I'd really, really milked the 'it's all going wrong' bit knowing I had a huge back-up, but now it really *was* all going wrong. I kept the T-shirt covered, denying its existence, and simply carried on with my act. Suffice to say that the result was a combination of looking like I was on the back foot and utter confusion. That feeling embedded itself so much in my brain, that from then on I felt I needed a back-up plan in case it happened again. So each night I would get the tour manager to write on my back, with a marker pen on my skin 'and one wanker always mentions the T-shirt', so that if it did crop up I would be ready.

For the remaining thirty odd gigs it only came up once that someone did shout it out again, but when they did, me ripping the T-shirt off and revealing the writing on my back was worth it. It made all those days of knowing hotel maids had been seeing the writing all over the bedsheets and assuming I was a crazy bloke, living a life like Guy Pearce in *Memento*, just a little less embarrassing.

The next tour happened in 2005. This third tour was better for two reasons:

Firstly, the numbers were starting to grow from simply going back to the same places again. A jump from about eighty a night on the last tour to about three hundred each night. This was starting to finally feel like

I was a proper touring comedian, and it was nice. Mainly because I didn't have to close the balcony as we had learned our lesson from last time and the venues were much more realistic in terms of size, about four hundred on average, and so there was often no balcony to close. I considered calling it the 'Look at Me, I Don't Need to Close the Balcony Any More Tour', but felt that might sound both conceited and confusing. Instead I once again went for the more imaginatively titled 'Lee Mack Live' tour.

There had also been a couple of notable TV appearances I'd made which were clearly helping the turn out. Months earlier I had been asked if I would like to do a screen test to host a new panel game called *Sporting Chance*. The rumour was that the BBC One panel game *They Think It's All Over* was, after eighteen series, about to be axed and they wanted a replacement show. It was so similar to its predecessor I did ask why they didn't just carry on with what they had. This question was answered a short time later when I was offered the job, but it wasn't going to be called *Sporting Chance*; it was going to be *They Think It's All Over*. Wow, this really was starting to look like its predecessor.

It was a hard decision to host that show. Nick Hancock had been doing it for about ten years and was totally synonymous with the show. I'd only met Nick once and so I'd be lying if I said my dilemma was born out of any sense of not wanting to tread on his toes. In fact, the one time I'd met him was actually when I was a guest on *They Think It's All Over* a few years earlier.

It was my first appearance on a panel game and, quite frankly, I was terrible. I was completely intimidated by the other more experienced comics on the show and made the ultimate error on any panel game – I clammed up. This is an awful feeling that thankfully doesn't happen to me any more, as once it happens it's very hard to break out of it. You end up sitting there watching the show happen around you as if you're watching it on the telly. Only you're watching yourself. And what's worse is that you're watching yourself saying nothing.

My dilemma about doing it was because I suspected that if the BBC felt the show wasn't right, then getting a different host wasn't really going to change anything. I felt like I was taking on a show that was already on its last legs. Plus I have to be completely honest with myself and say that I sort of knew in my heart of hearts that given my limited experience at that time, Nick was the better man for the job. However, it was a hard show to turn down. It was very well established and, more importantly, I would get to meet some pretty famous sports stars, especially footballers. That might sound like a bit of a basic and childish way to choose to do a show, but it really is what I felt. I remember during a recording break popping out to the toilet and Ian Wright, who was standing next to me, made some comment about how the show was going a bit pear-shaped due to some technical hitch. I said 'Yeah, but what does it matter, Ian? You scored in the FA Cup Final at Wembley.' As far as I was concerned he had lived the dream, this was all just nonsense.

I only did one series of the show, and then it was cancelled for good, but by doing it I got to meet Tony Woodcock. And as any TV critic will tell you, the real barometer of whether a show is any good or not is how many ex-Nottingham Forest and FC Köln strikers you get to meet. How many did Ricky Gervais meet in *The Office*? I rest my case.

The other TV show I did at that time, and which had even more effect on the number of people turning up to the tour, was *Live at the Apollo*. It was only the second series of the show, and at the time was hosted by Jack Dee. It's a great show, not least because of how much time you get on screen. To be able to do half an hour of stand-up on BBC One was unbelievable, and completely out of the question only a few years earlier. I'd been invited on as a fairly last-minute replacement for Roseanne Barr who had been unable to do the show due to her passing a Dunkin' Donuts on the way,* and, unlike the dilemma of doing *They Think It's All Over*, I grabbed this opportunity without a minute's thought. Although I'd done a few stand-up TV appearances at this point, including the Royal Variety Performance, this was different. Here was a one-off opportunity to do a proper substantial set, like I'd been doing for years. It went well, even though I say so myself, and the increase in my tour audience reflected that. Then again how

* This is a joke. I appreciate you already know this, but the legal team behind the book felt it needed pointing out just in case (honest). Thank God I didn't mention the story about Felicity Kendal and the strap-on (joke).

could it not have gone well? I was doing tried and tested material, stuff that had been tested over many, many nights, some of which had been performed over many, many years. They were bulletproof. Again, similar to the way an audience is seen as being 'killed' or the room 'destroyed' when it's going well, if it's not, then the audience are seen as having bullets to end your life. Odd job, isn't it?

I have mixed feelings about actually being on the road. Mostly it's great. Really great. After working on television I crave the freedom of it. If you suddenly want to add a joke about a woman riding naked on the back of a camel you can think of it at seven o'clock and be saying it at eight o'clock on stage. In television it's not so easy. You need to ask the producer if it's possible to squeeze the joke in on location, and even if it is, you then need to ask the broadcaster if you can do tasteful nudity. Then there's the camel, that needs to be booked, and that's at least a week's notice. Plus on top of all that you don't even know if it's funny, because you haven't tried it out on anyone. After last week's 'standing on a llama in my underpants' fiasco, which resulted in not one laugh, everyone is dubious. So it's a lot of work for a joke that may fail. And unlike stand-up, if it fails you can't make a joke about it failing.

Then there's the other side of touring. It's a hundred dates in, you first said some of these jokes two years ago, and you're sick of the sound of your own voice. You're really, really, really tired of all the travelling. Especially as you do all the driving yourself because you're a control freak. In fact, you're such a control freak, you're the only person in comedy that drives his tour manager round, when it should in fact be the other way round. You haven't seen your family for fifteen consecutive nights. Suddenly you can't wait to get back to television, because in telly it's a different show being made each week so there's more variety, you don't get sick of the gags, there's no travelling, and you get to see your family every day. What's more, you can think of a joke about a woman riding naked on the back of a camel, and suddenly it can actually come to life. An actress will be booked (you even get to choose her) and a camel (a real bloody camel!) will be hired. Not only that, it's not even your fault if it fails, it was a team decision. Even the broadcaster had to make a judgement call on whether it was worth it or not given the taste reasons, so if it fails the pressure's off because it wasn't just your decision. And let's face it, even if it doesn't work you've always got the edit to get rid of it, like you had to do last week after the 'standing on a llama in my underpants' gag failed.

Since 2005 I have toured twice more, and each time the audience numbers have grown steadily. I now perform to venues well into the thousands and what's more they sell out (thankfully no balconies need to be closed). I say this not to brag, but to try and express to you how odd that is for me.

In my job I have done many things over the years that have made me stop and have a reality check because of how strange they make me feel: appearing on a one-off remake of *Saturday Live* with Ben Elton, the show I watched when I was young that had made me want to do stand-up in the first place; playing football in front of thirty thousand spectators at Old Trafford alongside people like Ian Rush, John Beresford, Ole Gunnar Solskjaer and Ronan Keating (yes, honestly); shaking hands with and chatting to Prince Charles (three times, Liz, three times); being invited to 10 Downing Street and asking a woman loads of questions about the place, only to be told 'I don't know, I'm a bit new here myself', then realizing it was Sarah Brown, after hubby Gordon had just got the job; standing opposite Alice Cooper pretending to be my landlady in a sketch; making John Cleese laugh; going on *Who Wants to be a Millionaire?*, realizing I don't know the answer and hoping Stacey Solomon *does*; going on the *Jonathan Ross Show* and having Russell Crowe insist we've met before even though we haven't, so going along with it anyway; meeting Johnny Ball from *Think of a Number*; having a sitcom on telly. But nothing, absolutely nothing, makes me go 'Bloody hell, how did this happen?' more than peeking out from behind a curtain and seeing thousands of people waiting for me to come on and tell my jokes. It genuinely still feels crazy.

Of course, one of the reasons they're coming is because of *Not Going Out*.

PSYCHIATRIST'S OFFICE

BRIAN: Why do you think you do comedy?

LEE: I don't know. In fact, to be honest, I sometimes ask myself that.

BRIAN: What do you mean?

LEE: I suppose it's not exactly what I thought it was going to be when I started out. The reality is that sometimes it's actually quite hard work, certainly harder work than it looks. But you can't really ever say that because then it looks like you're moaning.

BRIAN: You certainly get the idea across that it's hard work in the book.

Brian laughs when she says this. Lee also laughs, but just to join in. He's not quite sure what the joke is. He then assumes that she means he goes on about it too much in the book. This worries Lee, and he wishes he'd written a bit more often words to the effect of 'however hard it is, at least it's not coal mining', which is what showbiz people are supposed to say when they are trying to look 'grounded'. Even though most don't know what coal mining, or indeed

*any manual labour, actually
entails. Lee makes a mental note
to start saying 'at least it's not
copper mining' from now on when
he's in social situations, for no
other reason than it will sound a
bit different as a phrase, and so
people will assume he must have
actually been a copper miner once.*

LEE: You see when I started out I
       wanted to be like the 'special'
       people who did comedy. But now I
       don't think they are special. In
       fact, to some degree I think the
       whole thing is a bit of a
       confidence trick. People often
       say . . .

       *Lee realizes he's doing the
       'people think' style of argument
       again. The idea that if you say
       'people think' it sounds like more
       of a credible fact than if you say
       'I think'. 'People think' suggests
       you've done market research. He
       wonders whether Brian will spot he
       is doing this style of argument,
       then realizes, again, that they
       are just talking and not actually
       having an argument. Lee often has
       to remind himself of this.*

LEE: People often say that comedy is
       for people with some sort of
       natural ability. But I don't buy
       that argument.

Lee realizes he is now having another 'argument'. This time with a fictional bunch of people who think that comedy is for those with natural ability. But Lee realizes that he's actually made those people up a few moments ago to suit his argument. So Lee is now not quite sure who he's arguing with, but decides to carry on arguing anyway.

LEE: Anyone can learn to do anything. If natural ability does come into it, then it's the natural ability to work hard as opposed to the natural ability to be funny. You see, my perception of this job has changed from when I started out. I used to think comedians were different to me. That they went on stage and made everything up on the spot, and this made them a rare breed. But I soon realized effort went into it. Basically there are three stages you go through when watching a comedian. The first time you see them say 'A funny thing happened to me on the way here tonight', you believe them. The second time you see them say 'A funny thing happened to me on the way here tonight', you don't believe it actually happened to them that night. The third time you hear them say 'A funny thing happened on the way here tonight', you don't believe it ever happened

at all. That's when people start
to understand the importance of
writing and hard work.

*Lee is pleased with this summary
of comedy, particularly as he's
just used the phrase 'people'
again, so she will see it as a
concrete fact. Lee feels he has
won the argument, even though,
again, they are not actually
having one.*

CHAPTER TWENTY

Bashing the Blu-tac

Even though stand-up is the thing that I consider my actual proper job, the thing that has actually dominated most of my waking hours over the last seven years is my sitcom, *Not Going Out*.* It started as a side-step from what I usually do, but ended more like a side-leap.

This first opportunity arose when my manager Rob told me that there had been an enquiry from the BBC about whether or not I had any sitcom ideas I would like to develop. On the face of it that sounds like a very exciting opportunity, and to a degree it is, but in the world of television being asked to 'develop' stuff can mean many, many things.

At its best it can mean a broadcaster has so much faith in a comedian that it gives them millions of pounds and a

---

* I only mean in relation to work. If I include everything it would be my kids. In fact not only have they dominated my waking hours, they've caused them.

guarantee of X amount of shows over the course of many years. Often known as a 'golden handcuff' deal. This was not what I was being offered. There was no gold, and certainly no handcuffs. It was more along the lines of tin-foil and a bit of sellotape.

At this point I'd had a couple of TV series under my belt and, more importantly, some stand-up tours and Edinburgh shows. In terms of TV people, I'd now done enough to be classed as a 'consideration', i.e. the person in the position to offer something had at least heard of me. Even better, maybe even seen me live.

This is a hurdle which is a lot harder to jump than you'd imagine. There are many, many comedians out there, and a lot of commissioners only see regular live comedy when they are at the annual Edinburgh Festival. Even then, there are hundreds of shows to see, so crossing the line of 'Oh yeah, I've seen him' can be a bit longer than you might first think. It still amuses me when comedians say things like 'So-and-so won't have me on their channel because they really don't like me', when in fact so-and-so hasn't actually heard of them.

So although I was being asked to 'develop' stuff, I was also aware that so were many other people.

Knowing what I'm like in terms of throwing myself into a project 100 per cent, and also being perfectly content as a stand-up comedian, I needed to know that the interest was real.

If you were in a long-term relationship and the person you were dating started hinting at marriage, you might start hearing wedding bells. If it turned out that they had been dating fifty others in the hope that one came up trumps, you might need to replace the word 'wedding' with 'alarm'.

The only real way of knowing if the interest is genuine is if they show you the cash (I mean TV, not relationships). There's often a lot of false enthusiasm and smiling in the world of showbiz about projects, but when you ask for money I find you get a much more honest assessment of the situation.

So, money was shown. This amount was, in the world of making TV shows, small. But in terms of knowing if people are genuinely interested in you in television, when it comes to money the difference between nothing and a little is a lot. It meant that the chances of me actually getting something eventually filmed had just gone from 'extremely unlikely' to 'slim', which I felt was a decent enough shift in the odds to warrant having a crack.

The first thing I needed was a deadline. Without that I'm always stuffed, as *not* writing is always much more fun than writing. As is watching the telly. Or reading emails. Or washing conkers.

So I booked the Latchmere in Battersea for a live read-through, the fringe theatre we'd used to test the material for *The Sketch Show*, and indeed all my previous work.

Actually 'work' is another word I struggle with when it comes to past projects, but I find it hard to think of an alternative (stuff?). The problem with 'work' is that it's advertising that the end product is exactly that, the fruition of work. Which, of course, it is. But I think that's giving away the magic, and comedy is much better suited to looking effortless. People want to see the swan gliding across the water, not the legs going thirteen to the dozen underneath. Which is massively hypocritical of me considering I've written so much about the writing in this book, but I'm hoping that you'll keep schtum so people will think I just make it up as I go along. Actually some of the critics of *Not Going Out* probably think we do.

I now had a deadline, but I still needed a script.

The only sitcom-type idea I had at the time was the small sketch set in a flat I had performed in my Edinburgh Festival show 'Lee Mack's Bits' around the start of the new millennium (I could have just written 'around 2000' but there's something very grand about talking in terms of 'millennia'. It implies that what you're talking about is monumentally important, like the ice age). Even that was a pretty small seed of a thought. It was after all a sketch. A series of jokes, with no real beginning or end. It wasn't really about anything other than 'man lives with woman, man is annoying woman'. In the words of Dominic Holland when I made *Gas*, there was clearly a lot of work to do.

I knew nothing about story lines, structure or characters, but when you've considered going to the moon or winning the British Open golf championship as realistic, this type of thing was bound to be a doddle. So in 2003 I sat down and wrote what little ideas I had on a piece of paper.

Firstly, the characters. In the sketch I had played 'Lee', Catherine Tate's boyfriend, and we lived together. So I wrote that down. Good, I'd started.

I'd annoyed her quite a lot in the sketch doing silly impressions and cracking gags, instead of getting off my arse and getting a job. I wrote that down. So not only did I now have two characters, one of them even had some sort of character 'trait'.

Blimey, this was easier than I thought. I made a start on my BAFTA speech, then got back to work.

Was that enough? Did I have enough of a situation? Maybe not, but if I came up with a good story maybe that would compensate for the lack of a really original dynamic.

What story? I didn't have a clue. After all, what did I know about writing stories? Nothing. Shit. I ripped up my BAFTA speech.

I started thinking about successful sitcoms. *Friends* was big at the time. That's it, I'll have a friend. Dan Antopolski played my mate in the sketch, he can be my mate in this. I wrote that down. Was that enough characters? In *Friends* there were loads, and half of them were women. I'd better get more women. I'll give Catherine a sister. She can be Dan's girlfriend. Yes, that's it, that all ties together neatly. I got the BAFTA speech back out of the bin.

I felt that I now had a basic 'situation' (with the emphasis on basic). But I still needed a story.

In the sketch I was a layabout. Maybe that's the story. Or is that a character trait? Maybe it's both. Does it matter? Who knows? I was starting to wonder if I was up to this.

I decided that maybe the story should introduce the character traits. So if I'm a layabout in the series, then the first story should be about that. So the story is 'Lee has to get a job'. Good. I wrote that down. Where do the others fit into that story? Maybe they don't. I'll give them their own stories. Catherine can think that her parents prefer her sister. Actually, that's a good character trait. That can be her 'thing'. I wrote it down.

So I now had a basic idea for a story, and a basic idea for a subplot. I now just needed the dialogue.

Having now had many more years of experience, this is a fatal error. The only plot I had was a vague notion that could be written down as one sentence. This wasn't even close to being ready for scripting, but what did I know?*

I had a few bashes at making a start but very soon decided it would be nice to have help so asked my old college mate Neil Webster, who had written with me on *Gas* and *The Sketch Show*. He too had never written a sitcom, so I thought he was perfect as we'd have a lot in common.

I was due to fly to Berlin to perform stand-up to loads of Germans who didn't fully understand what I meant by 'gymnastics', so we decided that he'd come with me and we'd lock ourselves away in the daytime and write the sitcom (we also took many *How to Write a Sitcom*-type books, which were both invaluable and useless in equal measure).

There's always the temptation when writing to go somewhere else to do it, the idea being that if you're somewhere different, especially if you're abroad or somewhere beautiful in the countryside, you'll somehow be

* Nowt.

more inspired and write better stuff. This is a lie that the brain tells you, to allow it to procrastinate. The reason why 'somewhere else' feels better to write is that it needs to be arranged, and arranging it is easier than writing. It's a way of putting off the inevitable; of just having to get on with it. I've tried every possible place there is when it comes to writing; I've done it from home, on a boat, in an office in Oxford Street, in bed, in a holiday cottage, going abroad, sat outside a tent. None of it helps. Unless you can just learn to get on with it, you've had it. Running up a hill is no easier abroad than it is round the corner. Unless you're in Holland.

We came back from Germany with at least the backbone of a script, and over the next few weeks I managed to bash it into some sort of shape that resembled a finished product. 'Bash it into shape' is an appropriate phrase when describing writing a script, as that's exactly how it feels for me.

I (genuinely) think of a *Not Going Out* script in terms of a massive sculpture I've been asked to make. Instead of soft malleable clay I've been given a massive six-foot lump of hardened Blu-tac. You know, the type that's been untouched for about a year and has gone rock hard. The only tool they've given me to fashion the thing is a shovel. I (genuinely) picture myself smacking it with the shovel over and over again until eventually there's a sort of vague resemblance to a person's face. There's a point, after a few weeks, when it goes from a big blob of hard blue nothingness to the vague look of a person, and that's when I know it's going to be OK. It still takes weeks of hitting it with the shovel, but eventually I get there and it finally looks like a reasonably well-sculpted, if somewhat battered, face. I (genuinely) need psychological help.

A few weeks later I was at the Latchmere with Catherine and Dan to try out the script (despite the fact that I'd run off to telly land without them to do *The Sketch Show*, they were thankfully still happy to be involved). I'd chosen to perform it live because, as ever, I didn't trust people would know it was funny by simply reading it.

Despite what anyone might say about understanding scripts, there is not one person in the world who can visualize how a script will actually turn out better than if you simply perform it to them. I wanted the BBC to see it would work. Although, to be honest, I wasn't even sure myself, but I knew doing it to a live audience would at least give it a fighting chance. Having a room full of people laughing at something massively influences decisions. The hard bit is getting them to laugh in the first place.

The story was that I was living with my girlfriend Catherine and she had decided enough was enough and I needed to go on a job centre training scheme to get me back to work. I had gone to the wrong room and ended up in room full of people with an addiction to internet pornography. Why they would be in the same building as a job centre training scheme is a detail that you don't need to worry about. We certainly didn't, and we wrote it. The upshot was that when I do eventually get an interview I recognize the man across the desk from the pornography meeting, and so as a way of keeping me quiet he offers me a job, and at my request agrees to sack me after a week so at least it would show I had made the effort. All very far-fetched, and a bit farcical, but it at least adhered to the rules of story telling I'd learned from the books.

Having just read it again many years later for the purposes of this book, I'm genuinely thinking of turning it into an episode for *Not Going Out*. I can't work out if that's a sign that my early efforts were better than I thought, or a sign that after more than forty episodes I'm running out of ideas. If you're from the BBC and you're reading this, it's the former.

I thought the show had gone fairly well, but I was told by the relevant powers that be that perhaps it needed a 'bit more development'. Basically they felt it wasn't good enough, but egos in showbiz are so brittle that the phrase 'no good' has never been said to the face of a writer or performer. Unless the conversation is about *other* people's work, in which case it gets said a lot.

That was that. I didn't really think much more of it. I'd had a go, and it hadn't quite happened. Back to the day job of stand-up. Well, night job.

Then, many months later, the sitcom was once again brought up and there seemed a renewed interest in it. This may have been because my management kept hammering away at it. It could have been because I was having a slight profile raise due to my forthcoming American TV show. It could literally be as simple as a new commissioner seeing me doing a gig and thinking 'Yeah, he's all right, I wonder if he's got any ideas.' How and why commissioners decide they like or indeed don't like you is as much a mystery now as it's ever been. Maybe they go by smell. I hope not.

But looking back I suppose one of the biggest factors in this renewed interest was that Catherine Tate had suddenly become very big (famous, not fat). The fact that she was in it, and was now doing very well, probably got it through the door.

So I was asked to do another script. But this time I decided I wanted to revamp the whole thing.

The first thing I wanted to do was give it a bit of depth.

Not much, I certainly didn't want to do anything 'realistic', which was suddenly the flavour of the month on telly, where studio audience sitcoms were seen as archaic and instead were being replaced with 'gritty realism'.

In my humble (right) opinion, reality is a very over-rated currency in comedy. 'Real' in comedy is seen as high-brow, well, certainly in comparison to the studio stuff which is seen as 'unreal'. Yet in an art gallery it's the other way round. Go to a Picasso exhibition and look at a picture of a horse. Then say really loudly 'That's crap, it looks nothing like a horse. I like my horses to look "real".' They'll look at you like you're an absolute heathen. Trust me, I know, I do it all the time.

I've always been a bit wary of the explosion of realism in comedy. It's not that I don't like those sorts of shows, it's just I always think they are more like comedy dramas than sitcom. It's almost like the industry got sick of trying and failing to get sitcom right so instead decided to take another genre, one that *was* working, and call *that* sitcom. That's like spending years trying to fix your fridge, giving up, then saying 'From now on we're calling the oven the fridge.'

Having said all that, in sitcom you do need *some* drama, not much, but some. And we had none.

So it was decided that maybe I should draft in some help from someone who *had* written something more dramatic: Andrew Collins. Andrew had written with Simon Day on a show called *Grass* and, more interestingly to me, *EastEnders*. My theory was that if he could write the drama, and I could do the jokes, we'd have a good show. Basically I thought that drama plus jokes equals sitcom. But it doesn't. It really doesn't.

Sitcom, real studio-based proper sitcom, is a unique stand-alone genre of comedy. The only people that can really write it well are people who have experience in it. All other experience of writing can only get you so far. But we only had a single script commission at that stage, we were way off this ever being on telly; so 'so far' was all we needed.

The first thing we decided, which was a pivotal moment in the show, was that Lee and Catherine were no longer a couple. They would be just flatmates. They would be 'not going out'. We decided this because during the previous incarnation of the show, I kept getting the feedback that people wondered why they were together. All they did was bicker and argue, and so why didn't they just split up? They said we needed to see the other side to their relationship, the loving side. I felt that there was then the danger of it being just a little cheesy. I didn't want to show the loving side because if you get it wrong, and let's face it that was very possible given the inexperience we had of writing a sitcom at that time, then it could look mawkish and sickly sweet. To me the loving side represented the dramatic side. I didn't want to do comedy drama, I wanted to do a sitcom. Plus 'love' isn't funny. Dogs saying 'sausages' is funny.

Looking back this was mainly driven from fear and inexperience, because actually you can show love on screen without it being too cheesy, but at the time it's just something I didn't want to risk. Plus it's not like I used to finish my stand-up routines about my girlfriend with 'But seriously, folks, I actually really love her. Goodnight', so I wasn't going to start doing it now.

So Catherine was now simply my landlady. Instead of asking 'Will they split up?' the audience would now hopefully ask 'Will they get together?' which was a much more positive feeling. 'Will they or won't they?' is much better for sitcom if it's followed by 'shag' rather than 'kill each other'.

The other big change was the character of 'Dan'. We decided to make the show into a bit of a love triangle by making this character not only my best mate, but also Catherine's ex-boyfriend. That way there would be a moral dilemma about whether Lee should be trying to get together with his best friend's ex. Although not everyone agreed it was a moral dilemma. A good friend of mine said he wouldn't hesitate for a second. In fact he'd still consider it if the best mate was still going out with her. Luckily he was just a good friend, as opposed to my best mate.

The main character trait of the person I was portraying is that he is a layabout. The best way to highlight that is to make his mate the opposite. Someone who is dynamic, successful and rich. We decided he was going to be a stockbroker who drove a Porsche and who was really sure of himself and cool (how the hell the part eventually went to Tim Vine is a mystery). The problem was the character of 'Dan' wasn't like that. He was kooky, off the wall, and basically everything that the real Dan Antopolski was in his stand-up act. Like me, Dan was a comedian not an actor, and could only really play himself. Although I soon regretted that decision after I saw his performance as the overweight Afro-American woman in the film *Precious*. Outstanding.

We also decided that we needed a bit of 'weight' to the story. The previous version about Lee needing to find a job just felt a little 'light'. I'd always had this feeling that what British studio-based sitcom had done in the past, which was possibly a mistake, was to avoid anything too 'heavy'. Perhaps this was one of the reasons why gritty realism was starting to take over? Studio sitcom was extremely safe, and I thought it would be interesting if on the face of it it looked like a traditional, warm, happy, brightly lit studio sitcom, but then suddenly from nowhere someone announced they'd been abused as a child.

Not a subject for comedy you might think, but you're wrong. You see, in my humble (i.e. correct) opinion, there is nothing that isn't a potential subject for comedy, in the same way there isn't anything you can't do a drama about, or write a song about, or paint a picture of. The key thing is that the joke has to be funnier than the subject is serious. The more heavy your subject matter is, the better the joke has to be, so the brain can shelve the trauma for a moment, and enjoy the joke. That's why comedy is so good, because it can make people park their fear/sadness/disgust for a moment, and instead laugh. Of course, this is the problem, because the joke has to be *really* good if the subject is *really* serious. The reason why comedians get lambasted for material that is deemed offensive is that quite simply the jokes are often just not good enough in relation to how heavy the subject is. So although everything in my opinion is a *potential* subject for comedy, the reality is that there are some things that are so serious that no one on earth can think of anything funny enough to shelve the dark thought. You're left reminded of the event, not the joke.

Plus, of course, we weren't intending doing jokes about child abuse. We were doing jokes about my character's inability to talk about child abuse, which is not the same thing.

So it was decided that the story was going to be about Lee meeting a woman who was too heavy for him (deep, not fat. Basically assume from now on I'm never calling anyone fat. Unless I say they are fat). This would show that Lee had a problem with being serious. This is what we would make the key element of the episode. In contrast to this, Catherine's character acted too seriously, for too much of the time, and had to learn how to joke around more. So we called it 'Serious' (seriously).

We wrote the script and for reasons I now find

inexplicable I broke my rule and didn't perform it live to prove it would work. I simply handed it in. Looking back I think this was probably because I felt it wasn't going to happen anyway, so why bother trying any more. A bit like that scene at the end of *The Shawshank Redemption* when Morgan Freeman stops trying to get parole and virtually tells them to get stuffed, but as a result then gets parole. Actually, the person who had to read our script might have a different take on events. They might think it was more like the bit when Tim Robbins' character has to wade through loads and loads of 'shit-smelling foulness most people couldn't even imagine'.

Against the odds, and, trust me, 'against the odds' is the right phrase when you're pitching an idea for a studio-based sitcom involving child abuse, we got a pilot.

This was unbelievably good news. There are many hurdles to jump getting a sitcom on telly, but the jump from script to pilot is the biggest. Suddenly the broadcaster is telling you they are (seriously) serious. They have to be, because before this point it's very cheap to show interest. Just a few thousand pounds to commission scripts etc., but now it was going to cost them a quarter of a million to actually film it. In relationship terms you've just gone from dating to living together. You're now just one step away from marriage (an actual series), providing you don't do something stupid like sleep with her sister (work for ITV).

The first thing we needed to do was find the person to play my mate 'Colin' (as he was called in the pilot). We cast many people for this role and just couldn't find the right person. He had to tick three boxes. One, was he a comedic contrast to me? Two, do we believe he is Catherine's ex-boyfriend? Three, can he deliver a joke? That last one might seem obvious, but it surprised me just how many people couldn't, for the simple reason that they'd never had to. We were seeing lots of actors because naturalism was now big in the world of comedy, and so the people dominating the screen, and thus the auditions, were from this world. When it came to comedy, actors were starting to take over.

I was sat at home watching the audition tapes and realizing that we still hadn't found 'Colin', when it dawned on me that with such a gag-driven script we should be seeing more stand-ups and fewer actors. But who? We'd seen a few, but what they gained in ability to tell a joke, they perhaps lacked in ability to act. And we already had someone on the show doing that.

Then I remembered Tim Vine. We'd done two series of *The Sketch Show* together, and I remember thinking at the time that, as comedians go, he was a decent actor. We had stayed mates, so I immediately rang him and asked if he'd like to read for the part. He couldn't have been any more indifferent. I thought he would have bitten my hand off to be in a BBC One sitcom, but actually he wasn't that fussed. He barely nibbled my fingernails. (I'm keeping the 'biting my hand off' metaphor going, that wasn't something I made people do to prove themselves to me.) Tim had always been a stand-up and solo performer and I suspect (well, know) that the thought of sharing the stage wasn't really his thing. It took a bit of persuasion but we finally got him to read for it, and he was great. We immediately offered him the part and he accepted. His reluctance to share the stage was outweighed by the fact that, like me, he's very competitive and by beating thirty other people to the role he felt he had effectively won something, so should at least collect his prize. And if there's one man who likes a prize it's Tim. He's the only man in showbiz who puts on his rider that he wants a wrapped present of any album of the theatre's choice in his dressing room when he turns up. Shameless.*

The only problem was, Tim was supposed to be a bit of a cool customer, a tough cookie, a bit of a rogue. For those who have seen Tim's act, they're not the immediate words that you would use to describe him. It was like giving the part of Scarface to Richard Briers. It still makes me laugh when I watch the pilot of *Not Going Out,* seeing Tim with shaven head, stubble and a leather jacket in some vain attempt we had made to roughen up his edges.

We finished our script and immediately read it out to the powers that be. Afterwards I was taken to one side by a BBC executive, and it was suggested to me that the script was a little bit too much about me, and not enough about Catherine. My management had (and rightly so) used Catherine's success to try and refuel interest in the thing in the first place, and so there was a chance that it had been sold as Catherine's new vehicle. She was brilliant in it of course, but there was no doubt about it, I was in the centre of the action and it was mainly about me. It was

* Or do I mean 'odd'?

made quite clear to me that this was 'not on' and I needed to address that. I completely agreed, said I would make some radical changes, then went away and didn't alter a word. After the pilot was filmed a few weeks later the same person thanked me for taking on board what they'd said, oblivious to the fact that nothing had changed whatsoever. The number one rule of business, as someone in my management team once told me, is to tell people exactly what they want to hear, then simply do whatever you want anyway.

The non-broadcast pilot was filmed on 2 October 2005 and it was one of those weird moments in this job when you think 'Bloody hell, how did this happen?' I was in a sitcom. That was odd. That wasn't what I'd intended when I started doing stand-up, but here I was, sat in a fictional flat, with a fictional mate, and a fictional girlfriend. And, more worryingly, with a fictional acting CV. I'd done sketches, but that was far more like stand-up than acting.

Could I do it? To be honest, it didn't really bother me, because if I couldn't then it would be rubbish, and if it was rubbish it was best to find out now, in a non-broadcast pilot, rather than with millions of people watching. If I could, then great. It felt win/win either way. As long as we'd had our shot, in front of a studio audience, then I was happy. So many potentially great pilot scripts are never made simply because the person reading it is not visualizing it the same way as the writer. They wouldn't have to visualize anything with this show, because it was actually being filmed. We were having a proper, decent crack and that was enough for me. Which are obviously easy words to write knowing it all panned out. If it hadn't, I may have been sat here now writing sentences involving words such as 'pearls' and 'swine'. Actually, I've always found that an odd expression. 'Casting pearls among swine' is supposed to mean you shouldn't give something of quality to those who don't understand its value, but actually a pig *does* know a pearl's value. To a pig, it's worthless, that's why the pig doesn't eat it. The expression should be 'Don't give your mouldy old potatoes to a pig that then won't eat them.' Luckily my mouldy old potatoes were devoured by the commissioner.

For the purposes of this book I dug out the old tape of the recording of that night and watched it. What struck me straight away was the pace. It was a lot slower than the way we do *Not Going Out* now, and this was mainly due to the way I delivered the lines. In sketches and stand-up I'd always been used to just belting out the lines at a fairly rapid pace. In the pilot it is clear that I'm not 100 per cent sure about combining what is supposed to be a 'real world' with the fact that four hundred people are laughing. I would say the gag, then there's a sort of frozen look on my face as I wait for the laughter to stop, then I say the next one. Nowadays we do what is called a 'laugh run' where our director, Nick Wood, will laugh in rehearsals at the place the laughter should happen on the night. That way we are so used to breaking up the dialogue we start adding our own little 'fillers' to allow for the time it takes for the laughs. Small facial ticks, looks of disgust, a bit of juggling, anything really, just as long as it's not the frozen look of a man waiting for the laughs to end. Then there's the problem of applause; that really breaks up the natural conversation. So much so that after the pilot was filmed I went into the edit and realized that a round of applause for a joke had actually been edited out. It was felt that having two characters on screen sitting and just waiting for the clapping to stop was 'unnatural'. I insisted it went back in. The fact that the characters are waiting for the applause to end shows that what we are doing is the filming of a live event, and that's vital for a sitcom. I didn't want to take out the applause or shrink the laughter any more than I would if it was a stand-up show. Some people might say 'Yes, but sitcom is different to stand-up as you are offering up a fictional world where the audience doesn't exist.' But these people are idiots (I argue like this for real by the way, it's not just in book form). If that's true then I don't want to hear any applause or laughter at a theatre play, because they too are in a fictional world. When you can get that sorted, get back to me, and I'll see what I can do.

You need applause and laughter in studio-based sitcom because, as the brilliant editor of *Not Going Out*, Richard Halliday, once told me 'real sitcom has as much to do with panto as it does drama'. Yet some people still seem really averse to the thought of hearing laughter on screen.

Whilst we're on this subject, let's get something cleared up once and for all. One of the biggest myths about studio-based sitcom is that they use canned laughter. There is this strange belief that in the edit a man sits there and presses a button to fill in where the laughs should be because no one actually laughed on the night. This is not what happens. Almost all of the laughs you hear, certainly on *Not Going Out*, are real. When I say 'real', I mean that's how they laughed on the night when we did the joke. The reason I say 'almost' is because there are times when something goes wrong and we have to use the second take. Maybe there was a shadow, or the camera wobbled, or my flies were undone, but for whatever reason we have to do a joke again. Now, the second time an audience hear a joke it doesn't get so much of a laugh, obviously. But the first laughs were more genuine, so they are the laughs we use. We take the laughter 'track' from that first reaction and put it on the end of the second take. Sometimes this is essential as it might be the fourth or fifth take, and then the reaction really is absolute silence. What happens if the first time we do the joke they don't laugh? Hand on heart this is extremely rare, because the scripts have been tried out already to an audience in a theatre. That's when a lot of the gags are met with silence. That's why we get rid of them before we get to the studio. What if a new, untested gag has been put in at the last minute and it doesn't get a laugh (good question, you're obviously very bright)? We edit it out. If four hundred people are not laughing at a joke, they won't be laughing at home either. The only exception to all of this is if an untested joke gets nothing, but because of the action on screen we have to keep it in. For example, if I'm in the kitchen and I say a punchline whilst moving to the living room, we obviously can't get rid of it otherwise I've magically appeared in another room. Even for someone like me who's not a massive believer in the necessity of realism in comedy, mysteriously transporting yourself to a different room is too much. So yes, on those occasions we do add a laugh from somewhere else in the show to cover it. But that is rare, once an episode, at most, which considering there are well over a hundred laughs an episode is pretty small. So, I don't want to hear any more talk of canned laughter, OK? Good, let's carry on. (I'm genuinely a bit angry after writing that. Like we've just had an argument. I would apologize, but I honestly think you were in the wrong.)

The pilot was filmed, edited, and handed in to the BBC. Then we waited for the big decision; did they want an actual series? Would anyone actually get to watch this thing, or was it to be put on the shelf with all the other non-broadcast pilots that have never actually gone to series? Trust me, there are loads of these. I've been involved in two myself.

The first was a show called *Put Your Money Where Your Mouth Is*, where myself and Alice Plunkett (now one of the faces of Channel Four horse racing) would sit on a sofa and introduce two guests. They would have a fantasy amount of money to bet with on various events, including everything from football to the Oscars, and each week we would see how the various people were getting on in the fantasy league.

The mistake we made with this show was that it was sometimes too simple, and sometimes too confusing. Explaining what 11 to 2 means is too patronizing for the serious gambler, and trying to explain spread betting is too much information for the once a year Grand National punter.

Looking back I'm actually relieved it never went on air, as now I'm a bit older and wiser (well older) I'm not sure I want to be responsible for some viewer living under a bridge because his gambling habit has got out of hand. Instead I prefer doing more spiritually enlightening programmes such as *Would I Lie to You?* which prove that to win in life you have to be as dishonest as possible.

The other pilot, however, felt like it had potential. It was a show where myself and Sean Lock provided the voices for a pair of puppets called *Gobo and Dipps*. The premise was that in the 1970s the two titular* characters, who were children's TV presenters, were taken off air because of their bad language and other general shenanigans. They had been put in a suitcase at the BBC, and left there for twenty-five years, but had recently been taken out, dusted off, and given their own show again.

The idea was aimed at adults, and the central idea was to spoof the then modern-day 'wacky' shows such as *The Big Breakfast*. I played the stupid one and Sean played the cynical one, which was typecasting that would haunt us for the rest of our careers.

The powers that be didn't pick up the show but we heard rumours that they might want to take the two puppets and use them on Saturday-morning television, which to a large extent was missing the point. I said if they offered I'd do it, Sean was less keen. Because I'm stupid and he's cynical.

* I hate writing words that I've never used before in my life, as I think it's false and pretentious. But I made an exception this time as I felt it was felicitous.

I would have actually quite liked to do a show like this, not least because I really like working with Sean. He's one of the few comedians I regard as a proper mate, and he's one of the most naturally funny people I've ever met. He also, like me, seems to have a natural suspicion of the world we are involved in, and I'm always drawn to people like that. And on top of all that, he's a wonderful kisser.

A month after making the pilot for *Not Going Out* I got the phone call to say they wanted to do an actual series.

I wanted to milk this bit of the book, slowly describing how the phone rang and I slowly picked it up, palms sweaty, knowing that the next few minutes could change my . . . etc., but I figured that if you're reading this book you probably know the result as you've probably seen the sitcom. Also I wasn't exactly screaming with delight when I heard the news, so it would lack dramatic tension as an anecdote.

Maybe I wasn't screaming with delight because I was still aware that we had lots to do yet and this was just the start. Or maybe I thought this was now going to take me away from stand-up and so it might not be a good thing. Maybe it was because me and Tara were expecting our second child and things like this didn't seem so important now. Maybe I was starting to feel that showbiz was a load of pretend bullshit, as I'd first learned at Pontin's, and so 'Big deal, I have a sitcom.'

Or maybe I was so utterly delighted at the prospect of doing something unbelievably amazing that I had to put a lid on the excitement for fear that it would all go tits up anyway.

I immediately rang Catherine. She was delighted for me. I said you mean 'us' surely. She said no, 'you'. She had decided she wasn't doing the series. Oh well, that was a quick celebration party, about thirty seconds.

Catherine had decided that she wanted to concentrate on her own thing, which looking back was fair enough. Her sketch show was going through the roof* and despite the fact that I had genuinely attempted to do a sitcom about 'us' rather than 'me', there was no escaping the fact that this was a show with me at the heart of it. I was asking a bigger name than me (albeit a mate) to slightly be my sidekick. So it was fair enough that she then said no. I told her I wasn't 'bovvered', and she laughed. Which shows you how long ago it was, because if I said that now, I'm guessing she'd cry and punch me in the face.

It's really great to see Catherine doing so well. The only thing I objected to seeing her doing was *Dr Who*, as this was my favourite show from childhood, and so the 'escapism' for me was difficult when I saw her in it. It's hard to feel like the universe is really in the hands of one woman, when the week before she has rung you asking what a Cyberman looks like.

I've heard her say in interviews that working with me at Edinburgh was a massive help in getting recognized in the industry, and there is some truth in that. Likewise, without her we wouldn't have got *Not Going Out* out of the

* Idea for a gag: people say that, when it comes to books, sequels never sell as well. But look at *Charlie and the Great Glass Elevator*, that went through the roof.

starting gate, and I'll always be grateful to her for that. She's one of the few famous people I know who I regard as a real mate, probably for the simple reason that she wasn't famous before I met her. I genuinely hope that one day we can play a married couple on screen as I'm convinced it will be really good. We've got years of good times behind us, we've had loads of arguments, and we've never had sex. See, perfect married couple.

So Catherine was gone, but as anyone in this industry will tell you, as one ginger door closes, another blonde American one opens.

We searched high and low for a replacement, and it was hard. The lead girl in our sitcom was very difficult to find (and trust me, I know, I've had to do it three times). The problem is they have to do so many jobs and tick so many boxes. They have to be the love interest, they need to be funny, they need to be the straight 'man', they need to be likeable, they need to be the 'mother' figure and so on and so on. Above all, they need to be able to deliver a gag. It's the constant dilemma, if we use stand-ups in the show often they can't act, if we use actors in the show often they can't deliver a gag. I tend to lean towards stand-ups who can act, rather than actors who can do gags. Particularly for the main characters, and sadly there are not that many female stand-ups to choose from, for the simple reason that there are fewer women doing stand-up.

Why is this? Well, funny you should ask, because I did my thesis on this at university, and the conclusion that some experts have come to is that when a group of men get together they take it in turns to show off rather than talk to each other the way women do. So one man does an anecdote, the next then does his, often trying to top each other. This type of showing off is perfect training for stand-up. When women get together they are far more interested in being interactive. One woman will talk, but will go out of her way to bring in another person by asking them a question. Basically they are less selfish about it and prefer chatting. This is obviously less conducive to them becoming a stand-up, where it's all about showing off as an individual. Something like that anyway, I was pissed when I wrote it. But I passed, so it must be right.

Anyway, eventually you find a woman who ticks all the boxes and you snap her up before someone else uses her and she becomes unavailable. In the first series this was Megan Dodds. As soon as she came in we pretty much knew we wanted her, but the battle was to convince the BBC, because she was American and the BBC wondered if the lead girl should be British. I liked the fact that she was American, because that's exactly how I wanted the show to look, American. Actually, I wanted the show to look good, but that was sort of the same thing.

When *Not Going Out* was starting out, traditional British studio-based sitcom was seen as dead. And no one wants to look like something that's dead, unless you're an extra in *Silent Witness* or you're on your way to a Marilyn Manson gig.

In fact so 'dead' was the genre of comedy we were doing, the night before we filmed our first episode of the series there was a Channel Four programme saying exactly that. *Who Killed the Sitcom?* was a ninety-minute talking-heads show in which stalwarts of the sitcom world, including Victoria Wood, said it was all over. Like most people on the show she said that due to the new gritty realism of *The Office* and *The Royle Family*, traditional sitcom was no longer relevant. I shouted at the telly 'But they're more like comedy dramas. You can't call the oven the fridge!' etc., but I couldn't sway them. It was clear that everyone felt it was game over for shows like mine, and I was filming episode one the next bloody day! Of course, I already knew that's what people were thinking and that's why we were going to try and do something about it.

The thing I could never quite understand was that although the industry's attitude was that the British sitcom was a thing of the past, everyone was still raving about the American sitcoms like *Seinfeld* and *Frasier*, which were still on the telly. It very quickly dawned on me that if the perception was that the Americans can get it right but we can't, then the simple answer is to do it like the Americans. It's not necessarily what I thought, but I knew the industry thought it. To be honest, I was so desperate to get it right, if the perception had been that it was the Taliban that were getting their sitcoms right, I'd have happily grown a beard and set it in a cave. And I could have still called it *Not Going Out*.

I sat down and watched everything I could from the States, and then sat and watched everything I could from here. I wanted to know what they were doing so right, and what we were doing so wrong. It was pretty obvious straight away (although I still sat and watched hundreds of hours of telly, because that's easier than getting on with work); the American ones were better written.

Much better jokes, and much more of them. There's an old saying I kept hearing when I started writing my sitcom, 'You need a joke a page.' But you don't, you need more. A lot more. Otherwise the whole thing is just too bloody slow. The Americans know this of course and they slave much more than we do over each line. It's not just the gags. Their attention to detail is in every aspect of the writing. Just watch the credits of an American sitcom. There will be a 'story supervisor', a 'story editor' a 'story creator', the list seems endless. What do we have? 'Written by . . .', that's it. And even then the credit for this job is buried away somewhere on the list next to 'tea maker' or 'fluffer'. The whole TV industry in America is just so much more writer-driven than over here. There are many more man-hours spent on writing in the States than over here.

Unfortunately we didn't have the manpower, but we did have the hours. Myself and Andrew Collins sat in our pokey little Oxford Street office and wrote and wrote and wrote. That's of course when we weren't spending hours staring quietly into space unable to think of anything. Our natural way of being with each other when working was fairly serious and quiet, whereas next door Matt Holness and the *IT Crowd*'s Richard Ayoade, who were working on a new Channel Four show, would be laughing their heads off and screaming with delight. Me and Andrew were like a middle-aged couple who no longer had sex, listening to the neighbours at it like rabbits.

By the end of six months there were Post-it notes

everywhere, filthy coffee* cups and, more importantly, six scripts. Our abstinence from sex had paid dividends, and we had written a series of a BBC One sitcom. The question was, was it any good?

The answer was: Yeah, not bad for a first effort, but room for improvement. Obviously everyone around me told me it was brilliant, but that's what happens in telly land. As ever the only opinions that were brutally honest were the critics, and they count for nothing. This was the first review I read:

> *'It had to happen sooner or later. BBC One has finally found a sitcom worth staying in for . . .* Not Going Out *looks like the perfect solution to Friday nights.' Jane Simon,* Daily Mirror

And this was the second:

> *'. . . you cannot have a terrible script and terrible acting and no story. Well you can, but then you end up with something like* Not Going Out, *a disastrous new six-part series that's calling itself a comedy but has forgotten the jokes.' Nicole Jackson,* Observer

It's obviously quite harsh for me to say 'the critics count for nothing' when someone like Jane Simon in the *Daily Mirror* has written such nice words about us, but you can't

---

* 100,000 words and, appropriately, I go for a coffee. If only the hundred-thousandth word would have been 'orgasm'.

have it both ways. If I embrace good reviews like that, and assume them to be factually correct, then clearly I have to be level-headed and mature about the situation and also take on board the comments of the thick bird from the *Observer*.

If I had to sum up the reaction to the first series, I'd say we did fine, but were largely ignored. We were doing a genre of comedy that was seen as being past its sell-by date and so to the fashion police we were largely seen as irrelevant. At the time it was hard to feel ignored because of the amount of work we did. Plus I always liked strong opinions, one way or the other. I liked the love/hate thing, it helped with gang membership, but 'ignored' was hard. They didn't want to be in *or* out of the gang. They didn't even know there *was* a gang.

After the first series had finished airing we were called in by the then head of BBC One, Peter Fincham, the man who subsequently had to step down after a BBC One documentary falsely suggested the Queen was miserable (you might want to start turning up at my gigs, Liz, if you want to shake off that tag, love). We were going in to find out if we had a second series.

It's impossible for me to go to these sorts of meetings without feeling like Alan Partridge. There is always loads of small talk and everyone is very tense, and I always want to shout 'Monkey tennis'. But we did get a second series so there was no need for me to shove a block of cheese into the controller's face and shout 'Smell my cheese!'

The second series began as the first one started. We needed to find a new leading lady. Megan had decided she no longer wanted to be in the show as she wanted to 'concentrate on other things'. Which I think was telly talk for 'If I have to spend another day with that ferret-faced Lancastrian I'll strangle him.' Looking back that was fair enough. I've mellowed a bit since (cue everyone that knows me: 'You've what?'), but at the time every single line had to be said exactly like I wanted it saying. That's quite a lot of pressure to put on anybody. And, again, it's back to the different psyches of different nationalities. She was American, and I was not. And I find that can cause all sorts of problems with Americans. Like wars and things.

So we needed to find a third lead girl, which must be some sort of record when you consider we'd only done one series. Once again we searched high and low to find the perfect woman who could tick all the usual boxes: she had to be able to play the love interest, the funny person, the straight 'man' etc. Plus there was now a new box to tick. She had to be able to tolerate me. This ruled out quite a few, but luckily I had already used this system in my real life to find a wife, so at least I was used to it.

After weeks of seeing more women than a cross-eyed man at a Siamese twins speed-dating convention, we saw Sally Bretton.

She seemed to tick every box, but there was so much riding on her being right we made the poor girl come back about five times. We couldn't afford to make any more major cast changes after this, so there was a good chance Sally could be around for a while (if the BBC wanted us around for a while, that is). It was because of this that I needed to know she was fairly normal. Trust me, being normal in showbiz is a rare commodity. She was talented, good-looking and an actress. This meant that the chances of her being a right pain in the arse were high.

I am delighted to say that far from being a right pain in the arse she is one of the most down-to-earth people imaginable, and I genuinely cannot remember one single time when she's moaned about a thing. 'What's she got to moan about, she's on a BBC One sitcom?' I hear you ask. Before I worked in telly I would have asked the same question, but, trust me, they can moan. I should know, I'm one of them.

Sally's involvement in the show has been a godsend, and without her positivity on set, to say nothing of her natural comic talent, I honestly think I'd have packed the show in years ago. Making a telly show sounds very glamorous, and to some extent it is, but it can also be mentally exhausting, especially when it comes to dealing with cast members who want to leave. You have moments when you start questioning yourself and, to be honest, sometimes ask if it's all worth it. So having someone around who also has an attitude of 'Wow, we're making a telly show, isn't that great!' is brilliant, and a reminder of just how lucky we all are. You'd be surprised how often people take this profession for granted. If you recorded a conversation between TV performers and played it back to someone who didn't know what job they did, I honestly believe that they would guess they were listening to the staff room at the armpit-sniffing department of a deodorant laboratory during a heatwave.

Like I say, the part she plays is extremely difficult to do

because she has to do so many things. Often it's comedically the least glamorous, because more than any other character she has to occasionally play the 'straight' role in a scene. I often call her the 'Gary Neville' of the show, and not just because of the startling resemblance. Despite the fact that players like David Beckham and Ryan Giggs got all the attention, it was actually Gary Neville that was more of the backbone of the team and the reason that Man Utd were . . . you know what, I'm starting to annoy *myself* with these football analogies.

There have been other cast members coming and going over the years. Miranda Hart was with us for two years as the inept cleaner, Barbara. She made a very small (well, very tall as it happens) appearance as an acupuncturist in the first series, and I thought she was so funny I decided to write a part for her as a regular cast member. But, like Catherine Tate, she soon hit the big time and felt it was time to concentrate on her own thing. This was annoying at the time as I felt we were just starting to get somewhere with the show, but looking back it was only a matter of time before Miranda got her own show. She's genuinely one of the funniest women I've met, and I'm really pleased she's doing well. Then again I have to say that, as she is the only woman I've worked with who can cause me physical harm.

Talking of funny women, there's only one other regular cast member left to mention: Katy Wix, who plays Tim's dippy girlfriend, Daisy. We first introduced Daisy in the second series in a speed-dating episode, and again she was so funny that I thought we needed to use her again. As each series has gone on she has become a bigger and bigger part of the show, and I'm delighted that she is now a permanent fixture. Having Katy on set is really great. I feel like an old man saying this, but there is something about being around her that makes you feel just that little bit younger. Oh, that's it, she's really immature.

And writing her lines is a delight, not only because they are easier to write than anyone else's (the 'dippy' character is always the easiest to write gags for), but because no matter how I write them Katy will always add some facial tic or bemused look that brings a whole new dimension to the gag. Knowing my luck she'll get her own TV series and I'll start getting worried that she'll leave us too. Hang on, she *has* just got her own TV series. Oh bollocks.

We've had ups and downs over the years, as all shows do, but the hard-core cast (I mean in a regular way, not a sexual way) of me, Sally, Katy and Tim are what I will always consider 'the show', and I can honestly say the four of us, combined with the other regular faces in the day-to-day rehearsal, Jamie the producer, Nick the director, Kendall the script supervisor and Sarah the stage manager, genuinely have a really good laugh at work, and there isn't one bad egg amongst them. The fact that the *Not Going Out* team are a bunch of 'normals' is something I will always be grateful for, because if it wasn't the case I wouldn't be able to spend months and months at home in my pyjamas, banging my head against the wall trying to think of ideas for the show. I need to have light at the end of the writing tunnel, and that light is the people I get to work with. In fact if it wasn't for these people, I don't think I would have had the stomach to try and fight to get the show back on air after it was cancelled.

We were about six episodes into the broadcast of the third series when I found out *Not Going Out* was, well, not going to be going out any more. Actually, I can't believe I've just played with the words 'not going out', as any time anyone else does it to me it makes me want to scream, especially reviewers. Good reviews always seem to end with 'a good reason to stay in' and bad reviews always seem to say something along the lines of 'Not Going Out? I will be next week.' Then there's the false smile I have to do when someone I've never met says 'Oh, so you *do* go out then.' It was mildly amusing the first eight hundred times, but due to my limited acting abilities I have been unable to keep faking it once it had reached a thousand.

I had just finished the recording of an episode of *Would I Lie to You?*, or WILTY as we like to call it, when my manager Rob asked if he could have a lift home in the car that was driving me back. Rob had never asked for a lift, so clearly there was something wrong. As soon as we set off he turned to me and said 'I'm afraid the BBC don't want any more of *Not Going Out.*' It was genuinely quite dramatic, not least because it was pitch black and we were driving through the woods at midnight. It was like some sort of gangster film, and I think I was slightly concerned that Rob was going to say 'you're no good to me now', then open the door whilst the car was still moving, kick me out, then drive another fifty yards and pick up John Bishop.

Suddenly, and without any warning whatsoever (and I mean none, as the show felt like it was really finding its feet), the main motivating factor in my work life was gone. It had dominated so much of the previous four years of my life and now it was finished.

My overriding initial feeling wasn't disappointment, or sadness, or anger. It was genuinely that someone had made a mistake. And when I say a mistake, I don't mean I felt someone had made the wrong decision in cancelling the show, I mean a mistake as in an admin error. Like Rob had got it wrong and he was mixing me up with Nicholas Lyndhurst, and he meant to say *Goodnight Sweetheart* had been axed.

I just couldn't get my head round why it had been dropped. If it had been after the first series, or even the second, then I would have understood. In fact I was sort of expecting it after those two series because I felt we were being ignored as a show, and I was slightly surprised each time we got re-commissioned. But something had happened during the third series which had made it clear the show had 'broken through'. I'm slightly reluctant to use that phrase as it was something that had been said to me early on in relation to the show by other people, and I never liked it. 'The show hasn't quite broken through yet.' Why couldn't they just say 'Not enough people are watching it'? Why couldn't TV people talk normally?

The truth is, something does happen when you make a telly show, a sort of tipping point where you feel there suddenly is an interest in it, and it's not just an increase in viewers. It's more a sense that people are watching it in a different way. It's like they used to watch it with the sound down, but now they've started turning the volume up. See, not really easy to describe, that's why it's better to say it's 'broken through'.

This increased interest was evident to me and Tara one day when we took the kids to the London Aquarium towards the end of the broadcast of Series Three, and people who I'd never met suddenly wanted to say hello and talk about the show. They seemed quite animated and passionate, but because people when they meet you will often say 'I really like your show', as opposed to actually naming it, I genuinely thought they were mixing me up with someone else. I simply wasn't used to this sort of reaction. My kids certainly weren't. For some reason I didn't want them to know the truth, so instead I told the kids people had been asking for photos because I looked like a famous fish expert and they were mixing me up.

Yet, despite this new-found interest, a week later we were cancelled.

The battle to get the show reinstated started immediately, and although credit for that fight has to be given mainly to Jon Thoday, the head honcho at Avalon TV, I was dragged along to various meetings and 'chats' to lend my support. The reason we were given was that the viewing figures weren't good enough, and yet I had been told by those around me they were great. Then again in telly land everyone tells you everything is great, so it's hard to get a clear perspective. I once rolled the trouser legs of a suit up to my knees to test this theory and asked the costume woman if it looked OK. She told me that it was 'great' but we should try them rolled down as well, to compare the two.

Viewing figures, on the face of it, should be an easy barometer of success. But like any statistic they can be presented to suit the argument of the person quoting them. If, for example, you're getting three million viewers, and the person who makes the decisions doesn't want your show on any more, then they can compare you to *My Family*, which gets twice as many. If, however, the person quoting them is trying to get you back on the telly, they will point out that *My Family* is losing figures and you are gaining, or that you've not been on for ten series, or that you get a higher ABC 1 demographic (don't ask), or that you're on at a time when the weather is warmer and so more people are out (honestly, that was said. Actually there is some truth in it). Or that Robert Lindsay has more friends than you, so he gets more of his mates watching. Everyone just stared at me when I presented that argument, so I shut up after that.

In fact, I didn't massively get involved in these debates as I'd sort of given up and felt it was game over. All I knew was that people were coming up to me in the street and were suddenly very interested in the show, so it was a slight surprise to have been given the axe. I even had a few people come up to me offering me their sympathy about the cancellation. I told my kids the fish expert I looked like had been sacked for eating the last remaining Goppler fish of Tanzania.

And I have to be honest and say that, in a weird sort of way, I wasn't actually that bothered. This is a hard thing to explain, as I was passionate about the show, but sometimes I feel some things are so beyond my control it makes me feel like I just don't care any more.

The process of trying to get the show back on telly dragged on for a year, by which time I had decided it was time to get back to doing what I do anyway, stand-up. I had all but given up ever getting the show back on, and so decided to book in a hundred-date tour. Two weeks later the BBC did a U-turn and we were back on air.

I went from unemployed to over-employed in the space of a phone call.

Despite me convincing myself I no longer cared, I actually found myself delighted to be back. Hopefully the increased viewing figures of the last two series have justified the decision (which is good considering it's been quite warm weather). But what this whole process did was cement in my head what I already sort of knew.

Being a stand-up comedian is the only really guaranteed job I have.

PSYCHIATRIST'S OFFICE

BRIAN: There are a lot of times in this book when you show ambivalence about your job.

Lee assumes this means he doesn't care about his job. Which he objects to, yet agrees with, at the same time. He feels like he wants to say 'What right have you got to say that? Apart from being right?'

LEE: I suppose sometimes I do worry that I care less than other comedians.

BRIAN: A lot of people think that ambivalence means you don't care. But in a psychodynamic sense it actually means you are torn. It means you care too much in opposite directions. You get torn between two things so end up in a state of ambivalence. This contributes to a feeling of restlessness.

Lee thinks that surely any restlessness would be because of his ADHD, a condition he now seems to not only accept he has, but is OK about. Although now he wonders if he isn't really OK with it at all. Maybe he just doesn't care

> *due to this new chronic sickness*
> *of 'ambivalence'.*

BRIAN: I think you care about your job really, but your ambivalence sometimes makes you think you don't.

LEE: So why me? Why have I got 'ambivalence'?

BRIAN: Well, sometimes you have to look at your primary relationships. Your mother, for example.

> *Lee wonders if Brian sends a*
> *'happy primary relationship day'*
> *card to her primary relation on*
> *primary relationships day.*

BRIAN: Many schools of thought believe that a lot of your personality is formed when you are very young.

LEE: 'Show me the seven-year-old and I'll show you the man.'

BRIAN: The Jesuits used to say that.

> *Lee has obviously heard of 'the*
> *Jesuits' and knows they are*
> *connected with religion, but he's*
> *never quite sure who they are*
> *exactly. He is, however, glad to*
> *feel like one of them in this*
> *incident, as it makes Lee feel*
> *like his previous sentence was of*
> *Biblical importance.*

BRIAN: If I was from the Melanie Klein
          school of thought . . .

          *Lee wonders if that's the woman
          who plays the piano that used to
          be in the band Hear'Say, then
          remembers that is Myleene Klass.
          His ADHD then makes him wonder
          what happened to the two blokes
          who were in Hear'Say, and wonders
          if maybe they share a flat with
          Frankie Marrow.*

BRIAN: . . . I would say much younger.
          Probably when you were a baby. She
          often spoke of the 'good breast'
          and the 'bad breast'.

          *Lee wonders if breasts can ever be
          bad.*

BRIAN: When a baby is fed the breast
          feels warm, and good. The baby is
          in a state of Nirvana . . .

          *Lee thinks about Kurt Cobain, and
          actually wonders if the word
          'nirvana' should no longer be
          associated with comfort and warmth
          given the rock star's tragic end.*

BRIAN: They are in a cocoon . . .

          *Lee thinks about the horror film
          Cocoon and wonders if this too is
          no longer a good word to suggest
          comfort and peace. Lee makes a
          mental note to use this as*

*potential material in his act, but
then realizes he's never actually
seen Cocoon, and in fact it might
not be a horror film after all.
Lee then decides probably best to
forget the idea, and instead
listen to Brian, seeing as he's
paying for these sessions.*

BRIAN: The breast is 'good'. But when the
          baby is hungry and their needs
          aren't being met, the breast
          becomes 'bad'. They then don't
          know how to feel about the breast
          and they can get torn between
          these two feelings, and end up
          stuck in a state of ambivalence.

          *Lee actually thought that the
          'good breast' or the 'bad breast'
          referred to which breast the baby
          chose. Like there is one good one
          and one bad one. Up until this
          explanation he had spent the last
          few seconds wondering if maybe he
          had chosen the wrong one when he
          was a baby. The middle one
          perhaps. That's always the wrong
          one.*

BRIAN: This state is also known as
          paranoid-schizoid.

          *Lee decides to push this no
          further. He can accept he has
          'ambivalence', he can also accept
          he has ADHD, but he's not
          accepting he has anything with*

'paranoid' and 'schizo' in the title.

LEE: So are you saying that by not engaging either way with my job it makes me less disappointed?

BRIAN: Possibly, yes.

LEE: Well, if this way of thinking is decided at such a young age, then there's not much I can do about it, is there?

BRIAN: Yes, there is. People used to think that life was about being on a train track, and that people couldn't change direction. That all of these things are decided at an early age. But psychotherapy has proved that you can change, and that these conditions can be managed. The Jesuits were wrong.

        Lee decides he no longer wants to be associated with the Jesuits if they keep getting things wrong. Before he liked them, now he doesn't. In fact, from now on he decides he will feel ambivalent about them, and go back to liking breasts.

CHAPTER TWENTY-ONE

How do you end a book?

As I sit here, starting to write this final chapter, it is 5.40 a.m. Even for me that is ridiculously early, but my six-month-old daughter has just woken me up. Well, she has half woken me up. The main jolt to actually get out of bed was the fact that I have to finish a book.

But how do you finish a book about yourself? I've never written an autobiography before so I'm not sure how you're supposed to end them.

I can hear my kids playing in the garden.

In case you're wondering why they are outside playing at 5.45 a.m., they're not. It is now 9 a.m. After I wrote the first two paragraphs of this final chapter I couldn't decide what to do next, so I made the fatal mistake of typing 'how do you end an autobiography' into Google. There was a suggestion to go back to your childhood and try and think what you thought your life would be like, and compare this with what actually happened. This led me to start thinking about my school, which in turn led me to start thinking about *Grange Hill*, and then about the character Trisha Yates. I then couldn't relax until I knew what had become of the actress that played her. It turns out, according to Wikipedia, that she works for a Dundee company called All Glass and Glazing (although why I trust Wikipedia I'm not sure. After all, they once said I was Russ Abbott's nephew). This got me wondering about the name of the company. Why call it All Glass and Glazing? Surely 'all glass' covers everything. What is it about 'glazing' that makes it not covered by 'all glass'? Surely that's a tautology. I then wonder if a tautology is in fact the right word, and look that up. But I don't spell it right, and before I know it I'm looking at Tortola Cruises, and wondering if I can overcome my seasickness, or should we simply go to Center Parcs this year. This type of thing carried on for about three hours and ended with me looking up the best way to wash a cat.

That's the internet for you. Never have so many known so much about so little.

Hearing my kids in the garden makes me wonder if I could do what other autobiographies do at the end and say something like 'As I sit here looking out of the window of my office and watch my children playing with gay abandon, their laughter echoing like the ghost of my own carefree innocent childhood, I wonder if they too will be lucky enough to see what I have seen, to learn what I have learned etc.' You know, all that sort of self-important crap. But that would be a lie. As any parent will know, what I'm really thinking when I hear them in the garden is 'Don't run on the slippery decking', 'Stop shouting "willy"' and 'Don't throw mud at the cat.'

Maybe I should just talk about the future and what I'm hoping to do next. But that feels wrong. I find it odd enough telling people about what I've done so far, never mind stuff that hasn't even happened yet. More importantly, I don't actually know what it is I do hope to be doing next. I don't even know what I'm doing tomorrow, never mind over the next few years. Actually, I do know what I'm doing tomorrow, trying to think of a way of ending this book. In fact, at this rate I'll be doing it for the next few years.

Then I have a brainwave. Well, a small one. Let's call it a microwave. If I can't think of an ending to the book, then maybe I shouldn't properly have one. Maybe I could make the book shorter, up to the point where I step on stage for my first ever gig at the Gong Show back in the mid-nineties. Then I could write something like 'What happened next? You'll just have to wait and see in my upcoming sequel *Mack the Life 2*.' That way, having an abrupt ending would feel appropriate, without any feelings of summary or conclusion. More of a cliff-hanger. With modern technology I could probably get a button attached to the end of the book that, when pressed, does the drum beats from the beginning of the *EastEnders* theme.

Plus there's also the lucrative 'second book deal'. Why use it all up now when I can shamelessly split it into two parts (even though most readers just want you to hurry up and get famous, so the first books are always crap).

I decide this is what I am going to do, and I tell my wife. She is a little disappointed. The book has now taken much longer than I originally told her, and now I'm talking about writing a second one, which will no doubt take up much of the next twelve months.

She reminds me that I said when I'd finished *this* book, I would start to lighten my load a little and spend less time sat in front of the computer. But now I'm saying I might do it all again.

This does not come as a complete shock to my wife, as she never believed me in the first place. I always tell her I will take it easier, and I mean it when I say it, but I always seem to take on more and more projects. I think this is because as soon as I've finished one, I forget how much time it took to do it and commit to something else. I never seem to be able to keep my promise to my wife to do 'dictionary corner'.

'Dictionary corner' is a phrase that is used in my house to represent 'taking it easy' work-wise. It comes from the TV show *Countdown*, and it's the role of the show that a guest presenter takes up, their job being to check the words in the dictionary. I appreciate you probably already know this, but this description is for anyone that isn't housebound or a student.

In the world of comedy careers 'dictionary corner' is totally unimportant, in helping you pay off your mortgage it is totally irrelevant, and in terms of artistic merit it is totally bereft. So to do it you would have to find it nothing but fun. That's what I mean by starting to do 'dictionary corner'.

As it happens, I have no interest whatsoever in making nine-letter words from random letters, so I personally wouldn't find it fun, and so would probably not do that particular show. But the principle still holds – to do stuff that is only a laugh, regardless of career, money or any of the other bullshit that, even with the best will in the world, starts to overtake your brain the more you do this job.

The comedians that I know who have done dictionary corner on *Countdown* did it because they like it. Nothing else. Despite the fact that many would see it as a slight down-step on the career ladder of success, they don't give a monkey's, because that's not the reason they're doing it. They're doing it for a bit of a laugh, and probably because they have an interest in the show. I happen to think that's very admirable.

It's like when Vic Reeves went into *I'm A Celebrity, Get Me Out of Here* with his wife Nancy Sorrell. Loads of comedians felt this was a bad idea because it affected his status as a comedian, especially given that he's very much a comic's comic and not one you'd expect to be involving himself in reality TV. But I quite admired him for it. It was like he just wanted to go camping for a week, and a bit like he was sticking two fingers up at the thinking classes, and I'm always a fan of that.

I'm not saying *I* would do reality TV, but what I *am* saying is that if I turn it down it will be because I don't think it will be fun, rather than being concerned about how it will affect my status as a comedian, or any fears that it will be artistically worthless.

Anyway, that's all irrelevant now because I'm not doing 'dictionary corner', I'm doing another book.

My wife then reminds me we have three children, and wonders how I will juggle the book with the kids. I tell her I'll use the Reverse Cascade system. She doesn't laugh. I don't know if this is because she is already well aware how difficult it has been to write the book at the same time as my sitcom, and thinks by doing it again it will send me over the edge, or because she doesn't realize that the Reverse Cascade is a juggling technique. She tells me it's the former (with her eyes).

She has a point of course. There's no getting away from the fact that writing already takes me away from the kids more than I would want. Not geographically, but mentally. Writing always seems to take for ever. If it wasn't for writing, this job would be the best job in the world. Instead it's the second best job in the world, behind professional footballer.

I have tried many, many systems of writing over the years and many, many writers. All of which have been with the aim to lessen the load. This is especially true with *Not Going Out*. The problem is, and I totally accept that it's mainly down to me being a control freak, I haven't been able to let go enough to ever feel like I'm truly ever relaxed about a script.

Having said that, we recently employed the services of Danny Peak to help, a scriptwriter who is not only great, but whose writing is the closest we've ever achieved in terms of matching my own style. This has been the number one problem in the past. All the writers we have used have been great, otherwise we wouldn't have used them. However, the rhythm and language of the writing has been sufficiently different to mine that it has still involved many, many hours of work by me to get the words to sound like they would come out of my mouth. It's no coincidence that Danny is from Manchester, a place that is very close to my hometown of Southport. Our accents are fairly similar, albeit Danny's is more Mancunian and therefore has a slightly more 'man complaining through a trumpet' quality.

My wife then reminds me that I can't write another book as I have other things I have to do. Apart from the obvious (family), I have to try and work on my new BBC One Saturday night entertainment show. This is a type of show I dabbled with recently in *Lee Mack's All Star Cast*, a show that myself and old college mate Neil Webster had devised based on my Radio 2 show from a few years earlier.

The idea was that we take all the elements of an entertainment show and combine them. Stand-up, chat show, sketch, music, audience participation, phone-ins; it was all there. We only did one series, and the people who liked it said they loved that there was so much going on. The people who didn't like it said they hated that there was so much going on.

Now I am working closely with the BBC to try and find another vehicle to take to Saturday night. 'Vehicle' is another word that I used to hate in this job, but now I've become inured to. Why can't people say 'programme'? I suppose it's because 'vehicle' suggests that it's a show that is there to promote the performer, rather than a show for its own sake. In the same way that a car is not as important as the passengers. Although after once seeing Piers Morgan in a secondhand rusty Vauxhall Nova I would dispute that.

I would love to get a big Saturday night TV show right. Some people say it's the hardest thing to crack. Then again, some people say that about sitcom. Someone even told me it's an autobiography that's the hardest. It's almost like I'm drawn to things that are as difficult as possible to get right. I'm not saying I love a challenge, I'm saying I'm an idiot. Still, however hard this job can be, at least it's not copper mining.

My wife also reminds me that if I write another book I won't be able to 'potter'. Pottering is something that my wife tells me I used to do all the time when we met, and now never seem to do. When we first met, before I got into comedy, I would walk round the house doing all sorts of inane projects to fill the day. Like the time I built 'Arthur'.

'Arthur' was a full-sized man I made from chicken wire and old clothes. Well, I say full-sized: he had no legs, hence the name 'Arthur' – he was 'alf a man. The purpose of 'Arthur' was so Tara could put him in the passenger seat of her car when driving at night. There had been a spate of car-jackings in the news, and I got it into my head that Tara needed protecting, so built 'Arthur' to look like she had a man in the car with her. After a while she decided that the looks she was getting from other drivers at traffic lights was too much, as when you got close it was clear that 'Arthur' wasn't real. I think it made Tara look a bit sad and lonely. Also, she kept forgetting to put him in the boot at night so he would sit there all night in the car and the neighbours started to find it odd. Plus, I was starting to get a little suspicious of 'Arthur'. He and Tara were spending just a little too much time together and I was starting to worry that, despite his lack of legs, they might run off together. So 'Arthur' was put in the bin, and Tara decided to employ the services of a proper, professional male escort.

Tara also tells me that if I decide to write another book it will prove what she has always suspected, that I will never be able to truly lighten my work load, which in turn means I will never actually retire. Something I often tell Tara I would eventually like to do. In fact she reminds me that very early on in our relationship one of the first things I said to her was that I was looking forward to getting old, shuffling down to the shops to buy a bar of chocolate, then sitting in my shed and eating it whilst listening to Radio 4. Tara reminds me that I told her this on our first date, and that it wasn't for comedy effect. I genuinely meant it. Looking back, I certainly knew how to woo the ladies with my get-up-and-go personality.

There is a lot of truth in the idea that I want to retire early.

Many years ago I was sat with Jimmy Carr having dinner at some comedy bash, and we saw Bruce Forsyth on a different table. Jimmy said 'It's great this job, isn't it? Look at Brucie, in his eighties and still going strong. This means we can be doing this job for years to come.' Jimmy had meant this as a positive, but I just thought 'You've got to be kidding!' I told him I wanted to retire at some point and tend to my allotment. Actually, I know nothing about gardening and probably didn't say that. I probably said to Jimmy something like 'I want to retire at some point and lie on a beach with a load of hookers', because I'm good at knowing my target audience.

Tara can't understand why I would consider writing another book given how much this has taken me away from the family. So I tell Tara the truth, which is that I can't think of a way of ending this one.

Tara tells me I should probably concentrate on thinking of a good ending to this one rather than thinking of starting a new one. After all, I'd still have the same problem next time. She tells me that would be like not being able to end a sentence, so starting a new one instead. Then she realizes that is what I do all the time and so is a bad example.

She then comes up with a solution. She tells me I should do what other people do at the end of books and have some sort of closure. I don't really know what she means by this, but Tara knows what she's talking about as she reads a lot more books than me. Actually, that would be true if she read one a year. Tara goes on to explain that most books have a journey, some sort of lesson that the protagonist has learned, often through finally obtaining something that they have chased throughout the story. She suggests I read the book back, from the beginning, and try and find out what it is I've been chasing. What the golden chalice is that has kept me going.

I read the book back and all I can come up with is 'I've always wanted to meet the Queen'. Tara tells me that as spiritual journeys go, this is probably not the most profound journey that anyone has ever been on, but it's a journey nevertheless.

So I think about doing this as an ending, then reject it on the basis that I *haven't* met her, so therefore I haven't obtained or achieved anything. This would have been perfect, a nice photo of me shaking hands with the Queen. That would tie up neatly what I wrote very early on in that first chapter about seeing comedians on the Royal Variety Performance. They met the Queen afterwards, which in my head proved they'd 'made it', so this would be like me going full circle. But I haven't, I've only met Prince Charles. Three times. Three bloody times. If only she'd turned up at the Royal Variety Performance. Just once. She's ruined my book. I am annoyed.

I then go away and write up a different ending, which has nothing whatsoever to do with the book. A rant about how I hate alcohol sponsorship in comedy, and how the TV channels that allow this to happen should be ashamed of themselves. I write about Foster's lager sponsoring Channel Four comedy and say things like 'It doesn't sponsor originality in comedy at all. It stifles it. Because to warrant the money it pays for these "stings" the shows then need to reach a specific demographic of people, and targeting specific marketplaces that suit a business plan is not in any way conducive to originality.

So it's not true. Then again "Foster's increases your chances of stomach cancer" isn't as catchy, I suppose.'

I show people connected with my book this ending, and they all agree it is a very odd way to end a book. I tell them I am a 'very odd' person so it's perfect, but they tell me I am not. They are right. I said it to make me sound interesting and kooky, as opposed to the truth, which is I am normal and unkooky. Better to be mad than boring as my Nan used to say, as she sat there naked eating a packet of custard powder.

The people connected to the book realize they are getting nowhere with the 'odd' argument, so instead tell me there is a danger of me being called a hypocrite. I have appeared on Foster's sponsored Channel Four shows in the past. Indeed my own sitcom, *Not Going Out,* is sponsored by booze companies on Dave, a situation I have tried to rectify and yet unfortunately have no control over, other than stopping making the show altogether. Sadly I don't currently have the moral backbone to make that decision, as the sitcom means too much to me. Although I may reconsider that in the future.

The hypocrite argument is enough to sway me, and so I delete what I've written (or my 'odd rant' as it became known). So now I am back to square one, and don't have an ending for my book.

Then a few weeks later, by almost unbelievable co-incidence, I get a phone call from my manager, Rob. I have been asked if I will be one of the co-hosts for the Queen's Diamond Jubilee concert outside Buckingham Palace. This is too good to be true. Not only will it be the most exciting gig I will ever do, performing live to tens of millions around the world and sharing the stage with the likes of Paul McCartney, Stevie Wonder and Elton John, but it means I will have a chance to meet the Queen. That means that I will be fulfilling a childhood dream, and more importantly, I will get a photograph of me shaking her hand.

Which means I will have an ending for the book.

Which means I won't have to do the sequel, which means my kids will have back their semi-retired, pottering father, and Tara won't get back in touch with 'Arthur'.

So on 4 June 2012, after one of the most surreal nights of my life, which ended with me wandering round Buckingham Palace being told by Prince William he loves *Not Going Out*, I met the Queen.

And here's the evidence . . .

So what have I learned from this? What knowledge have I garnered from finally obtaining the thing I dreamed of as a child?

I'd like to say something profound, something along the lines of realizing that fulfilling our dreams is not necessarily the key in the pursuit of happiness. That by reaching the top of the mountain I have learned that it is important that we enjoy the climb, as true fulfilment does not lie at the top of the peak. That finally meeting the person who represents your childhood dreams makes you realize that the only people that really matter are around us every day.

That's what I would like to say.

But actually what I've really learned is this: that Alfie Boe, Britain's leading operatic tenor, a man whose voice alone is so rich it can make ladies swoon, can't take photos to save his bloody life.

Either that, or he's a massive fan of Kylie Minogue.

PSYCHIATRIST'S OFFICE

*Lee and Brian are discussing his
final chapter.*

BRIAN: It's interesting that you were
contemplating having an ending that
wasn't actually an ending. Maybe
that's how you like to deal with
all 'endings'. Career changes,
relationships, deaths. Maybe you
like to pretend it isn't really
the end.

*Lee panics. Although this is his
last session with Brian, he lied
and told her he might need another
one next week. The reason he lied
is that Lee hates the awkwardness
of saying goodbye to people, so
instead will often pretend he will
see them again very soon so as to
avoid mawkish goodbyes. Or kisses
on the cheek, which he always
finds a bit odd and wishes it was
made illegal, unless you are
French. He now thinks that Brian
is on to him and decides to come
clean.*

LEE: I suppose I do sort of dislike
saying goodbye to people. It's
like after I finish a TV series. I
will often avoid saying goodbye to
a member of cast or crew by saying
'I'll see you in the bar', even

though I know full well they
aren't going to the bar.

Lee realizes that's a bad example.
*People in TV **always** go to the bar.*

LEE: And it's not just work. I will
         often say to people 'I'll see you
         tomorrow' even though I know I'm
         not seeing them for a long time.

         Lee realizes that actually that is
         utter nonsense and he has never
         said that in his life to anyone.
         It clearly wouldn't work. 'Right,
         I'll see you tomorrow' – 'No you
         won't' – 'Oh yeah, I won't will
         I.'

BRIAN: Maybe your reluctance to end
         things is because you need the
         uncertainty.

LEE: What uncertainty?

BRIAN: 'Has it ended or hasn't it?' 'What
         happens next?'

LEE: There is some truth in that.
         Traditionally I make my sitcom
         without knowing if we will be re-
         commissioned. Yet recently, for the
         first time ever, we got
         commissioned for two on the run,
         series five and six. I have to be
         honest and say, in a strange sort
         of way, I didn't enjoy making
         series five as much as I should

have done. Knowing we already had another one guaranteed, there wasn't the uncertainty any more, and I sort of missed the rollercoaster ride of not knowing. Having said that I would still like to be re-commissioned two at a time.

Lee never actually said that last sentence to Brian. He added it in case anyone from the BBC is reading this.

BRIAN: The other reason you may struggle to end things is your ADHD.

*Lee has noticed that Brian has started referring to it as **his** ADHD as opposed to **the** ADHD. Lee is not sure he likes that, as Lee is only used to hearing that type of phrasing in a negative sense. Like when his wife Tara says '**Your** cat has pissed on the rug.'*

BRIAN: We often use a self-assessment questionnaire to gauge whether someone may have ADHD or not. And the first question is 'How often do you have trouble wrapping up the final details of a project?'

LEE: Always. In my sitcom I will spend ages on the final scene, and even worse the final line. I can never think of a way of ending it.

Lee then has an idea.

LEE: Actually, could you send this
         questionnaire to me. I'll fill it
         in, and then not only will that
         prove one way or the other if I've
         got ADHD, it will also give me
         another ending, as to be honest
         I'm a bit fifty-fifty about the
         Queen idea.

BRIAN: OK.

LEE: Great. Right, I'll be off.

         *Lee stands up and heads for the
         door. He is about to say, as a
         joke, 'I'll see you in the bar',
         then remembers that in an earlier
         session he jokingly suggested she
         was a chronic alcoholic, and
         decides against it.*

LEE: Bye.

         Lee goes to exit then turns back.

LEE: Thanks, Eileen.

         Lee exits and closes the door.

Adult ADHD Self-Report Scale (ASRS-v1.1) Symptom Checklist

Today's Date

Patient Name	Never	Rarely	Sometimes	Often	Very Often
Please answer the questions below, rating yourself on each of the criteria shown using the scale on the right side of the page. As you answer each question, place an X in the box that best describes how you have felt and conducted yourself over the past 6 months. Please give this completed checklist to your healthcare professional to discuss during today's appointment.					
1. How often do you have trouble wrapping up the final details of a project, once the challenging parts have been done?					X
2. How often do you have difficulty getting things in order when you have to do a task that requires organization?			X		
3. How often do you have problems remembering appointments or obligations?			X		
4. When you have a task that requires a lot of thought, how often do you avoid or delay getting started?				X	
5. How often do you fidget or squirm with your hands or feet when you have to sit down for a long time?				X	
6. How often do you feel overly active and compelled to do things, like you were driven by a motor?					X
					Part A
7. How often do you make careless mistakes when you have to work on a boring or difficult project?					
8. How often do you have difficulty keeping your attention when you are doing boring or repetitive work?					
9. How often do you have difficulty concentrating on what people say to you, even when they are speaking to you directly?					
10. How often do you misplace or have difficulty finding things at home or at work?					

11. How often are you distracted by activity or noise around you?					X X X
12. How often do you leave your seat in meetings or other situations in which you are expected to remain seated?					X X X
13. How often do you feel restless or fidgety?					X X X
14. How often do you have difficulty unwinding and relaxing when you have time to yourself?	N/A I have 3 kids				X X X X
15. How often do you find yourself talking too much when you are in social situations?					X X X X
16. When you're in a conversation, how often do you find yourself finishing the sentences of the people you are talking to, before they can finish them themselves?					X
17. How often do you have difficulty waiting your turn in situations when turn taking is required?	N/A I am a queue jumper				
18. How often do you interrupt others when they are busy?					X X X X

Part B

* I left this blank as I wasn't sure if it was aimed at me

** During Skype meetings they always end up looking at my crotch

*** But it is my job

**** But I do a much better job

* * * * * But it's always more important

ACKNOWLEDGEMENTS

Thanks to Doug Young, Madeline Toy and everyone at Transworld, and to Rob Aslett, Alice Russell, Lucy Plosker and everyone at Avalon. Oh yeah, and to Granddad Joe as well, who, for some inexplicable reason, didn't get a mention in the book, even though he was always the 'head honcho'. And finally, thanks to the person who invented Tunnock's Caramel Wafers.

INDEX